COMPUTER - AIDED CONTROL SYSTEM DESIGN

COMPUTER - AIDED CONTROL SYSTEM DESIGN

H. H. ROSENBROCK

Control Systems Centre, University of Manchester
Institute of Science and Technology, Manchester, England

1974

ACADEMIC PRESS
LONDON   NEW YORK   SAN FRANCISCO
A Subsidiary of Harcourt Brace Jovanovich, Publishers

ACADEMIC PRESS INC. (LONDON) LTD.
24/28 Oval Road, London NW1

United States Edition published by
ACADEMIC PRESS INC.
111 Fifth Avenue, New York, New York 10003

Library of Congress Catalog Card Number: 74 5678
ISBN: 0 12 597450 7

Printed in Great Britain by
C. F. Hodgson & Son Ltd., 50 Holloway Road N7 8JL

Preface

This book is devoted to frequency-response and allied methods for designing control systems, because these at present are the only available methods which are suitable for interactive use with a computer. It therefore carries on a line of development which flourished between 1935 and 1960, and was highly successful for a well-defined class of problems. These were the servo following problem and the regulator problem, for linear time-invariant plants having only one input and out output.

After 1955 the demands of rocket guidance led to the development of state-space methods, which deal directly with the differential equations. These methods, referred to rather unfortunately as "modern control theory", were particularly appropriate for many aerospace problems, and they have also led to a much better understanding of some important aspects of control.

The sharp distinction which once existed between frequency-response and state-space methods is now beginning to disappear. When one deals with linear time-invariant systems, it is now recognized that most theoretical results can be obtained either by vector-space methods or by algebraic methods allied to the Laplace transform. There are seen to be alternative (and closely related) mathematical techniques which can be applied to the given problem. If state-space methods have a scope which extends far beyond the linear time-invariant problem, frequency-response methods on the other hand give an unmatched visual insight and are largely insensitive to small errors in the description of a system.

State-space methods have never succeeded in replacing frequency-response methods for the linear, time-invariant regulator or servo problem when there is only a single input and output. For multivariable problems, however, no very good methods existed when progress was interrupted about 1960. Accordingly an important objective of this book is to give an extension of frequency-response methods to multivariable regulators and servos.

In taking up again the earlier lines of work, there are two intervening developments which are of great importance. First, state-space theory and later developments have clarified some questions which were poorly understood in the earlier period, particularly questions of structure. Full advantage has been taken of this increased knowledge to give a better treatment of such questions as stability and the effect of redundancy ("uncontrollability" or "unobservability") in the system. It should be particularly noticed that frequency response methods can be used without difficulty for systems which do not have least order. The results needed are usually given here in an algebraic form as developed in an earlier book, "State-space and Multi-variable Theory", and are briefly recapitulated in Chapter 1. They can however be obtained in most cases by vector-space methods, and probably most will already be familiar to the reader.

The second development, which will have a profound and increasing influence on all engineering design, is the availability of computers with graphical display. This allows a complete re-evaluation of the existing frequency-response methods, so that the graphical features are used only for communication with the designer, and not to replace standard numerical procedures for root-solving etc. It also allows the development of graphical methods without that close attention to the computational burden which would be needed if they were to be used without a computer. The resulting design methods are believed to have a power and flexibility, for industrial problems, which cannot be matched at present by any alternative methods.

The resurgent interest in frequency-response methods would have permitted a wide scope. For example existing state-space methods could have been restated in frequency-response terms, methods for nonlinear systems based on the describing function could have been given, and most of the results given here could have been extended to sampled-data systems. However, it is important that any proposed design method should have been widely tested on real engineering problems. This has so far been done on a wide scale, and for multivariable problems, only within a limited area. The account given here has therefore been restricted to techniques which have been fully tested and which can be supported, as in Chapter 4, by a wide range of practical applications.

To a much greater extent than usual, this book is the result of a collaborative effort. Over a period of five years, colleagues and students have contributed to the development and application of the methods described. The first computer programme to implement the methods of Chapter 3 was written by Mr. I. Paul. The largest contribution in this area, and in the early applications, was however made by Dr. R. S. McLeod, with major contributions also by Dr. D. J. Hawkins and Dr. P. D. McMorran. Meanwhile the computer installation and graphic facilities were developed by Dr. G. C. Barney, Dr. J. M. Hambury and Dr. S. Karniel. Later development of the programmes was carried on under the direction of Dr. N. Munro by Mrs. B. J. Bowland and Mrs. L. S. Brown.

A major debt of gratitude is owed to the Science Research Council, which provided the specialized computer facilities. These had to be available before evidence for the success of the methods could be obtained, and their provision was therefore an act of faith in the team concerned which no thanks can adequately repay.

Many friends and colleagues have helped to improve the form and presentation of this book, and among these it is a particular pleasure to acknowledge the advice of Professors R. W. Brockett and A. G. J. MacFarlane. All graphical output from the computer used in the diagrams was obtained by Dr. N. Munro, whose invaluable help is most gratefully acknowledged. A similar debt is acknowledged to Mrs. L. E. Mann who turned an untidy manuscript into a neat and workmanlike typescript.

Finally I owe a personal debt to Sir Harold Hartley, who died while the manuscript was in preparation, for the generous encouragement which he gave many years ago to me and to the infant subject of automatic control. To him this book is gratefully dedicated.

September, 1974   H. H. ROSENBROCK

Contents

Use a hammer of ample weight, and
avoid a finicky manner of
tapping the nail

Stubbs and Reed
Practical Handywork for All

Chapter 1

Introduction and mathematical background

This chapter provides the setting within which the later discussion of control will take place. It also contains some definitions and results from the mathematical theory of dynamical systems which will be needed later in the book. These mathematical results are intended for reference purposes, and for the most part are summarized from the appropriate sections of an earlier book [State-space and multivariable theory, Rosenbrock, 1970] which will be referred to here as SSMVT.

The student who wishes to have a deeper grasp of the subject will benefit from a preliminary study of that volume; but it is also envisaged that this book will be used by students and engineers who are prepared to accept the necessary theorems, deferring details of the proofs for later study. Such readers need not delay over the mathematical preliminaries, but should turn after a brief study to Chapters 2 and 3. These will be found to be simple and easy to understand, regarded as working specifications of a design procedure. Mathematical details can then be followed back through this chapter to the earlier volume as desired.

1. System models

The situation of the engineer who has to design a control system will generally fall into one of two broad categories. First the plant may already exist and be accessible for measurement. Then it is usual to inject signals at the plant inputs and to measure the response at the plant outputs. From these measurements, if the plant can be regarded as linear and time-invariant, it may be characterized by a transfer function matrix $G(s)$. The injected signals may be steps, pulses, sine-waves, pseudo-random binary signals, or may have other forms. By processing the measurements, $G(s)$ may be obtained (or at least approximated) as a rational $m \times l$ matrix, or its elements may be found numerically for certain imaginary values of s.

Usually the assumption that the plant can be regarded as linear will be

1

valid only if the input signals are sufficiently small. The assumption of time-invariance may also be valid only over restricted time intervals, for example while the plant is run steadily at one operating point. Furthermore, the data may have to be treated by statistical techniques to eliminate the effects of noise. All these questions are outside our present consideration: we assume that the plant can be characterized by $G(s)$ which is known either algebraically, or numerically for imaginary s.

The alternative situation arises when the plant is not accessible for measurement, and it is necessary to obtain a mathematical model from theoretical grounds. This involves a consideration of the physical and chemical processes occurring, and may result in algebraic, differential, partial differential, or other types of equation, or in a mixture of these. However, by standard procedures (finite differences, "lumping", etc.) it is usually possible to represent the plant by algebraic equations, ordinary differential equations, and possibly time delays (in which case we have difference-differential equations).

Again the detailed procedures by which the model is obtained are outside our present scope. We assume for the most part, however, that the plant can be described adequately by algebraic and differential equations which are time-invariant but generally nonlinear. Then by standard perturbation techniques it is possible to linearize the equations for small departures from nominal operating condition. If D is the differential operator, the resulting equations can be written

$$\left. \begin{aligned} T(D)\,\xi &= U(D)\,u \\[2mm] y &= V(D)\,\xi + W(D)\,u \end{aligned} \right\} \tag{1.1}$$

Here u is an l-vector of *inputs* (or *manipulated variables*), y is an m-vector of *outputs* (or *measured variables*) and ξ is an r-vector of *system variables*. The physical devices which allow the elements of u to affect the plant are called *actuators*, and the elements of y are derived from *transducers* (or *measuring instruments*). The matrices T, U, V, W are real polynomial matrices, that is, their entries are polynomials in D with real coefficients, and we assume $|T(D)| \not\equiv 0$.

We assume that u in (1.1) obeys conditions which ensure that it has a Laplace transform [SSMVT, Chapter 2, Section 1] and we take the Laplace transform of (1.1) with zero initial conditions. The result is

$$\left. \begin{aligned} T(s)\,\bar{\xi} &= U(s)\,\bar{u} \\[2mm] \bar{y} &= V(s)\,\bar{\xi} + W(s)\,\bar{u} \end{aligned} \right\} \tag{1.2}$$

where s is the variable of the Laplace transformation, and $\bar{\xi}$, $\bar{u}$, $\bar{y}$ are the

Laplace transforms of ξ, u, y. By eliminating ξ from (1.2) we obtain the transfer function matrix

$$G(s) = V(s)\,T^{-1}(s)\,U(s) + W(s) \qquad (1.3)$$

Besides the two broad categories described above, there are other possible intermediate situations in which the engineer may be placed. For example parts of a system may be available for measurement, and other parts may be modelled theoretically and simulated on an analogue computer. Measurements may then be taken on the analogue computer while it is connected to the remaining available components.

2. System matrices

The previous Section defines the way in which our data arise. We assume now that we are given either (1.2) or (1.3). The first objective is to bring these apparently different ways of describing a system into a common framework. We do this by defining a *system matrix* $P(s)$,

$$P(s) = \left[\begin{array}{ccc|c} I_{n-r} & & 0 & 0 \\ 0 & & T(s) & U(s) \\ \hline 0 & & -V(s) & W(s) \end{array}\right] \qquad (2.1)$$

Here n is the degree $\delta(|T(s)|)$ of $|T(s)|$, and is known as the *order* of the system. If $r \geqslant n$ (where T is $r \times r$) the identity matrix I_{n-r} in (2.1) is omitted. By defining

$$T_1 = \begin{bmatrix} I_{n-r} & 0 \\ 0 & T \end{bmatrix}, \quad U_1 = \begin{bmatrix} 0 \\ U \end{bmatrix}, \quad V_1 = (0 \quad V) \qquad (2.2)$$

we may write P in the form

$$P(s) = \begin{bmatrix} T_1(s) & U_1(s) \\ -V_1(s) & W(s) \end{bmatrix} \qquad (2.3)$$

in which T_1 is $r_1 \times r_1$ with $r_1 \geqslant n = \delta(|T_1(s)|)$. A system matrix in this form will be called a *polynomial system matrix*.

As a special case we may have

$$T(s) = sI_n - A, \quad U(s) = B, \quad V(s) = C, \quad W(s) = D(s) \qquad (2.4)$$

Here A, B, C are real matrices independent of s, and $D(s)$ is again a real polynomial matrix. The corresponding system matrix is

$$P(s) = \begin{bmatrix} sI_n - A & B \\ -C & D(s) \end{bmatrix} \tag{2.5}$$

which is said to be a *state-space system matrix*. The transfer function matrix is then

$$G(s) = C(sI_n - A)^{-1} B + D(s) \tag{2.6}$$

which if $|sI_n - A| = s^n + a_{n-1} s^{n-1} + \ldots + a_1 s + a_0$ is given more explicitly by the formula

$$\begin{aligned} G(s) = \{ & (s^{n-1} + a_{n-1} s^{n-2} + \ldots + a_1) CB \\ & + (s^{n-2} + a_{n-1} s^{n-3} + \ldots + a_2) CAB \\ & + \ldots + CA^{n-1} B\} \div (s^n + a_{n-1} s^{n-1} + \ldots + a_0) + D(s) \end{aligned} \tag{2.7}$$

The special forms of this equation when $C = I_n$ or $B = I_n$ are also important.

If $D(s) \equiv 0$, then $G(s) \to 0$ as $s \to \infty$: $G(s)$ is then said to be *strictly proper*. We normally assume that $G(s)$ is strictly proper, when the differential equations corresponding to (2.5) are simply

$$\left.\begin{aligned} \dot{x} &= Ax + Bu \\ y &= Cx \end{aligned}\right\} \tag{2.8}$$

in which x is the *state* of the system. These equations are often taken as the starting-point when describing a system, but usually a good deal of manipulation is needed to reach this form. By adopting the more general description (2.1), this manipulation can be systematized.

An important formula, which will be needed in the analysis of stability, connects the transfer function matrix $G(s)$ with the system matrix $P(s)$ giving rise to it [SSMVT, Chapter 2, Section 1]. Let the $(r+m) \times (r+l)$ polynomial system matrix

$$P(s) = \begin{bmatrix} T(s) & U(s) \\ -V(s) & W(s) \end{bmatrix} \tag{2.9}$$

give rise to

$$G(s) = V(s) T^{-1}(s) U(s) + W(s) \tag{2.10}$$

Then

$$G^{i_1, i_2, \ldots, i_q}_{j_1, j_2, \ldots, j_q} = P^{i_1, i_2, \ldots, i_q}_{j_1, j_2, \ldots, j_q}) \div P), \quad q \leqslant l, m \tag{2.11}$$

where $G^{i_1, i_2, \ldots, i_q}_{j_1, j_2, \ldots, j_q}$ is the minor formed from rows $i_1, i_2, \ldots, i_q$ and columns $j_1, j_2, \ldots, j_q$ of G; $P^{i_1, i_2, \ldots, i_q}_{j_1, j_2, \ldots, j_q})$ is the minor formed from rows $1, 2, \ldots, r$,

$r+i_1, r+i_2, ..., r+i_q$, and columns $1, 2, ..., r, r+j_1, r+j_2, ..., r+j_q$ of P; and $P) = |T|$. In particular $g_{ij} = G_j{}^i = P_j{}^i) \div |T|$ and, when $l = m$, $|G| = G_{1;2;...;m}^{1;2;...;m} = |P| \div |T|$. These formulae also apply, of course, if the polynomial matrices have the special form (2.4).

Even though our plant is described by differential equations, we may wish to restrict attention to discrete instants of time. This is particularly true when a digital computer is used for control. The variables then are sampled at discrete times $0, T, 2T, ...$ which by a change of time scale can be represented by $0, 1, 2, ...$ The computer processes the measurements and produces a control signal u which is constant between sampling times. In this way equations (2.8) are replaced by

$$\left.\begin{aligned} x_{k+1} &= A_1 x_k + B_1 u_k \\[2mm] y_k &= C x_k \end{aligned}\right\} \tag{2.12}$$

where (SSMVT, Chapter 4, Section 9)

$$\left.\begin{aligned} A_1 &= e^{AT} \\[2mm] B_1 &= \int_0^T e^{A\tau}\, d\tau\, B \end{aligned}\right\} \tag{2.13}$$

and

$$u(t) = u_k, \quad kT < t \leqslant (k+1)T \tag{2.14}$$

Under appropriate conditions, and when $x_0 = 0$, equations (2.12) may be z-transformed to give

$$\left.\begin{aligned} z\tilde{x} &= A_1 \tilde{x} + B_1 \tilde{u} \\[2mm] \tilde{y} &= C\tilde{x} \end{aligned}\right\} \tag{2.15}$$

where $\tilde{x}, \tilde{u}, \tilde{y}$ are the z-transforms of the sequences $\{x_k\}, \{u_k\}, \{y_k\}$, and $\{x_k\}$, for example, stands for the set $\{x_0, x_1, ...\}$. Corresponding to (2.15) is the system matrix

$$\tilde{P}(z) = \begin{bmatrix} zI_n - A_1 & B_1 \\[2mm] -C & 0 \end{bmatrix} \tag{2.16}$$

More generally, a discrete-time system may be represented by a system matrix

$$\tilde{P}(z) = \begin{bmatrix} \tilde{T}(z) & \tilde{U}(z) \\[2mm] -\tilde{V}(z) & \tilde{W}(z) \end{bmatrix} \tag{2.17}$$

in which as before $\tilde{T}$ is $r \times r$ with $r \geqslant n = \delta(|\tilde{T}(z)|)$.

B

All purely algebraic properties of system matrices are clearly independent of the symbol (s or z) given to the variable occurring in them. Differences arise when we interpret the algebraic results in terms of their physical significance. The significance of a given algebraic result will usually be different according to whether the system matrix arose by Laplace transformation or by z-transformation.

2.1 Generation of system matrices

Equations (1.2) can be written

$$
\begin{bmatrix} T(s) & U(s) \\ -V(s) & W(s) \end{bmatrix} \begin{bmatrix} \bar{\xi} \\ -\bar{u} \end{bmatrix} = \begin{bmatrix} 0 \\ -\bar{y} \end{bmatrix}
\tag{2.18}
$$

and provided that $r \geq n$ the matrix in (2.18) is a polynomial system matrix. When we wish to generate a system matrix for a new system, all we have to do is to write down an equation in the form of (2.18). Provided that $\bar{\xi}$ is a vector of system variables, $\bar{u}$ is the input, and $\bar{y}$ is the output, we then have ensured that the matrix is a system matrix.

Suppose, for example, that (2.18) relates to an open-loop system. Let $l = m$, so that $\bar{u}$ and $\bar{y}$ are both m-vectors. Close m loops around the system by putting

$$
\bar{u} = \bar{v} - \bar{y}
\tag{2.19}
$$

where $\bar{v}$ is an m-vector of reference inputs. The closed-loop system now satisfies the equations

$$
\left.\begin{array}{c} T(s)\,\bar{\xi} = U(s)\,\bar{u} \\ \bar{y} = V(s)\,\bar{\xi} + W(s)\,\bar{u} \\ \bar{u} = \bar{v} - \bar{y} \end{array}\right\}
\tag{2.20}
$$

or

$$
\begin{bmatrix} T(s) & U(s) & 0 & 0 \\ -V(s) & W(s) & -I_m & 0 \\ 0 & I_m & I_m & -I_m \\ \hline 0 & 0 & I_m & 0 \end{bmatrix} \begin{bmatrix} \bar{\xi} \\ -\bar{u} \\ -\bar{y} \\ \hline -\bar{v} \end{bmatrix} = \begin{bmatrix} 0 \\ 0 \\ 0 \\ \hline -\bar{y} \end{bmatrix}
\tag{2.21}
$$

which with the partitioning shown can be written

$$
\begin{bmatrix} T_1(s) & U_1(s) \\ -V_1(s) & 0 \end{bmatrix} \begin{bmatrix} \bar{\xi}_1 \\ -\bar{v} \end{bmatrix} = \begin{bmatrix} 0 \\ -\bar{y} \end{bmatrix}
\tag{2.22}
$$

This is in the form of eqn. (2.18) and provided that $|T_1(s)| \not\equiv 0$ and

$\delta(|T_1(s)|) \leqslant r_1 = r+2m$, it follows that the matrix in (2.22) or (2.21) is a polynomial system matrix for the closed-loop system.

Similar remarks apply to the generation of system matrices obtained by z-transformation.

3. Least order

Suppose that equations (1.2) are given and that there exists a polynomial matrix $Q(s)$ such that

$$
\left.\begin{array}{c}
T(s) = Q(s)\,T_1(s) \\[2mm]
U(s) = Q(s)\,U_1(s)
\end{array}\right\} \tag{3.1}
$$

Then Q is called a *common (left) divisor* of $T(s)$ and of $U(s)$. On forming $G(s)$ as in (1.3) we have

$$
G(s) = V(s)\,T_1^{-1}(s)\,Q^{-1}(s)\,Q(s)\,U_1(s)+W(s) \tag{3.2}
$$
$$
= V(s)\,T_1^{-1}(s)\,U_1(s)+W(s) \tag{3.3}
$$

If $\delta(|Q(s)|) \geqslant 1$, it follows that $G(s)$ arises not only from (1.2), in which $\delta(|T(s)|) = n$, but also from

$$
\left.\begin{array}{c}
T_1(s)\,\bar{\xi}_1 = U_1(s)\,\bar{u} \\[2mm]
\bar{y} = V(s)\,\bar{\xi}_1+W(s)\,\bar{u}
\end{array}\right\} \tag{3.4}
$$

because (3.4) gives rise to (3.3). Then since $\delta(|T(s)|) = \delta(|T_1(s)|)+\delta(|Q(s)|)$ it follows that

$$
n_1 = \delta(|T_1(s)|) < \delta(|T(s)|) = n \tag{3.5}
$$

Consequently there is a system (3.4) of lower order than (1.2) which also gives rise to $G(s)$.

In the same way, if $T(s)$ and $V(s)$ in (1.2) have a common (right) divisor $Q(s)$, with $\delta(|Q(s)|) \geqslant 1$, then again there is a system with lower order than (1.2) which also gives rise to $G(s)$.

When $T(s)$ and $U(s)$ have no common (left) divisor $Q(s)$ with $\delta(|Q(s)|) \geqslant 1$, they are said to be *relatively (left) prime*. Relative (right) primeness of $T(s)$ and $V(s)$ is defined in a similar way. Then if and only if

(i) $T(s)$ and $U(s)$ are relatively (left) prime, and

(ii) $T(s)$ and $V(s)$ are relatively (right) prime

it follows [SSMVT, Chapter 3, Section 3] that there is no system of lower order giving the same $G(s)$. The system is then said to have *least order*. The order of such a least-order system giving rise to $G(s)$ is a property of the rational matrix $G(s)$ and is written $v(G)$.

A test for relative primeness is the following. The matrices $T(s)$ and $U(s)$

are relatively (left) prime if and only if the $r \times (r+l)$ matrix

$$(T(s) \quad U(s)) \qquad (3.6)$$

has rank r for all s. If this matrix has rank less than r for some $s = s_0$, then $|T(s_0)| = 0$: consequently we need only check the rank of (3.6) at the roots of $|T(s)| = 0$. A similar test, using the matrix

$$\begin{bmatrix} T(s) \\ V(s) \end{bmatrix} \qquad (3.7)$$

shows whether $T(s)$ and $V(s)$ are relatively (right) prime.

If T, U, V, have the particular forms given in (2.4), we may use the following alternative test. The matrices $sI_n - A$ and B are relatively (left) prime if and only if the $n \times nl$ matrix

$$(B \quad AB \quad \cdots \quad A^{n-1} B) \qquad (3.8)$$

has rank n. Similarly, $sI_n - A$ and C are relatively (right) prime if and only if

$$\begin{bmatrix} C \\ CA \\ \vdots \\ CA^{n-1} \end{bmatrix} \qquad (3.9)$$

has rank n.

3.1 Decoupling zeros

The property of "least order" has been introduced above in a purely algebraic way. In Section 6 it will be linked with the properties of "controllability" and observability from which it is usually derived. For many industrial control problems, however, the algebraic treatment is more natural because it is closely related to transfer-function ideas and to the characteristic modes of the system, as will now be shown.

From the algebraic point of view, the question of least order is bound up with the possibility that zeros of a system may coincide with poles and cancel them. The idea will already be familiar for single-input single-output systems. For example if a system has

$$A = \begin{bmatrix} 1 & 0 \\ 0 & -1 \end{bmatrix}, \quad B = \begin{bmatrix} 1 \\ 1 \end{bmatrix}, \quad C = (0 \quad 1) \qquad (3.10)$$

then from (2.7)

$$G(s) = \frac{s-1}{(s-1)(s+1)} = \frac{1}{s+1} \qquad (3.11)$$

Cancellation of the pole at $s = 1$ indicates that the system does not have least order, and evaluation of (3.9) confirms this.

However, some care is needed in extending this familar idea to multivariable systems. These may have coincident poles and zeros which do not cancel when the transfer function matrix is formed: a simple example would be a plant giving

$$G(s) = \begin{bmatrix} \dfrac{s-1}{(s+1)^2} & 0 \\ 0 & \dfrac{1}{s-1} \end{bmatrix} \tag{3.12}$$

Here the zero at $s = 1$ coincides with the pole at $s = 1$, but they do not cancel. Accordingly we must distinguish those poles and zeros which cancel from those which do not.

We define the *poles of the system* given in (1.2) as the n zeros of $|T(s)|$, which we write $\eta_1, \eta_2, ..., \eta_n$. When $T(s) = sI_n - A$, as in (2.4), the poles of the system are the zeros of $|sI_n - A|$: that is, they are the eigenvalues of A. The *zeros of the system* are defined in the following way. Consider all minors of the form $P_{j_1, j_2, ..., j_q}^{i_1, i_2, ..., i_q}$ in which q has the largest value for which a nonzero minor of this form exists. The zeros of the system are the zeros (counted according to their multiplicity) of the greatest common divisor of all these minors.

On the other hand, having formed $G(s)$ we may define the *poles of G*. To do this we form all minors of all orders in G, and find their least common denominator: the zeros of this polynomial are the poles of G, which we denote by $\alpha_1, \alpha_2, ..., \alpha_q$. An alternative way of phrasing the definition is that the poles of G are all the zeros of the denominator polynomials in its McMillan form (Section 4, below). Similarly we can define the *zeros of G*. These are all the zeros of the numerator polynomials in the McMillan form of G. They will be denoted $\zeta_1, \zeta_2, ..., \zeta_z$. Notice that the zeros of G, as we have defined them, are not the same as the zeros occurring in the individual entries of G. For example

$$G(s) = \begin{bmatrix} \dfrac{1}{s} & \dfrac{1}{s^3} \\ 0 & \dfrac{1}{s} \end{bmatrix} \tag{3.13}$$

has McMillan form

$$\begin{bmatrix} \dfrac{1}{s^3} & 0 \\ 0 & s \end{bmatrix} \tag{3.14}$$

and so has a zero at $s = 0$.

When the poles of G are evaluated, it will be found that they coincide with poles of the system, but may be less in number. That is, some of the poles of the system may be lost when G is formed. Similarly, some of the zeros of the system may be lost when forming G. Moreover, the set of missing poles is the same as the set of missing zeros. These missing poles and zeros have cancelled, and they are called the *decoupling zeros* of the system. The reason for the name will be given in Section 3.2 below.

The set of decoupling zeros may be further subdivided. Any one of the decoupling zeros may be associated only with the input, or only with the output, or with both input and output. Those which are associated with the input (whether or not they are also associated with the output) are called *input decoupling (i.d.) zeros*. Similarly, those which are connected with the output (whether or not they are also connected with the input) are called *output decoupling (o.d.) zeros*. Those which are connected with both input and output are called *input–output decoupling (i.o.d.) zeros*. The set of all decoupling zeros is therefore the i.d. zeros together with the o.d. zeros less the i.o.d. zeros.

To find the i.d. zeros, we examine the $r \times (r+l)$ matrix (3.6). Those values of s, evaluated according to their multiplicity, for which this matrix has rank less than r are the i.d. zeros $\beta_1, \beta_2, ..., \beta_b$. Similarly, the o.d. zeros, $\gamma_1, \gamma_2, ...,$ γ_c are those values of s, evaluated according to their multiplicity, for which the $(r+m) \times r$ matrix (3.7) has rank less than r.

If the system has one or more i.d. zeros, it follows from what has been said above that $T(s) = Q(s)\,T_1(s)$, $U(s) = Q(s)\,U_1(s)$, where the zeros of $|Q(s)|$ are $\beta_1, \beta_2, ..., \beta_b$. The matrix $T_1(s)$ can in fact be found fairly readily by an algorithmic procedure [SSMVT, Chapter 2, Section 4]. Then we may consider the $(r+m) \times r$ matrix

$$\begin{bmatrix} T_1(s) \\ V(s) \end{bmatrix} \tag{3.15}$$

Suppose that this has rank less than r for $s = \theta_1, \theta_2, ..., \theta_r$, the zeros being evaluated according to multiplicity. Then if $\{\gamma_i\}$ is the set of o.d. zeros, it can be shown that the set $\{\theta_i\}$ is included in $\{\gamma_i\}$. The set

$$\{\delta_i\} = \{\gamma_i\} - \{\theta_i\} \tag{3.16}$$

is the set of i.o.d. zeros, d in number. In words, the i.o.d. zeros are those o.d. zeros which disappear when the i.d. zeros are removed. The set $\{\alpha_i\}$ of poles of G is given by

$$\{\alpha_i\} = \{\eta_i\} - \{\beta_i, \gamma_i\} + \{\delta_i\} \tag{3.17}$$

where $\{\eta_i\}$ is the set of poles of the system, and $\{\beta_i, \gamma_i\}$ is the set consisting of all i.d. zeros and all o.d. zeros.

EXAMPLE 3.1 The system matrix

$$P(s) = \begin{bmatrix} I_2 & 0 & 0 & | & 0 \\ 0 & s^2(s+1) & s(s+2) & | & -s \\ 0 & 0 & s+2 & | & 1 \\ \hline 0 & 0 & -1 & | & 0 \end{bmatrix} \qquad (3.18)$$

has

$$\{\eta_i\} = \{0, 0, -1, -2\}$$
$$\{\beta_i\} = \{0\}$$
$$\{\gamma_i\} = \{0, 0, -1\}$$
$$\{\theta_i\} = \{0, -1\}$$
$$\{\delta_i\} = \{0\}$$
$$\{\alpha_i\} = \{-2\}$$

The zeros of the system are $\{0, 0, -1\}$ while the transfer function is $1/(s+2)$, which has no zero and the single pole $\alpha = -2$.

From the above definitions it follows that $T(s)$ and $U(s)$ are relatively (left) prime if and only if the system has no i.d. zero. Similarly $T(s)$ and $V(s)$ are relatively (right) prime if and only if the system has no o.d. zero. The system has least order if and only if it has no decoupling zero, that is no i.d. zero and no o.d. zero.

If feedback is applied to the system (1.2) by putting $\bar{u} = \bar{v} - F\bar{y}$, where F is any real $l \times m$ matrix such that

$$\begin{bmatrix} T & U & 0 \\ -V & W & -I_m \\ 0 & I_l & F \end{bmatrix} \not\equiv 0 \qquad (3.19)$$

then the i.d., o.d. and i.o.d. zeros of the closed-loop system are precisely those of the open-loop system [compare SSMVT, Chapter 5, Section 1]. Further, the zeros of the closed-loop transfer function are precisely those of the open-loop transfer function [compare SSMVT, Chapter 5, Section 1]. From these facts it follows that the zeros of the closed-loop system are precisely those of the open-loop system. In particular, if the open-loop system has least order, then so also does the closed-loop system, and the zeros of the determinant (3.19) are then the poles of the closed-loop transfer function. More general results of this type are given in Chapters 2 and 3.

If equations (2.15) arise by sampling a system of least order, then the system (2.15) is itself of least order provided that the sampling interval T

satisfies the following condition.

Im $(\alpha_i - \alpha_j)\ T/2\pi$ is not a nonzero integer for any α_i, α_j having
Re $(\alpha_i - \alpha_j) = 0$.

3.2 Modes of the system

Consider a system in state-space form

$$\left.\begin{array}{l} \dot{x} = Ax + Bu \\[2mm] y = Cx \end{array}\right\} \tag{3.20}$$

and suppose for simplicity that all the eigenvalues η_i of A are distinct. Then
if $u = 0$, the solution of the differential equation can be written

$$x(t) = \sum_{j=1}^{n} q_j\, v_j\, e^{i\eta_j t} \tag{3.21}$$

Here the q_j are complex constants depending on the initial condition $x(0)$,
while the v_j are the corresponding eigenvectors of A. Each term $v_j\, e^{i\eta_j t}$ in the
sum (3.21) is called a *mode* of the system.

Now suppose that $x(0) = 0$, and that u can be chosen as desired on the
interval $[0, t_0]$; that is, for $0 \leqslant t \leqslant t_0$; but is zero outside this interval. Can
we choose u on this interval in such a way that the response $x(t)$ for $t > t_0$
has $q_k \neq 0$ for some given k? The answer is no if η_k is an i.d. zero of the
system, and otherwise yes. When multiple eigenvalues are admitted the
situation is less simple, but an appropriate generalization can be stated.

Returning to the situation when $u(t) = 0$ for all t, we find from (3.20) and
(3.21)

$$y(t) = \sum_{j=1}^{n} q_j\, Cv_j\, e^{i\eta_j t} \tag{3.22}$$

Given k, is the vector Cv_k zero? The answer is yes if η_k is an o.d. zero, but
otherwise no. Again a generalization can be stated when multiple eigenvalues
occur.

What has been said can be summarized (for distinct eigenvalues) in the
following way. No mode $v_k\, e^{i\eta_k t}$ can be excited from the input if η_k is an i.d.
zero: the mode is decoupled from the input. No mode $v_k\, e^{i\eta_k t}$ can be detected
at the output if η_k is an o.d. zero: the mode is decoupled from the output.
This explains the name "decoupling zero" which was given above. The i.o.d.
zeros correspond, as would be expected, to modes which are decoupled both
from input and from output.

If a mode is decoupled from the input, or from the output, it is clear that it
can make no contribution to the transfer function matrix. It is also intui-
tively obvious that the corresponding eigenvalue cannot be changed by
output feedback.

4. System transformations

Let $P(s)$ be defined by (2.5), and let $P_1(s)$ be defined in the same way with A_1, B_1, C_1 and $D_1(s)$. Then if H is a nonsingular $n \times n$ real or complex matrix, and if

$$\begin{bmatrix} H^{-1} & 0 \\ 0 & I_m \end{bmatrix} P(s) \begin{bmatrix} H & 0 \\ 0 & I_l \end{bmatrix} = P_1(s) \tag{4.1}$$

we say that P and P_1 are *system similar*. Two matrices P and P_1 related in this way have the same order, the same i.d., o.d. and i.o.d. zeros, and give the same $G(s)$. The transformation (4.1) amounts to a change of basis (that is, of coordinate axes) in the state space.

More generally, let $P(s)$ be a polynomial system matrix,

$$P(s) = \begin{bmatrix} T(s) & U(s) \\ -V(s) & W(s) \end{bmatrix} \tag{4.2}$$

as defined above. Let $P_1(s)$ be another polynomial system matrix with submatrices $T_1(s)$, $U_1(s)$, $V_1(s)$ and $W_1(s)$. Then if $P(s)$ and $P_1(s)$ are related by

$$\begin{bmatrix} M(s) & 0 \\ X(s) & I_m \end{bmatrix} P(s) \begin{bmatrix} N(s) & Y(s) \\ 0 & I_l \end{bmatrix} = P_1(s) \tag{4.3}$$

we say that P and P_1 are *strictly system equivalent*. In (4.3), $M(s)$, $N(s)$, $X(s)$ and $Y(s)$ are polynomial matrices, respectively $r \times r$, $r \times r$, $m \times r$, $r \times l$. In addition $M(s)$ and $N(s)$ are *unimodular*; that is, their determinants $|M(s)|$ and $|N(s)|$ are nonzero and independent of s. Two matrices P and P_1 related by (4.3) have the same r, the same n, the same i.d., o.d. and i.o.d. zeros, and give rise to the same $G(s)$.

The transformation of strict system equivalence can be generated by the following *elementary operations*.

(i) Multiply any one of the first r rows (resp. columns) by a nonzero constant.

(ii) Add a multiple, by a polynomial, of any one of the first r rows (resp. columns) to any other row (resp. column).

(iii) Interchange any two among the first r rows (resp. columns).

A fundamental result is the following [SSMVT, Chapter 2, Section 3]. If P and P_1 in (4.3) happen to be in state-space form, then the fact that they are strictly system equivalent implies that they are system similar. Conversely (and trivially) if P and P_1 are system similar they are also strictly system equivalent. This shows that strict system equivalence is a natural generalization of system similarity.

A second fundamental result [SSMVT, Chapter 3, Section 3] is the following. Let P and P_1 be two $(r+m) \times (r+l)$ polynomial system matrices having least order. Then P and P_1 are strictly system equivalent if and only if they give the same $G(s)$. If P and P_1 are in state-space form (still with least order) then by the previous paragraph it follows that they are system similar if and only if they give the same $G(s)$.

4.1 McMillan form

Strict system equivalence leaves $G(s)$ unchanged. Another interesting transformation is defined by

$$G_1(s) = M(s)\, G(s)\, N(s) \tag{4.4}$$

where $M(s)$ and $N(s)$ are unimodular polynomial matrices. For convenience we assume $G(s)$ to be square, $m \times m$, and we achieve this if necessary by augmenting it with zeros. The transformation (4.4) does not leave G invariant. A standard form for G under the transformation is the McMillan form,

$$G_1(s) = \begin{bmatrix} \dfrac{\varepsilon_1(s)}{\psi_1(s)} & 0 & \cdots & 0 & 0 & \cdots & 0 \\[2ex] 0 & \dfrac{\varepsilon_2(s)}{\psi_2(s)} & \cdots & 0 & 0 & \cdots & 0 \\[1ex] \vdots & \vdots & & \vdots & \vdots & & \vdots \\[1ex] 0 & 0 & \cdots & \dfrac{\varepsilon_p(s)}{\psi_p(s)} & 0 & \cdots & 0 \\[2ex] 0 & 0 & \cdots & 0 & 0 & \cdots & 0 \\[0.5ex] \vdots & \vdots & & \vdots & \vdots & & \vdots \\[0.5ex] 0 & 0 & \cdots & 0 & 0 & \cdots & 0 \end{bmatrix} \tag{4.5}$$

in which the $\varepsilon_i(s)$ and $\psi_i(s)$ are polynomials, $\varepsilon_i(s)$ and $\psi_i(s)$ are relatively prime, $\varepsilon_i(s)$ divides $\varepsilon_{i+1}(s)$, $\varepsilon_{i+2}(s)$, ..., $\varepsilon_p(s)$, and $\psi_i(s)$ divides $\psi_{i-1}(s)$, $\psi_{i-2}(s)$, ..., $\psi_1(s)$. The zeros of the $\varepsilon_i(s)$, taken all together, are the zeros of G as defined in Section 3.1. The zeros of the $\psi_i(s)$, taken all together, are the poles of G, which were also defined in Section 3.1. Note that although $\varepsilon_i(s)$ and $\psi_i(s)$ are relatively prime, $\varepsilon_i(s)$ and $\psi_j(s)$ may have a common factor when $i > j$.

5. Reduction to least order

When the plant description arises in the form of a transfer function (usually by measurement as in Section 1) we may wish to obtain from this a description in terms of differential equations, which for simplicity we usually wish to have in state-space form, equation (2.8). For example these equations are the most convenient point of departure if we wish to compute the time-response of a system.

Given a strictly proper $G(s)$ it is very easy to write down state-space equations in the following way. We first find the monic common denominators $d^{(i)}(s)$ of the rows of $G(s)$, and write

$$G(s) = \begin{bmatrix} g^{(1)}(s)/d^{(1)}(s) \\ g^{(2)}(s)/d^{(2)}(s) \\ \vdots \\ g^{(m)}(s)/d^{(m)}(s) \end{bmatrix} \tag{5.1}$$

where the $g^{(i)}(s)$ are polynomial row vectors. We write the polynomials $d^{(i)}(s)$ in full

$$d^{(i)}(s) = s^{p_i} + d^{(i)}_{p_i-1} s^{p_i-1} + \ldots + d_0^{(i)} \tag{5.2}$$

and similarly the polynomial vectors $g^{(i)}(s)$ are

$$g^{(i)}(s) = g^{(i)}_{p_i-1} s^{p_i-1} + g^{(i)}_{p_i-2} s^{p_i-2} + \ldots + g_0^{(i)} \tag{5.3}$$

in which the $g_j^{(i)}$ are real row vectors. Then a state-space system matrix giving rise to $G(c)$ is

$$P(s) = \left[\begin{array}{cccc|c} sI_{p_1} - A_1 & 0 & \cdots & 0 & B_1 \\ 0 & sI_{p_2} - A_2 & \cdots & 0 & B_2 \\ \vdots & \vdots & & \vdots & \vdots \\ 0 & 0 & \cdots & sI_{pm} - A_m & B_m \\ \hline -C_1 & -C_1 & \cdots & -C_m & 0 \end{array} \right] \tag{5.4}$$

in which the A_i are *companion matrices*,

$$A_i = \begin{bmatrix} 0 & 0 & \cdots & 0 & 0 & -d_0^{(i)} \\ 1 & 0 & \cdots & 0 & 0 & -d_1^{(i)} \\ \vdots & \vdots & & \vdots & \vdots & \vdots \\ 0 & 0 & \cdots & 1 & 0 & -d^{(i)}_{p_i-2} \\ 0 & 0 & \cdots & 0 & 1 & -d^{(i)}_{p_i-1} \end{bmatrix} \tag{5.5}$$

while the matrices B_i are

$$B_i = \begin{bmatrix} g_0^{(i)} \\ g_1^{(i)} \\ \vdots \\ g^{(i)}_{p_i-1} \end{bmatrix} \tag{5.6}$$

and C_i has every element zero except for a 1 in position (i, p_i).

Equation (5.4) gives the state-space equations at once: a similar development can be made in terms of the columns of $G(s)$, and may sometimes be simpler. Though we can in this way easily generate state-space equations for the system, they do not generally have least order, and most of the computing effort is required to go from (5.4) to a least-order system. This effort is justified chiefly by the reduction of further effort to which it leads in the subsequent use of (5.4).

Most methods available for reduction of a system to least order are too slow for interactive use on a computer. The following method is relatively fast, and can be used interactively.

The system matrix in (5.4) has no o.d. zero. It usually has i.d. zeros, and these can be eliminated by the following algorithm. We first define two types of operation on P.

(i) Interchange rows p, q in P to give P_1, where $\alpha \leqslant p \leqslant \beta, \alpha \leqslant q \leqslant \beta$, and α, β are specified integers between 1 and $n = p_1 + p_2 ... + p_m$. Follow this immediately by interchanging columns p, q in P_1 to give P_2.

(ii) Add to row p in P a multiple by γ of row q to give P_1, where $p \leqslant q \leqslant n$ and γ is a real number. Follow this immediately by subtracting from column q in P_1 a multiple by γ of column p to give P_2.

In terms of these operations the required algorithm is as follows [SSMVT, Chapter 2, Section 7]

(1) Set indices $i = 0, j = 0$ and go to (2).

(2) If every element in positions $(1, n+l-i)$, $(2, n+l-i)$, ..., $(n-j, n+l-i)$ is zero, go to (6). Otherwise go to (3).

(3) Bring a nonzero element to position $(n-j, n+l-i)$ by operation (i) with $\alpha = 1, \beta = n-j$. Go to (4).

(4) By operations of type (ii) add such multiples of the element in position $(n-j, n+l-i)$ to the elements in positions $(1, n+l-i)$, $(2, n+l-i)$,..., $(n-j-1, n+l-i)$ that these last are reduced to zero. Go to (5).

(5) Increase i by 1 and j by 1. If $j = n$ the process terminates. If $j < n$, go to (2).

(6) Increase i by 1. If $i-j = l$ the process terminates. If $i-j < l$, go to (2).

When this process terminates, let $j = n-b$. Then $P(s)$ will have taken the form

$$\begin{bmatrix} sI_b - A_{11} & 0 & | & 0 \\ -A_{21} & sI_{n-b} - A_{22} & | & B_2 \\ \underline{\hspace{1cm}} & \underline{\hspace{1cm}} & | & \underline{\hspace{1cm}} \\ -C_1 & -C_2 & | & 0 \end{bmatrix} \tag{5.7}$$

and a least-order system matrix giving $G(s)$ is

$$\begin{bmatrix} sI_{n-b} - A_{22} & B_2 \\ -C_2 & 0 \end{bmatrix} \tag{5.8}$$

The procedure given resembles the standard procedures of numerical analysis for Gaussian elimination or (more closely) for reduction to Hessenberg form. It can be modified to include *partial pivoting* if required. To do this, replace (3) by:

(3a) Find the element with greatest absolute value among those in positions $(1, n+l-i)$, $(2, n+l-i)$, ..., $(n-j, n+l-i)$ and bring this to position $(n-j, n+l-i)$ by operation (i).

6. Controllability and observability

The controllability of a plant, in engineering terms, expresses in some way the ease or difficulty which it offers to our efforts to control it. Different aspects of this idea have been isolated and given mathematical expression. Unfortunately this process has introduced some confusion. We shall distinguish three types of controllability [SSMVT, Chapter, 5 Section 2]. Systems described by differential equations and those described by difference equations must now be considered separately.

For the system described by equations (2.8) we make the following definitions:

(i) The system is pointwise-state controllable, or *controllable (p.s.)* for short, if given any two states c_0 and c_1, there exists a time $t_1 > 0$ and a control u defined on $[0, t_1]$ which takes the state from $x(0) = c_0$ to $x(t_1) = c_1$.

(ii) The system is functionally controllable, or *controllable (f)*, if given any suitable vector y of putput functions defined for $t > 0$, there exists a vector u of inputs defined for $t > 0$ which generates the output vector y from the initial condition $x(0) = 0$. Here a "suitable" vector y is one which is sufficiently smooth to be generated without delta functions in u, and which has a Laplace transform. These conditions on y are a matter of convenience, and are given in mathematical form in SSMVT [Chapter 5, Section 2.5].

(iii) The system is *controllable (l)* if it is controllable (f) and if in addition all the zeros of $G(s)$ lie in the open left half-plane. The zeros of $G(s)$ were defined in Section 3.1.

These different kinds of controllability are appropriate in different circumstances. Controllability (p.s.) is appropriate in rocket guidance problems, and in some problems of batch-processing or start-up or grade-change in industrial plants. Controllability (f) is appropriate for the usual servo following problem, or for the regulator problem of industrial control in which the elements of the vector y must approximate to constant desired output values. Controllability (l) ensures that difficulties associated with non-minimum phase response do not arise [Chapter 2, Section 10.1; also SSMVT, Chapter 5, Section 2.6].

It is important to note that controllability (p.s.) is usually called just "controllability" in the literature. This leads to a presumption that it implies controllability (f), which is not true. Controllability (p.s.) and controllability (f) are distinct properties, and either can exist without the other [SSMVT, Chapter 5, Section 2.5].

For the discrete-time system of equation (2.11) the definitions take the following forms:

(i) The system is *controllable* (*p.s.*) if given any two states c_0 and c_1, there exists a positive integer p and a sequence $u_0, u_1, ..., u_{p-1}$ such that x is taken from $x_0 = c_0$ to $x_p = c_1$.

(ii) The system is *controllable* (*f*), if given any suitable output sequence $y_0, y_1, y_2, ...$ there exists a sequence $u_0, u_1, u_2, ...$ which generates the output sequence from the initial condition $x_0 = 0$. A "suitable" sequence $y_0, y_1, y_2, ...$ is now one which does not ask for a nonzero output in less time than the inherent time delay of the system, and which also has a z-transform [SSMVT, Chapter 5, Section 2.5].

(iii) The system is *controllable* (*l*) if it is controllable (f) and none of the zeros of $\tilde{G}(z)$ lies on or outside the unit circle.

Tests for controllability (p.s.) or controllability (f) are essentially the same for systems (2.8) and (2.12).

(i) A system is controllable (p.s.) if and only if it has no i.d. zero. This leads to algebraic tests as in (3.6) and (3.8).

(ii) A system having $l = m$ is controllable (f) if and only if its transfer function matrix $G(s)$ or $\tilde{G}(z)$ is nonsingular: that is if $|G(s)| \not\equiv 0$ or $|\tilde{G}(z)| \not\equiv 0$.

The system (2.8) is called *observable* if there exists a $t_1 > 0$ such that given u and y on the interval $[0, t_1]$ it is possible to deduce $x(0)$. The system (2.12) is called observable if there exists an integer $p > 0$ such that given $u_0, u_1, ..., u_{p-1}$ and $y_0, y_1, ..., y_{p-1}$ it is possible to deduce x_0. In either case a necessary and sufficient condition for observability is that the system has no o.d. zero.

Again confusion sometimes arises. Even when a system is unobservable, it is possible to obtain an asymptotically correct estimate of the state, provided that the system is stable. It is not possible, for an unobservable system, to compute the state accurately from observations on a finite interval, nor is it possible to construct an asymptotic observer which has its poles in arbitrary locations [SSMVT, Chapter 5, Section 3].

6.1 Decomposition of the state space

By an extension of the procedure given in Section 5, we may reduce a system matrix

$$P(s) = \begin{bmatrix} sI_n - A & B \\ -C & D(s) \end{bmatrix} \qquad (6.1)$$

to the form [SSMVT, Chapter 2, Section 7.1]

$$\begin{bmatrix} sI_d - A_{11} & -A_{12} & 0 & 0 & | & 0 \\ 0 & sI_{b-d} - A_{22} & 0 & 0 & | & 0 \\ -A_{31} & -A_{32} & sI_{c-d} - A_{33} & -A_{34} & | & B_3 \\ 0 & -A_{42} & 0 & sI_a - A_{44} & | & B_4 \\ \hline 0 & -C_2 & 0 & -C_4 & | & D(s) \end{bmatrix} \qquad (6.2)$$

The state vector can then be written

$$x = \begin{bmatrix} x_1 \\ 0 \\ 0 \\ 0 \end{bmatrix} + \begin{bmatrix} 0 \\ x_2 \\ 0 \\ 0 \end{bmatrix} + \begin{bmatrix} 0 \\ 0 \\ x_3 \\ 0 \end{bmatrix} + \begin{bmatrix} 0 \\ 0 \\ 0 \\ x_4 \end{bmatrix} \qquad (6.3)$$

where the partitioning conforms with the partitioning in (6.2). The subspaces spanned by the four vectors on the right-hand side of (6.3) are then called respectively:

uncontrollable and unobservable   (dimension d)
uncontrollable but observable   (dimension $b-d$)
controllable but unobservable   (dimension $c-d$)
controllable and observable   (dimension $a = n-b-c+d$)

The number b of i.d. zeros of a system is equal to the dimension of the uncontrollable subspace in any such decomposition of its state space. The number c of o.d. zeros similarly is equal to the dimension of the unobservable subspace, and the number d of i.o.d. zeros is equal to the dimension of the subspace which is both uncontrollable and unobservable [SSMVT, Chapter 5, Sections 2, 3]. Moreover, the values of the i.d., o.d. and i.o.d. zeros give the eigenvalues associated with these subspaces.

The number b of i.d. zeros of $P(s)$, equation (6.1), is equal to the *rank defect* of the matrix

$$(B \quad AB \quad \ldots \quad A^{n-1} B) \qquad (6.4)$$

that is, to the number by which the rank of this matrix falls short of its maximum possible value n. Similarly the number c of o.d. zeros is the rank defect of

$$\begin{bmatrix} C \\ CA \\ \vdots \\ CA^{n-1} \end{bmatrix} \qquad\qquad (6.5)$$

7. Stability

There are a number of possible ways in which stability may be defined. The commonest is *Liapunov stability*. This is applicable to differential equations or difference equations in the form

$$\dot{x}(t) = f[x(t), t]; \quad f[0, t] \equiv 0 \qquad\qquad (7.1)$$

or

$$x_{k+1} = f_k[x_k]; \quad f_k[0] \equiv 0 \qquad\qquad (7.2)$$

That is, there is no arbitrarily manipulated input u, no output y, and the equations are in state-space form with the origin as an equilibrium point. It is assumed that f in (7.1) obeys conditions which ensure that there is a unique solution $\phi(t; c, t_0)$ starting from every $x(t_0) = c$ with $\|c\| \leqslant R$, and that every such solution can be carried forward to any $t > t_0$.

Roughly speaking, Liapunov stability requires that solutions of (7.1) or (7.2) starting in a small enough neighbourhood of the origin remain in some other neighbourhood of the origin for all later time. Specifically, the solution $x = 0$ of (7.1) is *stable* if, given any t_0 and any $\varepsilon > 0$, there exists a $\delta(\varepsilon, t_0) > 0$ such that $\|x(t_0)\| < \delta$ implies $\|x(t)\| < \varepsilon$ for all $t \geqslant t_0$. Here $\|x\|$ is the Euclidean norm,

$$\|x\| = \sqrt{\{x_1^2 + x_2^2 + \ldots + x_n^2\}} \qquad\qquad (7.3)$$

In addition we may require that solutions starting near the origin tend to the origin as $t \to \infty$. Specifically, the solution $x = 0$ of (7.1) is *asymptotically stable* if it is stable and if in addition there is an $r(t_0) > 0$ such that $\|x(t_0)\| < r$ implies $\|x(t)\| \to 0$ as $t \to \infty$. The solution $x = 0$ is *asymptotically stable in the large* (or *globally asymptotically stable*) if the condition $\|x(t_0)\| < r$ can be dropped. These definitions extend in an obvious way to (7.2).

The solution $x = 0$ is *uniformly stable* if $\delta(\varepsilon, t_0)$ in the definition of stability can be chosen independent of t_0. This solution is *uniformly bounded* if there exists a bound $B(x_0)$, independent of t_0, such that if $x(t_0) = x_0$, then $\|x(t)\| < B$ for all $t \geqslant t_0$. The solution $x = 0$ is *uniformly asymptotically stable in the large* if it is uniformly stable, uniformly bounded, and every solution converges uniformly to 0 as $t \to \infty$.

For a system with an input and an output, a quite different type of stability can be defined. Let

$$\left.\begin{array}{l} \dot{x}(t) = f[x(t), t; u(t)]; \quad f[0, t; 0] \equiv 0 \\[8pt] y(t) = g[x(t), t; u(t)] \end{array}\right\} \tag{7.4}$$

where u is an l-vector of input functions and y is an m-vector of output functions. We require as usual that u should satisfy suitable conditions ensuring that a solution of (7.4) exists [Rosenbrock and Storey, 1970, Chapter 6]. This system is said to be *input–output stable* if, given any $x(t_0) = c$ and any $M_1 > 0$, there exists an $M_2(c, M_1)$ such that

$$\|u(t)\| < M_1 \tag{7.5}$$

for all $t \geqslant t_0$ implies

$$\|y(t)\| < M_2 \tag{7.6}$$

for all $t \geqslant t_0$, where y is the output obtained by solving (7.4) with $x(t_0) = c$ and with the given u:

$$y(t) = g[x(t; c, t_0), t; u(t)] \tag{7.7}$$

The system (7.4) has $x = 0$ as an equilibrium state. The *equilibrium state* is said to be *input–output stable* if (7.5) implies (7.6) when $x(t_0)$ is equal to the equilibrium state. This is clearly a weaker condition than input–output stability of the system, for which we require that (7.5) implies (7.6) for any $x(t_0)$.

Input–output stability guarantees that we can find a bound for the output knowing only a bound for the input. There is a weaker variant called *bounded input–bounded output stability*, in which the bound for the output may depend on the particular input applied. These ideas again carry over to systems governed by difference equations.

In general the relation between asymptotic stability and input–output stability is complicated [Willems, 1970]. Fortunately the situation is much simpler for systems which are linear and time-invariant. We have the following result [Willems, 1970, Chapter 3].

THEOREM 7.1.   The system

$$\left.\begin{array}{l} \dot{x} = Ax + Bu \\[8pt] y = Cx + Du \end{array}\right\} \tag{7.8}$$

is asymptotically stable and input–output stable if every eigenvalue of A lies in the open half-plane. Conversely every eigenvalue of A lies in the open left half-plane if (7.8) is asymptotically stable, or if (7.8) has least order and is input–output stable.

Notice that when we say (7.8) is asymptotically stable we mean that the equilibrium state $x = 0$ of $\dot{x} = Ax$ is asymptotically stable. If y depends also on derivatives of the output, say

$$y = Cx + D_0 u + D_1 \frac{du}{dt} + \dots + D_p \frac{d^p u}{dt^p} \qquad (7.9)$$

then references to asymptotic stability in the theorem are unaffected, because this type of stability does not involve y. References to input–output stability require amendment, however, because the derivative of a bounded function need not be bounded.

For the system

$$\left.\begin{array}{c} x_{k+1} = Ax_k + Bu_k \\[2mm] y_k = Cx_k + Du_k \end{array}\right\} \qquad (7.10)$$

Theorem 7.1 is true with "open left half-plane" replaced by "open disc of unit radius".

8. Complex functions

We collect here a few results which are required later. If f is a complex-valued function of the complex variable s, then f has a derivative $f'(s_0)$ at s_0 if the limit

$$\lim_{s \to s_0} \frac{f(s) - f(s_0)}{s - s_0} \qquad (8.1)$$

exists and is finite, and the limit is then equal to $f'(s_0)$. If f is defined on an open set S in the complex plane, and if f' exists everywhere in S, then f is said to be *analytic on* S. If f is analytic in some neighbourhood of s_0, it is said to be *analytic at* s_0.

THEOREM 8.1. If f is analytic inside and on the boundary of the annulus $r \leqslant |s - s_0| \leqslant R$, then $f(s)$ is given, for any s inside the annulus, by the *Laurent series*

$$f(s) = \sum_{n=0}^{\infty} a_n (s - s_0)^n + \sum_{n=1}^{\infty} b_n (s - s_0)^{-n} \qquad (8.2)$$

Proof. See Rosenbrock and Storey, 1970, Chapter 7, Section 4.

Let R now be chosen, if possible, so that f is analytic everywhere inside and on R, except perhaps at s_0. If f is analytic at s_0, every b_i is zero and the Laurent series is called a *Taylor series*. Then if $a_0, a_1, \dots, a_{m-1}$ are zero, but $a_m \neq 0$ for some $m > 0$, f is said to have a *zero of order m* at s_0. If f is not analytic at s_0, and if in the Laurent series $b_m \neq 0$ but $b_{m+1}, b_{m+2}, \dots$ are all zero, then f is said to have a *pole of order m* at s_0. A *closed elementary contour* C is a curve, made up of straight-line segments and of circular arcs, which does not cross itself but divides the complex plane into two regions, interior and exterior to the contour.

THEOREM 8.2 (*"Principle of the argument"*). Let f be analytic inside and on a closed elementary contour C, except for a finite number of poles inside C, and have no zero on C. As s goes once clockwise round C let $f(s)$ trace out the closed curve Γ. Then Γ encircles the origin $Z-P$ times clockwise, where Z is the number of zeros of f inside C and P is the number of poles of f inside C (each pole or zero of order m being counted m times).

Proof. See SSMVT, Chapter 1, Section 8.

THEOREM 8.3. Let f and g be two functions, each analytic inside and on a closed elementary contour C, except for a finite number of poles inside C. Let g have no zero on C; and let $|g(s)| > |f(s)|$ on C. Let g and $f+g$ have respectively Z_g, Z_{f+g} zeros inside C and P_g, P_{f+g} poles inside C. Then $Z_{f+g} - P_{f+g} = Z_g - P_g$.

Proof. Let the function

$$\psi(s) = \frac{f(s)+g(s)}{g(s)} = 1 + \frac{f(s)}{g(s)} \qquad (8.3)$$

map C into Γ. Then ψ has no ~~place~~ ^poles^ on C, and because

$$\left| \frac{f(s)}{g(s)} \right| < 1 \qquad (8.4)$$

for all s on C, ψ has no zero on C. By Theorem 8.2, the number of encirclements of the origin by Γ is $Z_{f+g} + P_g - (P_{f+g} + Z_g)$. But by (8.4), Γ cannot encircle the origin, which completes the proof.

COROLLARY (*Rouché's theorem*). If f and g are analytic inside C, g and $f+g$ have the same number of zeros inside C.

If f is analytic on the open region S, it maps S *conformally* into the complex plane. That is, the mapping preserves the sign and magnitude of the angle at which any two smooth curves in S intersect. For let t be a parameter, and let the two curves be $s = g(t)$, $s = h(t)$, meeting at $t = 0$. Where they meet the curves have direction respectively dg/dt, dh/dt, each evaluated at $t = 0$. The curves map into $f[g(t)]$, $f[h(t)]$ having direction at the common point

$f[g(0)] = f[h(0)]$ respectively

$$f'[g(0)]\frac{dg}{dt}\bigg|_{t=0} \quad \text{and} \quad f'[h(0)]\frac{dh}{dt}\bigg|_{t=0} \tag{8.5}$$

That is, the direction in each case is related to the original direction by the same complex factor $f'[g(0)] = f'[h(0)]$.

The following theorem belongs in the theory of the Laplace transform, through we prove only a rather special case.

THEOREM 8.4.   Let the system

$$\dot{x} = Ax + bu \tag{8.6}$$
$$y = cx$$

where b is a column vector and c a row vector, be asymptotically stable and have transfer function $g(s)$. Then when $u = \alpha U(t)$, with α a real constant and $U(t)$ the unit step, the output y tends as $t \to \infty$ to the value $g(0)\alpha$.

Proof. Because the system is asymptotically stable, every eigenvalue of A lies in the open left half plane, whence A is nonsingular and the equation

$$Ax + b\alpha = 0 \tag{8.7}$$

has the unique solution

$$x = A^{-1}b\alpha \tag{8.8}$$

That is, the differential equation has a unique equilibrium. It follows from the asymptotic stability and linearity that solutions starting from all initial values tend to this equilibrium. Hence y tends to $cA^{-1}b\alpha = g(0)\alpha$.

9. Matrices and determinants

A few of the less well-known results are given here for reference. They hold unless otherwise stated for matrices over any field: specifically the fields of real numbers, complex numbers and rational functions.

THEOREM 9.1 (*Laplace's expansion* of a determinant).   The determinant of the $n \times n$ matrix A can be written

$$|A| = \sum_j (-1)^{i_1 + i_2 + \cdots + i_r + j_1 + j_2 + \cdots + j_r} A_{j_1, j_2, \ldots, j_r}^{i_1, i_2, \ldots, i_r} A_{j_1', j_2', \ldots, j_{n-r}'}^{i_1', i_2', \ldots, i_{n-r}'} \tag{9.1}$$

where $i_1 < i_2 \ldots < i_r$ and $i_1' < i_2' < \ldots < i_{n-r}'$ form a complete set of indices $1, 2, \ldots, n$; $j_1 < j_2 < \ldots < j_r$, and $j_1' < j_2' < \ldots < j_{n-r}'$ form another such set; $A_{j_1, j_2, \ldots, j_r}^{i_1, i_2, \ldots, i_r}$ is the minor formed from rows $i_1, i_2, \ldots, i_r$, and columns

$j_1, j_2, ..., j_r$ of A; and the summation in (9.1) extends over all choices of the r indices $j_1, j_2, ..., j_r$.

Proof. See SSMVT, Chapter 1, Section 1.

THEOREM 9.2.   The partitioned square matrix

$$P = \begin{bmatrix} T & U \\ -V & W \end{bmatrix} \qquad (9.2)$$

in which T is square and $|T| \neq 0$, has determinant

$$|P| = |T||VT^{-1}U + W| \qquad (9.3)$$

Proof. See SSMVT, Chapter 1, Section 1.

THEOREM 9.3 (*Gershgorin's theorem*).   The eigenvalues of an $m \times m$ complex matrix Z lie in the union of the discs

$$|s - z_{ii}| \leqslant \sum_{\substack{j=1 \\ j \neq i}}^{m} |z_{ij}|, \quad i = 1, 2, ..., m \qquad (9.4)$$

and also in the union of the discs

$$|s - z_{ii}| \leqslant \sum_{\substack{j=1 \\ j \neq i}}^{m} |z_{ji}|, \quad i = 1, 2, ..., m \qquad (9.5)$$

Proof. See Rosenbrock and Storey, 1970, Chapter 5, Section 8.

COLOLLARY.   If the intersection of the two sets of discs (9.4), (9.5) excludes the origin, $|Z| \neq 0$.

Proof. $|Z| = \lambda_1 \lambda_2 ... \lambda_m$, where the λ_i are the eigenvalues of Z.

THEOREM 9.4.   Let $Z(s)$ be an $m \times m$ rational matrix and let C be a closed elementary contour having on it no pole of $z_{ii}(s)$, $i = 1, 2, ..., m$. Let there exist $\varepsilon > 0$ such that for each s on C either

$$|z_{ii}(s)| - \sum_{\substack{j=1 \\ j \neq i}}^{m} |z_{ij}(s)| > \varepsilon, \quad i = 1, 2, ..., m \qquad (9.6)$$

or

$$|z_{ii}(s)| - \sum_{\substack{j=1 \\ j \neq i}}^{m} |z_{ji}(s)| > \varepsilon, \quad i = 1, 2, ..., m \qquad (9.7)$$

Let $z_{ii}(s)$ map C into Γ_i, $i = 1, 2, ..., m$, and let $|Z(s)|$ map C into Γ_Z. Let Γ_i encircle the origin N_i times, and let Γ_Z encircle the origin N_Z times (all encirclements being clockwise). Then

$$N_z = \sum_{i=1}^{m} N_i \tag{9.8}$$

Proof. By (9.6) or (9.7), there is no pole of $z_{ij}(s)$ on C, $i, j = 1, 2, ..., m$, nor is there any zero of $z_{ii}(s)$ on C, $i = 1, 2, ..., m$. Moreover, by Gershgorin's theorem there is no zero of $|Z(s)|$ on C. Let $Z(\alpha, s)$ be the matrix having

$$\left.\begin{aligned}z_{ii}(\alpha, s) &= z_{ii}(s) \\[1em] z_{ij}(\alpha, s) &= \alpha z_{ij}(s), \quad j \neq i\end{aligned}\right\} \tag{9.9}$$

where $z_{ii}(s), z_{ij}(s)$ are the elements of $Z(s)$ and $0 \leqslant \alpha \leqslant 1$. Then every element of $Z(\alpha, s)$ is finite on C, and so therefore is $|Z(\alpha, s)|$. Consider the function

$$\beta(\alpha, s) = \frac{|Z(\alpha, s)|}{\displaystyle\prod_{i=1}^{m} z_{ii}(s)} \tag{9.10}$$

which is finite for $0 \leqslant \alpha \leqslant 1$ and all s on C, and which satisfies $\beta(0, s) = 1$. Let $\beta(1, s)$ map C into Γ. For given s on C, $\beta(\alpha, s)$ defines a continuous curve $\gamma(s)$ joining the point $\beta(0, s) = 1$ to the point on Γ corresponding to s. As s goes round C, $\gamma(s)$ sweeps out a region of the complex plane and returns at last to its original position.

Suppose, contrary to what is to be proved, that Γ encircles the origin. Then the region swept out by $\gamma(s)$ as s goes round C must include the origin. That is, there is some α in the interval $[0, 1]$ and some s on C for which $\beta(\alpha, s) = 0$. But the z_{ii} are all finite on C and so $|Z(\alpha, s)| = 0$. By Gershgorin's theorem and (9.6) or (9.7) this is impossible. Then from (9.10) the number of encirclements of the origin by Γ is

$$0 = N_Z - N_1 - N_2 - ... - N_m$$

which proves the theorem.

THEOREM 9.5. Let the $m \times m$ complex matrix Z satisfy

$$\sum_{\substack{k=1 \\ k \neq i}}^{m} |z_{ik}| = \theta_i |z_{ii}| \quad (\text{resp. } \sum_{\substack{k=1 \\ k \neq i}}^{m} |z_{ki}| = \theta_i |z_{ii}|) \quad \text{where } 0 \leqslant \theta_i < 1$$

for $i = 1, 2, ..., m$. Then Z has an inverse $\hat{Z} = Z^{-1}$ satisfying

$$|\hat{z}_{ji}| \leqslant \theta_j |\hat{z}_{ii}| \quad (\text{resp. } |\hat{z}_{ij}| \leqslant \theta_j |\hat{z}_{ii}|) \tag{9.11}$$

for $i = 1, 2, ..., m$ and $j = 1, 2, ..., i-1, i+1, ..., m$.

Proof. See SSMVT, Chapter 5, Section 6.1.

THEOREM 9.6 (*Ostrowski's theorem*). Let Z satisfy the conditions of Theorem 9.5 and write

$$\phi_i = \max_{k \neq i} \theta_k \qquad (9.12)$$

Then

$$|z_{ii} - \hat{z}_{ii}^{-1}| \leqslant \theta_i \phi_i |z_{ii}| \qquad (9.13)$$

Proof. See SSMVT, Chapter 5, Section 6.1.

Chapter 2

Single-input single-output systems

1. Introduction

As a preparation for Chapter 3, in which multivariable systems are discussed, this chapter deals with single-input single-output control systems. As much of the material is well known, the treatment will be brief, but more attention than usual will be given to stability and the effects of structure. These become particularly important when we progress to multivariable systems.

The chief difference between this account and earlier ones is, however, that we assume a computer to be available with graphical display. This changes our viewpoint very greatly, as will be explained.

1.1 Pencil, paper and computers

The traditional methods of servo theory grew out of the work of Nyquist, Bode, Evans and many others, and had reached their final form by about 1960. The methods were therefore adapted to hand calculation, and they had two functions.

The first function was to provide insight and to guide the design procedure. This was accomplished chiefly by graphical techniques such as the Bode diagram, Nyquist diagram, root locus, etc.

The second function was to give simple approximate methods suitable for pencil-and-paper investigations, which would avoid the heavy computing load of a direct analysis. For example, calculation of time responses was almost always avoided by the use of approximate correlations between time response and frequency response, or between time response and pole- and zero-locations.

Both functions were implicit in all the usual techniques, though some were aimed more at one function or more at the other. Mitrovic's method for example [Thaler and Brown, 1960] is chiefly a graphical means for finding the roots of a polynomial.

With the advent of large-scale digital computers, the second function of these methods is now largely obsolete. If we wish to know the time response of a system, the best approach is to compute it by standard numerical techniques. The same applies to finding roots of polynomials. The only exception is that for instructional purposes it is useful to go through a few very simple examples by hand. Even then, however, students will soon reach a point where they must go to the computer if their progress is not to be impeded by tedious details.

On the other hand, the first function remains vital. There has in the past ten years been a tendency to use the computer in a somewhat pedestrian manner—for analysis or at best synthesis, but not for design. Only with the availability of graphical output has it become possible for the designer to interact effectively with the computer.

Our outlook in this book will be the following. We assume that the designer will have available a digital computer with graphical output. He will communicate with the machine through a keyboard, entering numerical data and logical decisions. The machine will communicate with the designer both alphanumerically and graphically. In this situation we distinguish three modes of operation.

(i) *Analysis*. An engineering situation is specified in full mathematical detail by the designer, and the computer draws certain further mathematical consequences. An example is the calculation of time response, for a given servo system subjected to a step input.

(ii) *Synthesis*. The designer specifies in detail the properties which his system must have, to the point where there is only one possible solution. The computer finds this solution. An example is optimal control.

(iii) *Design*. This is the creative act of a designer, guided by calculations on the computer and interacting with them in a sequential manner to produce a satisfactory solution. This is intended as a description rather than a definition: definitions of design are notoriously unsatisfactory. The description will probably not be very meaningful before experience has been gained, after which it will no doubt seem self-evident. As further guidance, the design procedure is characterized by new situations to which no standard response is appropriate. Solutions are constrained by so many requirements that it is virtually impossible to list them all. The designer finds himself threading a maze of such requirements, attempting to reconcile conflicting demands of cost, performance, easy maintenance, safety, and so on. A good design usually has strong aesthetic appeal to those who are competent in the technology.

Of these three modes of operation, we regard the third as the most fruitful. The second can sometimes be used as an ingredient of the third, but by itself it has little power. If the real requirements are posed, synthesis is usually impossible. If simplified requirements are posed, the solution is usually worthless. Moreover, the act of specifying the requirements in detail implies the final solution, yet has to be done in ignorance of this solution, which can then turn out to be unsuitable in ways that were not foreseen. The first mode is, of course, basic to the other two.

With this outlook, we shall restate much of the traditional servo theory in this chapter. We shall free it from the second function—that of allowing analysis with pencil and paper—with which it has been traditionally associated. We shall show how its first function makes it a powerful assistant in design. In Chapter 3, these traditional methods will be greatly extended, still in the same spirit.

2. Notation

The system which will be considered in this chapter is shown in Fig. 2.1. The plant is linear and time-invariant, and has one input and one output.

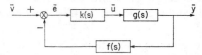

FIG. 2.1.   The general single-loop control system.

It is described by the transfer function $g(s)$, which is assumed to be rational unless otherwise stated. The compensator $k(s)$ is also rational, and is to be designed so that the closed-loop system performs satisfactorily.

The rational transfer function $f(s)$ in the feedback path is in most applications simply $f(s) = 1$. This corresponds to the situation in which we wish the output y to be equal to the input v. In the *servo problem* (or the *servo following problem*) v is some function of time specified either statistically, or, more usually, by means of a suitable test input such as a step. In the *regulator problem*) v is some function of time specified either statistically, or, more chosen arbitrarily.

Although we usually have $f(s) = 1$ in the actual system, it is convenient to keep the more general form during the design procedure. By manipulating the block diagram in Fig. 2.1 we can obtain the diagram shown in Fig. 2.2.

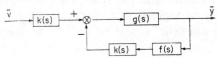

FIG. 2.2.   System giving the same closed-loop transfer function as the system of Fig. 2.1.

Alternatively if we write

$$k(s) = k_1(s) k_2 \tag{2.1}$$

where k_2 is a constant, independent of s, we may manipulate the system into the form shown in Fig. 2.3.

In Fig. 2.3, k_2 acting on $\bar{v}$ outside the loop simply changes the input from $\bar{v}$ to $k_2\bar{v}$, and for most purposes we need not be concerned about this change of scale. Certainly the shape of the transient response and the stability of the

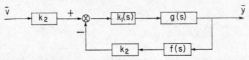

Fig. 2.3. If $k(s)$ in Fig. 2.1 can be written $k(s) = k_1(s)\, k_2$ then the system shown here gives the same closed-loop transfer function.

system are unaffected by it. If $f(s) = 1$, as usual, we may assimilate $f(s)$ and k_2 in the feedback path. Then with a change of notation we may replace Fig. 2.3 again by Fig. 2.1, in which now $k(s)$ is replaced by $k_1(s)$ and $f(s)$ is replaced by k_2. That is to say, we may move the gain k_2 into the feedback path, remembering that in doing so we are making an implicit change in the input $\bar{v}$.

EXERCISE 2.1. Show that "moving the gain into the feedback path" is the same thing as changing the point at which the input is injected into the system.

The transformation just considered is convenient in two ways. First, in an analogue simulation we may wish to study the behaviour of the system as we change the gain k_2. It is also convenient to be able to change easily from the open-loop to the closed-loop condition. If we move the gain into the feedback path, the open-loop condition is represented simply by putting the gain equal to zero. The penalty for this convenience is that we have to adjust the input v (usually a step function) as we change the gain: but such changes are usually necessary to preserve accuracy and avoid overloading even with the original configuration.

The second advantage of the transformation in Fig. 2.3 will become clear later: it allows us to see the effect of changing the gain, in an inverse Nyquist plot, in a very simple way. Similarly, the transformation of Fig. 2.2 allows us, in an inverse Nyquist plot, to analyse the effect of a dynamic compensator very easily.

This account of a simple transformation may seem laboured: such transformations are made in practice without any conscious analysis. However, when we come to multivariable systems the matter is less simple, and it is as well to be clear about the simpler case before going on to the more difficult one.

In general there are l inputs to a plant and m outputs. When, as in Fig.

2.1, $l = m = 1$, the system is *single-input single-output*. If $l > 1$ or $m > 1$ the system is *multivariable*. However, the case where $l = 1, m > 1$ is a special one which can be treated not only by the methods of multivariable theory, but

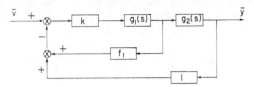

Fig. 2.4. A multiloop system.

also by an extension of the single-input single-output theory: it is then known as a *multiloop system*. The commonest example arises as in Fig. 2.4, which is easily put into the form of Fig. 2.5, when it can be treated as in Fig. 2.1.

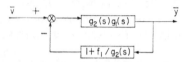

Fig. 2.5. System giving the same closed-loop transfer function as the multiloop system in Fig. 2.4.

EXERCISE 2.2. Suppose that Fig. 2.4 represents an electrical system for positioning a shaft. Let the input to g_1 be a torque, let $g_2(s) g_1(s) = a/s^2$, representing an inertia, and let $\bar{y}$ be position. Let the signal fed back through f_1 be obtained from a tachometer and represent speed. Compare what happens in the actual system (a multivariable system with two outputs) with the representation in Fig. 2.4 in which $g_2(s) = 1/s$. Consider the implications for noise in the system. Write down the differential equation governing the system and consider the effect of changing f_1.

EXERCISE 2.3. Consider the physical dimensions of the constants a and k in Exercise 2.2 and also the dimensions of the feedback coefficients f_1 and 1. Reconcile these dimensions with the way in which the system would be implemented. [Notice that the gain taken right round a loop is always dimensionless.]

Another example of a multiloop system is *cascade control*, which is common in the control of process plant. Suppose, for example, that the temperature of the fluid at the outlet of a steam-heated heat exchanger is to be regulated. The outlet temperature is measured, but it is not used directly to control the flow of steam. If it were, changes in pressure of the steam supply would disturb the control system, which would be too slow-acting to deal with them.

Instead, the pressure in the steam-side of the exchanger is measured, and a control loop is set up which manipulates the steam flow in order to keep the pressure in the exchanger at its desired value. This loop will be fast-acting, and will eliminate the effect of steam supply pressure variations. The pressure in the exchanger fixes the condensation temperature, and therefore the rate of heat supply. A *cascade loop* is now set up: it measures the fluid outlet temperature and generates (usually by a standard process controller) a signal which changes the desired value in the steam pressure control loop. Usually the cascade loop has integral action (Section 6.2, below) but the inner loop controlling pressure does not.

EXERCISE 2.4. Sketch the cascade control system just described and show that it is a multiloop system. [Divide the plant transfer function into two sections: one generating steam pressure from steam flow, the other generating fluid outlet temperature from steam pressure.]

EXERCISE 2.5. What would be the merits of a cascade system with the inner loop controlling steam flow (not pressure) for the duty just described. [Consider cost of measurement; effect of steam supply pressure variations on flow measurement.]

3. System specification

We shall be in a better position to consider the specification which a control system must satisfy when we have analysed its stability and sensitivity. For the present we write down some obvious requirements in qualitative terms. The importance of these requirements will vary from system to system, but all of them will usually be regarded as significant. Any particular system will also have its own special requirements: these can be very diverse and are difficult to codify.

(i) *Stability*. The closed-loop system should be asymptotically stable. That is, all poles of the closed-loop system should lie in the open left half-plane. As will be shown, decoupling zeros (Chapter 1, Section 3.1) of the open-loop system remain unchanged when feedback is applied. It is only the poles of the open-loop transfer function (Chapter 1, Section 3.1) which can be moved by feedback. In some servo problems the open-loop system is unstable and must be stabilized. In most regulator problems arising in process control, however, the open-loop system is highly stable and control encroaches on the margin of stability (below).

(ii) *Stability margin*. If there are poles of the closed-loop system Chapter 1, Section 3.1) at $s = \sigma \pm i\omega$, the angle $\theta = \tan^{-1} \sigma/\omega$ shown in

Fig. 2.6 is taken as a measure of *stability margin*. The output corresponding to such a complex pair of poles when the input is constant is

$$ae^{-\sigma t} \cos (\omega t + \phi) \tag{3.1}$$

This represents a damped oscillation having a *decrement*, over one period $2\pi/\omega$, equal to $e^{-2\pi\sigma/\omega}$. In servo practice θ is usually not allowed to be less than 45°. In process control, on the other hand, θ is allowed to be as small as 10°, corresponding to a decrement of about 1/3 in one period. A sufficient

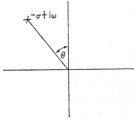

FIG. 2.6.   The angle θ measures the stability margin of a complex pole pair.

margin of stability is demanded partly to ensure that the response is sufficiently damped, but also partly to ensure that changes in the parameters of the system do not carry a risk of instability. This second reason is related to sensitivity (below).

(iii) *Overshoot.* When a step input is applied to the system, the output will usually overshoot its final value, settling to it with a damped oscillation as described in (ii). In some applications overshoot cannot be tolerated: for example a copy-milling machine.

(iv) *Decay rate.* Even when θ is large enough, if there is a pole at $s = -\sigma + i\omega$ with σ very small, the corresponding response will decay too slowly.

(v) *Transient frequency.* A pair of complex poles, having satisfactory values of θ and of σ, may still be unsatisfactory if ω is too large. The corresponding high frequency transient oscillation could impose high stresses on the system, or could coincide with structural resonant frequencies.

(vi) *Speed of response.* The time taken for the system to respond to a step input is an important indication of the effectiveness with which the system will follow changes of the input, or annul output changes caused by disturbances (for example, load changes). The speed of response depends on the location of those poles of the transfer function contributing significantly to the output: these poles must not be too close to the origin.

(vii) *Conditional stability.* Systems which are open-loop stable, and closed-loop stable with their designed loop gain, may nevertheless be unstable for some lower loop gain. They are said then to be *conditionally stable*, and among single-input single-output systems are rare and pathological: among multivariable systems we shall see in Chapter 3 that the condition is much more likely to occur. Because aging or failure of components is likely to reduce loop gain, conditional stability is generally undesirable.

(viii) *Sensitivity*. Disturbances entering the system must not have a large effect on the output. Equally, the system behaviour should be as little affected as possible by likely changes in system parameters. These are two aspects of sensitivity. Usually, low sensitivity demands high loop gains.

(ix) *Offset*. If the desired value of the output is changed to a new value, the output (provided that the system is asymptotically stable) will eventually be close to this value. It may not exactly reach it, in which case there is said to be *offset*. This is often undesirable.

(x) *Bandwidth*. The output will usually follow a sinusoidal input faithfully when its frequency is low, but not when its frequency is high. The *bandwidth* is the range of frequencies over which the system (in some suitable sense) will respond accurately to the input. It should be adequately wide: wide bandwidth implies high speed of response.

(xi) *Linearity*. Our analysis is linear, and if signals within the system become too large the assumption of linearity fails. The behaviour of the system usually deteriorates in these circumstances. These considerations sometimes restrict the loop gain which can be used.

(xii) *Noise*. Random disturbances (noise) acting on the system may cause large signals of high frequency at some points in the system. These may cause problems as in (xi), or they may lead to undue wear. This second consideration, for example, restricts the gain and bandwidth which can be used in flow control systems, which typically give a noisy measurement signal. Too fast a response of the system will rapidly wear the gland of the control valve.

Some of these requirements can be met, at least within a tolerable margin, during the design procedure. Others can only be checked by subsequent simulation or full-scale trials.

4. Stability

Let the plant transfer function $g(s)$ in Fig. 2.1 arise from the equations

$$T_g(s)\, \bar{\xi}_g = U_g(s)\, \bar{u}$$

$$\bar{y} = V_g(s)\, \bar{\xi}_g + W_g(s)\, \bar{u} \qquad (4.1)$$

Here, as in Chapter 1, Section 1, T_g, U_g, V_g and W_g are polynomial matrices, and we assume as in Chapter 1, Section 2, that $T(s)$ is $r \times r$ with $r \geqslant n$, where n is the degree of $|T(s)|$. In particular we may have

$$T_g(s) = sI_n - A_g, \quad U_g(s) = b_g, \quad V_g(s) = c_g, \quad W_g(s) = 0 \qquad (4.2)$$

where b_g is a column vector and c_g is a row vector. A system matrix for (4.1) is

$$P_g(s) = \begin{bmatrix} T_g(s) & U_g(s) \\ -V_g(s) & W_g(s) \end{bmatrix} \qquad (4.3)$$

The poles of the plant are the zeros of $|T_g(s)|$. If $P_g(s)$ has decoupling zeros, these will appear among the poles of the plant, but will be absent from the poles of the transfer function $g(s)$.

EXAMPLE 4.1. The system matrix

$$P_g(s) = \left[\begin{array}{ccc|c} I_3 & & 0 & 0 \\ 0 & (s+1)^2 \, (s-2)(s+3) & & s-2 \\ \hline 0 & & -(s-2) & 0 \end{array} \right] \qquad (4.4)$$

gives

$$g(s) = (0 \quad s-2) \begin{bmatrix} I_3 & 0 \\ 0 & (s+1)^2 \, (s-2)(s+3) \end{bmatrix}^{-1} \begin{bmatrix} 0 \\ s-2 \end{bmatrix} \qquad (4.5)$$

$$= \frac{(s-2)^2}{(s+1)^2 \, (s-2)(s+3)} \qquad (4.6)$$

$$= \frac{s-2}{(s+1)^2 \, (s+3)} \qquad (4.7)$$

so that $s = 2$ is a pole of the system (that is, a zero of $|T_g(s)|$) but not a pole of $g(s)$. Notice that (4.6) and (4.7) represent the same transfer function: two rational functions $p_1(s)/q_1(s)$ and $p_2(s)/q_2(s)$ are equal by definition if $p_1(s)q_2(s) = p_2(s)\,q_1(s)$. On the other hand $P_g(s)$ is not the same system matrix as

$$\left[\begin{array}{ccc|c} I_3 & & 0 & 0 \\ 0 & (s+1)^2 \, (s+3) & & 1 \\ \hline 0 & & -(s-2) & 0 \end{array} \right] \qquad (4.8)$$

or

$$\left[\begin{array}{ccc|c} I_3 & & 0 & 0 \\ 0 & (s+1)^2 \, (s+3) & & s-2 \\ \hline 0 & & 1 & 0 \end{array} \right] \qquad (4.9)$$

The system matrix $P_g(s)$ has one i.d. zero $s = 2$, one o.d. zero $s = 2$, and this zero is also an i.o.d. zero [Chapter 1, Section 3.1]. In (4.8) the i.d. zero has been removed, while in (4.9) the o.d. zero has been removed. Both (4.8) and (4.9) are least-order system matrices giving rise to the transfer function (4.7).

EXAMPLE 4.2. The system matrix

$$P_g(s) = \begin{bmatrix} I_4 & 0 & \vline & 0 \\ 0 & (s+1)^2\,(s-2)^2\,(s+3) & \vline & s-2 \\ \hline 0 & -(s-2) & \vline & 0 \end{bmatrix} \tag{4.10}$$

has one i.d. zero $s = 2$, one o.d. zero $s = 2$, but no i.o.d. zero. It gives rise to the transfer function $1/(s+1)^2\,(s+3)$.

EXAMPLE 4.3. A system matrix in state-space form which is strictly system equivalent to the $P_g(s)$ given in (4.4) is

$$\begin{bmatrix} s & 0 & 0 & -6 & \vline & -2 \\ -1 & s & 0 & -11 & \vline & 1 \\ 0 & -1 & s & -3 & \vline & 0 \\ 0 & 0 & -1 & s+3 & \vline & 0 \\ \hline 0 & 0 & -1 & 5 & \vline & 0 \end{bmatrix} \tag{4.11}$$

This again has one i.d. zero $s = 2$, one o.d. zero $s = 2$, and one i.o.d. zero $s = 2$, but these facts are now much less obvious. The system corresponding to (4.11) has an uncontrollable subspace of dimension 1, an unobservable subspace of dimension 1, and an uncontrollable and unobservable subspace of dimension 1. It has a controllable (p.s.) and observable subspace of dimension 3 (compare Chapter 1, Section 6.1).

EXERCISE 4.1. For the system corresponding to (4.11) form the matrices

$$(B \quad AB \quad \ldots \quad A^{n-1}\ B) \quad \text{and} \quad \begin{bmatrix} C \\ CA \\ \vdots \\ CA^{n-1} \end{bmatrix}$$

and investigate their rank. [Compare Chapter 1, Section 6.1.]

EXERCISE 4.2. Find a system matrix in state-space form which is strictly system equivalent to $P_g(s)$ defined by (4.10). What are the dimensions of its uncontrollable subspace, unobservable subspace, and unobservable and uncontrollable subspace?

Now let $k(s)$ and $f(s)$ in Fig. 2.1 arise from the systems

$$T_k(s)\,\bar{\xi}_k = U_k(s)\,\bar{e}$$
$$\bar{u} = V_k(s)\,\bar{\xi}_k + W_k(s)\,\bar{e} \qquad (4.12)$$

and

$$T_f(s)\,\bar{\xi}_f = U_f(s)\,\bar{y}$$
$$\bar{v} - \bar{e} = V_f(s)\,\bar{\xi}_f + W_f(s)\,\bar{y} \qquad (4.13)$$

Here we have used the symbols shown in Fig. 2.1 for the signals $\bar{e}$ and $\bar{u}$ which form the input and output of the system giving rise to $k(s)$, and similarly $\bar{y}$ and $\bar{v} - \bar{e}$ for the input and output of the system giving rise to $f(s)$. Each of the systems (4.12) and (4.13) may in general have decoupling zeros, though as these systems are specified by the system designer it is usually possible to avoid such zeros.

The equations of the total system corresponding to Fig. 2.1 can now be written in a single equation:

$$
\begin{bmatrix}
T_k & U_k & 0 & 0 & 0 & 0 & \vline & 0 \\
-V_k & W_k & 0 & -1 & 0 & 0 & \vline & 0 \\
0 & 0 & T_g & U_g & 0 & 0 & \vline & 0 \\
0 & 0 & -V_g & W_g & 0 & -1 & \vline & 0 \\
0 & 0 & 0 & 0 & T_f & U_f & \vline & 0 \\
0 & 1 & 0 & 0 & -V_f & W_f & \vline & -1 \\
\hline
0 & 0 & 0 & 0 & 0 & 1 & \vline & 0
\end{bmatrix}
\begin{bmatrix}
\bar{\xi}_k \\
-\bar{e} \\
\bar{\xi}_g \\
-\bar{u} \\
\bar{\xi}_f \\
-\bar{y} \\
\hline
-\bar{v}
\end{bmatrix}
=
\begin{bmatrix}
0 \\
0 \\
0 \\
0 \\
0 \\
0 \\
\hline
-\bar{y}
\end{bmatrix}
\qquad (4.14)
$$

This equation has been written in such a way that the matrix appearing in it is a system matrix for the closed-loop system [Chapter 1, Section 2.1]. If we write this matrix in the abbreviated form

$$P_h(s) = \begin{bmatrix} T_h(s) & U_h \\ -V_h & 0 \end{bmatrix} \qquad (4.15)$$

it follows that the poles of the closed-loop system are the zeros of $|T_h(s)|$. Furthermore, the closed-loop transfer function $h(s)$ is given by the formula

$$h(s) = \begin{vmatrix} T_h(s) & U_h \\ -V_h & 0 \end{vmatrix} \div |T_h(s)| \qquad (4.16)$$

This follows from Chapter 1, equation (2.11), because the 1×1 matrix $h(s)$ is equal to its own determinant. In the same way we have, from (4.1) and (4.12)

$$g(s) = \begin{vmatrix} T_g(s) & U_g(s) \\ -V_g(s) & W_g(s) \end{vmatrix} \div |T_g(s)| \tag{4.17}$$

$$k(s) = \begin{vmatrix} T_k(s) & U_k(s) \\ -V_k(s) & W_k(s) \end{vmatrix} \div |T_k(s)| \tag{4.18}$$

The preceding equations allow us to determine the poles of the closed-loop system, and so to investigate its stability. We have the following theorem:

THEOREM 4.1. The poles of the closed-loop system are the zeros of the polynomial $\phi(s)$ which is given by the formulae

$$\phi(s) = |T_h(s)| = [1 + g(s)\, k(s)\, f(s)]\, |T_g(s)|\, |T_k(s)|\, |T_f(s)| \tag{4.19}$$

$$= \frac{g(s)\, k(s)}{h(s)} |T_g(s)|\, |T_k(s)|\, |T_f(s)| \tag{4.20}$$

Proof.   From (4.16) and (4.14)

$$|T_h(s)| = \frac{1}{h(s)} \begin{vmatrix} T_k & U_k & 0 & 0 & 0 & 0 & 0 \\ -V_k & W_k & 0 & -1 & 0 & 0 & 0 \\ 0 & 0 & T_g & U_g & 0 & 0 & 0 \\ 0 & 0 & -V_g & W_g & 0 & -1 & 0 \\ 0 & 0 & 0 & 0 & T_f & U_f & 0 \\ 0 & 1 & 0 & 0 & -V_f & W_f & -1 \\ 0 & 0 & 0 & 0 & 0 & 1 & 0 \end{vmatrix} \tag{4.21}$$

Expanding the determinant on the right-hand side in terms of its last column we find that it is equal to

$$-(-1) \begin{vmatrix} T_k & U_k & 0 & 0 & 0 & 0 \\ -V_k & W_k & 0 & -1 & 0 & 0 \\ 0 & 0 & T_g & U_g & 0 & 0 \\ 0 & 0 & -V_g & W_g & 0 & -1 \\ 0 & 0 & 0 & 0 & T_f & U_f \\ 0 & 0 & 0 & 0 & 0 & 1 \end{vmatrix} \tag{4.22}$$

$$
= \begin{vmatrix}
T_k & U_k & 0 & 0 & 0 \\
-V_k & W_k & 0 & -1 & 0 \\
0 & 0 & T_g & U_g & 0 \\
0 & 0 & -V_g & W_g & 0 \\
0 & 0 & 0 & 0 & T_f
\end{vmatrix}
\tag{4.23}
$$

$$
= |T_f| \begin{vmatrix}
T_k & U_k & 0 & 0 \\
-V_k & W_k & 0 & -1 \\
0 & 0 & T_g & U_g \\
0 & 0 & -V_g & W_g
\end{vmatrix}
\tag{4.24}
$$

$$
= |T_f| \begin{vmatrix}
T_k & U_k \\
-V_k & W_k
\end{vmatrix}
\begin{vmatrix}
T_g & U_g \\
-V_g & W_g
\end{vmatrix}
\tag{4.25}
$$

by successive Laplace expansions in terms of rows or sets of rows. Using this together with (4.17) and (4.18) in (4.21) gives (4.20). We also have, from Fig. 2.1,

$$
\bar{y} = g(s)\,k(s)[\bar{v} - f(s)\,\bar{y}]
\tag{4.26}
$$

whence

$$
h(s) = \frac{\bar{y}}{\bar{v}} = \frac{g(s)\,k(s)}{1 + g(s)\,k(s)\,f(s)}
\tag{4.27}
$$

Using this in (4.20) we obtain (4.19). This completes the proof.

The quantity $1 + gkf$ which occurs in Theorem 4.1 is of basic importance. It is called the *return difference*, for the following reason. If the closed loop in Fig. 2.1 is broken just before f in the feedback path, and a signal $\bar{w}$ injected into f, the signal which returns to the other side of the broken loop is $-gkf\bar{w}$. The difference between the injected and the returned signal is therefore $(1 + gkf)\,\bar{w}$. Equation (4.27) shows that if $q(s) = g(s)\,k(s)$ is the transfer function in the forward path, another way of writing the return difference is $q(s)/h(s)$.

This theorem has been proved in its most general form. In special cases it can be simplified. For example, if $f(s)$ is a constant f independent of s we can give* to (4.13) the special form

$$
\xi_f = f\bar{y}
$$
$$
\bar{v} - \bar{e} = \xi_f
\tag{4.28}
$$

---

* We assume, in accordance with earlier remarks, that f is implemented by a system of least order, namely zero order.

with system matrix

$$\begin{bmatrix} 1 & f \\ -1 & 0 \end{bmatrix} \tag{4.29}$$

so that $|T_f(s)|$ in (4.19) or (4.20) is just 1.

EXAMPLE 4.4. For the system given by (4.4), with $k(s) = 1, f(s) = 1$, we have

$$1 + g(s)\,k(s)\,f(s) = 1 + \frac{s-2}{(s+1)^2\,(s+3)} \tag{4.30}$$

$$= \frac{s^3 + 5s^2 + 8s + 1}{(s+1)^2\,(s+3)} \tag{4.31}$$

and

$$|T_g(s)| = (s+1)^2\,(s-2)(s+3) \tag{4.32}$$

while $|T_k(s)| = |T_f(s)| = 1$. Then from (4.19)

$$|T_h(s)| = (s^3 + 5s^2 + 8s + 1)(s - 2) \tag{4.33}$$

so that the closed-loop system is unstable. From (4.27) we find

$$h(s) = \frac{s-2}{s^3 + 5s^2 + 8s + 1} \tag{4.34}$$

so that the unstable pole is absent from $h(s)$ as well as from $g(s)$.

Theorem 4.1 can be restated in a form which shows very clearly the role of $1 + gkf$ or gk/h. We assume for simplicity that gkf is strictly proper; that is, $g(s)\,k(s)\,f(s) \to 0$ as $s \to \infty$.

THEOREM 4.2. If gkf is strictly proper,

$$1 + g(s)\,k(s)\,f(s) = \frac{g(s)\,k(s)}{h(s)} = \frac{\displaystyle\prod_{i=1}^{n} (s - \alpha_i')}{\displaystyle\prod_{i=1}^{n} (s - \alpha_i)} \tag{4.35}$$

where $\alpha_1, \alpha_2, ..., \alpha_n$ are the open-loop poles (that is, the zeros of $|T_g(s)|$, $|T_k(s)|$ and $|T_f(s)|$, taken all together) and $\alpha_1', \alpha_2', ..., \alpha_n'$ are the closed-loop poles (that is, the zeros of $|T_h(s)|$).

Proof. If gkf is strictly proper, $1 + g(s)\,k(s)\,f(s) \to 1$ as $s \to \infty$. By (4.19) it follows that in

$$\frac{|T_h(s)|}{|T_g(s)|\,|T_k(s)|\,|T_f(s)|} \tag{4.36}$$

the numerator and denominator have the same degree, and have the same coefficient for the highest power of s appearing. This gives (4.35).

4.1 Decoupling zeros

An important fact follows at once from the form of the closed-loop system matrix in (4.14). Let the system (4.12) have an i.d. zero s_0. Then $(T_k(s_0) \quad U_k(s_0))$ has less than full rank. As one block row of (4.14) is just $(T_k(s) \quad U_k(s))$ followed by zeros, this system also has s_0 as an i.d. zero. Similar remarks apply to i.d. zeros of (4.1) and (4.3), and to o.d. zeros of (4.1), (4.12), (4.13). We conclude that if any of these three subsystems has a decoupling zero in the closed right half plane, then the closed-loop system also has a decoupling zero there. Such a decoupling zero is necessarily a zero of $|T_h(s)|$, and therefore is a closed-loop pole.

In particular, if (4.1) has such a decoupling zero, no way of stabilizing the closed-loop system by means of $k(s)$ or $f(s)$ exists. In simple terms, what this means is the following. The plant (4.1) has a pole in the right half-plane, and also a zero coincident with it. These cancel when we form $g(s)$, but are still physically present. Nothing that we can do by compensation and feedback from "outside" the plant (that is, using the specified input and output only) can affect the internal pole. Only by getting "inside" the plant (by using other inputs or outputs or both) can we affect it.

Notice that though decoupling zeros of (4.1), (4.12), (4.13) are decoupling zeros of the system (4.14) the converse need not be true. If a zero of $k(s)$ cancels a pole of $g(s)$, this introduces an extra decoupling zero in (4.14) which was absent in (4.1) or (4.12).

In the special case (4.2), another way of saying that (4.1) has an o.d. zero is to say that the plant is unobservable, and another way of saying that it has an i.d. zero is to say that it is not controllable (p.s.). The last of these statements, in particular, is open to misinterpretation. We are not interested, in the servo or regulator problem, in controllability (p.s.) as such: that is, in the ability to take the state from any one point to any other in the state space. Rather we are interested in controllability (f) which here expresses the relevant engineering content of the term "controllability".

EXAMPLE 4.5. Let a plant consist of two stirred vessels in series, in which the pH of a solution is to be adjusted. The pH is measured before the first vessel and acid is injected into this vessel which will bring the pH nearly down to its desired value (this is *feed-forward* control and is open-loop). Then the pH of the solution leaving the second vessel is measured, and used to control a flow of acid which trims the pH to its final value. Should this trimming flow go into the first or the second vessel? If it goes into the first, we introduce greater phase lags into the control loop, and shall have a slower response.

If it goes into the second we get better control, but the plant is not then controllable (p.s.) from the trimming flow, because no change of this flow can affect the pH in the first vessel. Both arrangements are controllable (f), and clearly controllability (p.s.) is not important in such an application.

5. Nyquist diagram

From Theorem 4.1 a graphical test for stability can be obtained. Let D be a large contour in the complex plane consisting of the imaginary axis from $s = -iR$ to $s = iR$, together with a semicircle of radius R in the right half-plane. The radius R is chosen large enough to ensure that every finite zero of the polynomial $\phi(s)$ in equation (4.19), if it lies in the open right half-plane, is inside D. If $\phi(s)$ has zeros on the imaginary axis, D is indented into the left half-plane to include them, and R is taken large enough to ensure that all are inside D. The contour D will always be traversed clockwise.

Let the polynomial $\phi(s)$ map D into the closed contour Γ_ϕ, and as s goes once round D let Γ_ϕ make N_ϕ clockwise encirclements of the origin. By Theorem 4.1 and the "principle of the argument" [Chapter 1, Section 8], it follows that the closed-loop system is asymptotically stable if and only if $N_\phi = 0$. A more convenient result is obtained in the following way. Write $q(s) = g(s) k(s)$, and let $q(s)$ map D into Γ_q. Assume for simplicity that $|T_f(s)| = 1$ and $f(s) = f$, a constant. We assume that $f \neq 0$, as otherwise the loop is open. Let D be large enough to include every finite pole and zero of $f^{-1} + q(s)$ lying in the closed right half-plane: D is indented into the left half-plane if necessary to include imaginary poles or zeros.

THEOREM 5.1.   Let $f(s) = f \neq 0$ and $|T_f(s)| = 1$, and let the open-loop system have p_0 poles in the closed right half-plane: that is, let $|T_g(s)||T_k(s)|$ have p_0 zeros there. Let $q(s)$ map D into Γ_q, and let Γ_q make N_q clockwise encirclements of the point $(-1/f, 0)$. Then the closed-loop system shown in Fig. 2.1 and described by equation (4.14) is asymptotically stable if and only if

$$N_q = -p_0 \tag{5.1}$$

Proof.   By equation (4.19)

$$\frac{\phi(s)}{f |T_g(s)||T_k(s)|} = f^{-1} + q(s) \tag{5.2}$$

The number of clockwise encirclements of the origin by the map of D under $f^{-1} + q(s)$ is the number of clockwise encirclements of the point $(-1/f, 0)$ by Γ_q, which is N_q. By the principle of the argument, this is the number z of zeros of $\phi(s)$ inside D, less the number p of zeros of $|T_g(s)||T_k(s)|$ inside D,

$$N_q = z - p \tag{5.3}$$

Now let R be increased until D includes all finite right half-plane zeros of $|T_g(s)||T_k(s)|$ (these are p_0 in number) and all finite right half-plane zeros of $\phi(s)$, z_0 in number. This increase of R does not change N_q, because D already included all finite poles and zeros of $f^{-1}+q(s)$ lying in the closed right half-plane. Hence

$$N_q = z_0 - p_0 \tag{5.4}$$

The closed-loop system is asymptotically stable if and only if $z_0 = 0$, whence the result.

The only subtlety in the proof lies in showing that $z-p = z_0-p_0$. This allows us to decide the necessary size of D from $q(s)$ alone: D is increased in size until N_q is unchanged by further increase. It may happen that at this point D fails to include a right half-plane zero of $\phi(s)$, but the proof shows that this does not invalidate the test. In fact such a zero will be a decoupling zero of the system giving rise to $q(s)$. If it is a decoupling zero of the system giving rise to $g(s)$, then no $k(s)$ can be found to stabilize the system.

EXAMPLE 5.1.   Let $g(s)$ arise from the $P_g(s)$ given in equation (4.10), so that there are two open-loop poles at $s = 2$ which do not appear in $g(s)$. Let $f(s) = f$, and try to choose $k(s) = a(s)/b(s)$ to stabilize the system, where $a(s)$ and $b(s)$ are polynomials. We have

$$\frac{1}{f}+g(s)\,k(s) = \frac{b(s)(s+1)^2\,(s+3)+fa(s)}{fb(s)(s+1)^2\,(s+3)} \tag{5.5}$$

The map of D under this function is to encircle the origin counter-clockwise p_0 times, where p_0 is two more than the number of right half-plane zeros of $b(s)$. But this would require $(s+1)^2\,(s+3)$ to have at least two right half-plane zeros, and so is impossible. Hence no rational $k(s)$ can be found which will stabilize the system.

EXERCISE 5.1.   The constant f in Theorem 5.1 may represent a gain which has been moved into the feedback path. By putting $f(s) = 1$, $k(s) = k_1(s)f$, derive the same stability criterion and so justify the procedure of moving a gain into the feedback path.

EXERCISE 5.2.   Let $f(s)$ arise from (4.13), and let $|T_g(s)||T_k(s)||T_f(s)|$ have p_0 zeros in the closed right half-plane. Let $g(s)\,k(s)\,f(s)$ map a suitable contour D into Γ, which encircles the point $(-1, 0)$, N times clockwise. It is clear (by moving $f(s)$ into the forward path and using Theorem 5.1) that the closed-loop system is asymptotically stable if and only if $N = -p_0$. Give a direct proof. What is a "suitable contour D"?

EXERCISE 5.3.   Let $f(s)$ arise from (4.13) and be nonzero for all s on D, and write

$$P_f(s) = \begin{bmatrix} T_f(s) & U_f(s) \\ -V_f(s) & W_f(s) \end{bmatrix} \qquad (5.6)$$

Prove that the closed-loop system is asymptotically stable if and only if the vector joining $1/f(s)$ to $q(s)$ makes as many net counterclockwise revolutions, when s goes round D, as there are zeros of $|T_g(s)||T_k(s)||P_f(s)|$ in the closed right half-plane.

Theorem 5.1 gives the usual *Nyquist criterion* for stability. To use it, we start with $k(s) = 1$ and inspect Γ_q, which is just the map of D under $q(s) = g(s)$. This will have some such form as is shown in Fig. 2.7, in which AB is the map of the imaginary axis from 0 to iR, BC is the map of the semi-circular arc of D, and CA is the map of the imaginary axis from $-iR$ to 0. Notice that because $q(s)$ gives a conformal mapping, the angles at B and C are right-angles preserving the sense of the corresponding angles of D. Usually only the portion AB is drawn: this is called the *Nyquist diagram*.

If $p_0 = 0$, that is if $q(s)$ arises from an asymptotically stable system, Fig. 2.7 shows asymptotic stability for all f such that the critical point $(-1/f, 0)$

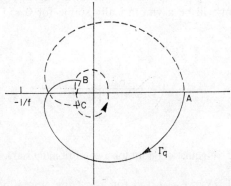

FIG. 2.7.   The contour D is mapped by $q(s)$ into the closed curve $ABCA$, which is Γ_q. The curve AB is the map of the upper half of that part of the imaginary axis which is included in D, and is called the Nyquist diagram.

is not encircled by the contour Γ_q. This will be true, for the contour shown, whenever f has a numerically small enough positive or negative value. If f is small and positive, and is gradually increased, there will come a point when $(-1/f, 0)$ lies on Γ_q: in fact it will lie on both branches AB and CA. At this point two poles are about to cross the imaginary axis and enter D. The closed-loop system then has two poles on the imaginary axis, at frequencies

$\pm \omega$ which can be found by noting the value of ω for which the curve AB crosses the negative real axis. Notice that if f is negative, and $-1/f$ is made smaller, then $(-1/f, 0)$ will cross Γ_q at a point corresponding to $\omega = 0$. The closed-loop system will then have a pole at the origin. In practice, of course, f will be positive.

The contour Γ_q in Fig. 2.7 does not encircle the origin. Consequently it might seem that the system would be asymptotically stable for large enough positive or negative f. However, as R is increased, the contour BC round the origin shrinks. The apparent anomaly is caused by failing to make D large enough to include all right half-plane zeros of $f^{-1} + q(s)$.

If $p_0 > 0$, Theorem 5.1 would require us, in order to stabilize the system corresponding to Fig. 2.7, to make N_q negative. That is, Γ_q would have to go round the point $(-1/f, 0)$ anticlockwise. Clearly there is no value of f for which this is true. If we are allowed to change $k(s)$, we may be able to modify the system so that it is asymptotically stable for some f. This will not be possible if one or more of the p_0 poles is a decoupling zero. If on the other hand the open-loop system has least order, it is known that a $k(s)$ can always be found to stabilize the system, though it may be excessively complicated or otherwise unsuitable (compare Problems 3, 5).

EXAMPLE 5.2.   If Γ_q has the shape shown in Fig. 2.8, with $p_0 = 0$, the closed-loop system will be asymptotically stable for $0 < f < 1.25$ and for

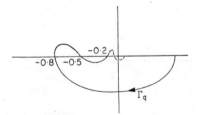

FIG. 2.8.   Nyquist diagram for a conditionally stable system.

$2 < f < 5$. For $1.25 < f < 2$ and for $5 < f$ the closed-loop system is unstable. Such a system is said to be *conditionally stable*: when $2 < f < 5$, it can be destabilized by reducing the gain. Such systems are theoretically interesting but rare. Conditionally stable multivariable systems, on the other hand, can arise quite easily [Chapter 3, Section 2].

5.1 Inverse Nyquist diagram

If $q(s)$ were identically zero, there would be little to say about the system. Consequently we assume $q(s) \not\equiv 0$, which means that the system is controllable (f). Then Theorem 5.1 can be restated in an alternative form.

For convenience write

$$\hat{q}(s) = q^{-1}(s), \quad \hat{h}(s) = h^{-1}(s), \quad \text{etc.} \tag{5.7}$$

and let $\hat{q}(s)$ map D into $\hat{\Gamma}_q$, which encircles the origin $\hat{N}_q$ times clockwise. From equation (4.27) we have

$$\hat{h}(s) = \frac{1+q(s)f(s)}{q(s)} = f(s)+\hat{q}(s) \tag{5.8}$$

Let $\hat{h}(s)$ map D into $\hat{\Gamma}_h$, which encircles the origin $\hat{N}_h$ times clockwise. The contour D is now taken large enough to enclose all finite poles and zeros, of $\hat{q}(s)$ and of $\hat{h}(s)$, lying in the closed right half-plane.

THEOREM 5.2.   Let the open-loop system have p_0 poles in the closed right half-plane: that is, let $|T_g(s)||T_k(s)||T_f(s)|$ have p_0 zeros there. Then the closed-loop system shown in Fig. 2.1 and described by equation (4.14) is asymptotically stable if and only if

$$\hat{N}_q-\hat{N}_h = p_0 \tag{5.9}$$

Proof.   By equation (4.20)

$$\frac{\hat{h}(s)}{\hat{q}(s)} = \frac{\phi(s)}{|T_g(s)||T_k(s)||T_f(s)|} \tag{5.10}$$

The function on the left-hand side maps D into a contour which goes $\hat{N}_h-\hat{N}_q$ times clockwise round the origin. This must equal the number z of zeros of $\phi(s)$ in D less the number p of zeros of $|T_g(s)||T_k(s)||T_f(s)|$ in D. But as D is increased to include all z_0 zeros of $\phi(s)$ and all p_0 zeros of $|T_g(s)||T_k(s)||T_f(s)|$ in the closed right half-plane, the number of encirclements by the function on the left-hand side is unchanged, whence

$$\hat{N}_h-\hat{N}_q = z_0-p_0 \tag{5.11}$$

The closed-loop system is asymptotically stable if and only if $z_0 = 0$, whence the result.

COROLLARY.   If $|T_f(s)| = 1$ and $f(s) = f$, a constant, then $\hat{N}_q$ is the number of times $\hat{\Gamma}_q$ encircles the origin, and $\hat{N}_h$ is the number of times $\hat{\Gamma}_q$ encircles the point $(-f, 0)$. If and only if the difference $\hat{N}_q-\hat{N}_h$ between these numbers is p_0, the closed-loop system is asymptotically stable.

The *inverse Nyquist diagram* is the part of $\hat{\Gamma}_q$ corresponding to the imaginary axis from $s = 0$ to $s = iR$. It is obtainable at once from the Nyquist diagram by taking reciprocals of the distances from the origin, and reflecting in the real axis. Figure 2.9 is obtained in this way from Fig. 2.7. The critical point is now $(-f, 0)$, and when $f = 0$ the critical point is the origin. If for Fig. 2.9, $p_0 = 0$, then stability is maintained as f increases from zero, until the critical point meets AB where that curve crosses the negative real axis.

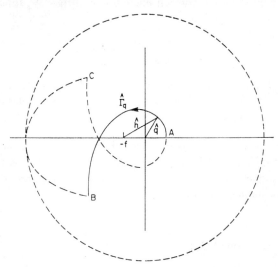

FIG. 2.9.   Inverse Nyquist diagram for the same system as in Fig. 2.7.

Each crossing of $\hat{\Gamma}_q$ by the critical point "from left to right" (counting all branches of the complete contour $\hat{\Gamma}_q$) represents the gain of a pole in the right half-plane. Each crossing "from right to left" represents the loss of a pole in the right half-plane. Here "left to right" means with respect to the direction in which $\hat{\Gamma}_q$ is traversed. For example, in Fig. 2.9, two poles move into the right half-plane when f is increased so that the critical point crosses $\hat{\Gamma}_q$. They form a complex pair, and cross the imaginary axis at the frequency for which $\arg \hat{q}(i\omega) = -\pi$.

Inverse plots have several advantages over direct plots. The open-loop situation is represented by the critical point $(0, 0)$, and as the gain f increases the critical point moves away from the origin. The closed-loop inverse transfer function $\hat{h}(s)$ is given (when $f(s) = f$) by the same diagram with the origin shifted to $(-f, 0)$: though if f represents a gain which has been moved into the feedback path $\hat{h}(s)$ must be suitably scaled. When $|T_f(s)|$ is a polynomial, the situation is simpler than the one shown by Exercises 5.2 and 5.3, and this is helpful in considering the effect of compensators (Section 6). The really important point, however, is that it is the inverse theorem which can be extended most profitably to multivariable systems, as will be shown in Chapter 3. Consequently we shall prefer the inverse diagram to the direct diagram in this chapter.

One objection which is sometimes raised to the inverse plot arises from a different way of stating Theorem 5.2. Let $q(s)$ have p_q poles and z_q zeros in the closed right half-plane and let $|T_f(s)| = 1$. Then $\hat{N}_q = p_q - z_q$, and (5.9) becomes

$$\hat{N}_h = p_q - p_0 - z_q \qquad (5.12)$$

which clearly requires more algebraic information about q for its application. This, however, is an objection to the alternative statement (5.12), rather than to inverse plots as such.

EXERCISE 5.4. Show that if $q(s)$ arises from a least-order system and $|T_f(s)| = 1$, (5.12) becomes $\hat{N}_h = -z_q$. [For then $p_q = p_0$].

EXERCISE 5.5. Show that

$$P_q(s) = \begin{bmatrix} T_k & U_k & 0 & 0 & | & 0 \\ -V_k & W_k & 0 & -1 & | & 0 \\ 0 & 0 & T_g & U_g & | & 0 \\ 0 & 1 & 0 & 0 & | & -1 \\ \hline 0 & 0 & -V_g & W_g & | & 0 \end{bmatrix} \qquad (5.13)$$

is a system matrix corresponding to (4.1) and (4.12), and giving rise to $q(s)$. [Show that P_q operating on $(\bar{\xi}_k^T, -\bar{e}, \bar{\xi}_g^T, -\bar{u}, -\bar{e})^T$ gives rise to $(0, 0, 0, 0, -\bar{y})^T$].

EXERCISE 5.6. Show that if $|T_f(s)| = 1$, then $p_q - p_0 - z_q = -z_0$; where z_0 is the number of zeros of $|P_q(s)|$ lying in the closed right half-plane. [Use equation (2.11) of Chapter 1 to show that $q(s) = |P_q(s)| \div |T_q(s)|$, with P_q given by (5.13). Then show that $|T_q(s)| = |T_g(s)||T_k(s)|$].

5.2 Practical application

The stability theorems as we have stated them are mathematically satisfactory, but they have the following defect when used for practical purposes. If we wish to obtain N_q (for Theorem 5.1) or $\hat{N}_h$ and $\hat{N}_h$ (for Theorem 5.2) we have to plot the whole of the contour Γ_q or $\hat{\Gamma}_q$. The part corresponding to the imaginary axis can be obtained by measurement on the open-loop system, if this is asymptotically stable. The part corresponding to the semicircular arc of D, however, cannot be obtained by measurement.

One way of avoiding this difficulty is to fit a rational transfer-function to the measurements. Then the whole of Γ_q or $\hat{\Gamma}_q$ can be drawn. This procedure however, involves greater difficulties than might be thought, as is shown by

Example 5.5 below. It is therefore desirable to use only the response for imaginary s, which is permitted by the following result.

THEOREM 5.3. Let $q(s)$ be strictly proper, and let $f(s) = f$, independent of s. Then given any $f_1 > 0$, the radius R of the semicircle in the contour D can be chosen large enough to ensure that no zero of $|T_h(s)|$ lies on this semicircle for any f satisfying $0 \leqslant f \leqslant f_1$.

Proof. Write $q(s) = g(s) \, k(s) = n(s)/d(s)$ where $n(s)$ and $d(s)$ are polynomials. By (4.19)

$$|T_h(s)| = \left[\frac{d(s)+n(s)f}{d(s)} \right] |T_g(s)| |T_k(s)| \tag{5.14}$$

The right-hand side is a polynomial, and because $d(s)$ has higher degree then $n(s)$, the term of highest degree in s is independent of f. That is, for all f satisfying $0 \leqslant f \leqslant f_1$, $|T_h(s)|$ has the same number of zeros, and these are continuous functions of f. Let these zeros be $s_1(f), s_2(f), ..., s_p(f)$, and write

$$m(f) = \max_i \{|s_i(f)|\} \tag{5.15}$$

Then $m(f)$ is a continuous function of f on the compact interval $0 \leqslant f \leqslant f_1$, and so has an absolute maximum m_0 on this interval [Rosenbrock and Storey, 1970, Chapter 4, Section 7.1]. It is sufficient to choose $R > m_0$.

As a consequence of this theorem, the number $\hat{N}_h - \hat{N}_q$ can only change (when R is sufficiently large) by passage of the critical point $(-f, 0)$ across that part $\hat{\Gamma}_q$ corresponding to the imaginary axis. The value of $\hat{N}_h - \hat{N}_q$ can therefore be evaluated by counting the number of such crossings as f increases from zero to the design value, as explained in Section 5.1. For any practical system $q(s)$ will be strictly proper, though sometimes this fact is concealed by using a $q(s)$ which is valid only for small values of $|s|$. Without the condition that $q(s)$ is strictly proper, $\hat{N}_h - \hat{N}_q$ could change by passage of a pole across the semicircular arc of the contour D.

EXAMPLE 5.3. Let $q(s) = (1-s)/(1+s)$ arise from a least-order system. Then

$$f + \hat{q}(s) = \frac{(1+f)+(1-f)\,s}{1-s} \tag{5.16}$$

This has a zero at

$$s = \frac{f+1}{f-1} \tag{5.17}$$

which is therefore a pole of the closed-loop system. As f goes from 0 to 1 −, this pole goes from -1 to $-\infty$, and as f goes from $1+$ to 2 the pole goes from $+\infty$ to 3. For any given $f > 1$, we may choose R large enough to ensure that the pole is inside D, but no R however large will prevent the pole from crossing the semicircular arc of D as f increases from $1+$. Though a system might be well represented by $q(s) = (1-s)/(1+s)$ when $|s|$ is small, this representation must be inaccurate for $s = i\omega$ and ω sufficiently large. For if the transfer function were valid, sinusoidal inputs of arbitrarily high frequency would give sinusoidal outputs with the same amplitude as the input. No physical system behaves in this way.

EXERCISE 5.7. Plot $\hat{\Gamma}_q$ for Example 5.3 and show that the critical point $(-f, 0)$ does not lie on that portion of $\hat{\Gamma}_q$ which maps the imaginary axis, for any $f \geqslant 0$ and any finite R.

EXERCISE 5.8. When $f = 1$, equation (5.16) shows that the closed-loop system has no pole. Investigate this anomalous behaviour by considering the state-space representation

$$\left. \begin{array}{l} \dot{x} = -x + 2u \\ y = x - u \\ u = v - y \end{array} \right\} \qquad (5.18)$$

[Note that x is determined by the algebraic equations independently of the differential equation.]

EXERCISE 5.9. Write down a system matrix for equations (5.18) and show that $|T(s)|$ is independent of s. [Note that the input is v and the output is y, and compare Section 2.1 of Chapter 1].

EXERCISE 5.10. Consider the application of Theorem 5.3 to Γ_q.

In applications, Theorem 5.3 is combined with an assumption about the system which we state formally in these terms.

ASSUMPTION 5.1. Those poles which determine stability cross the segment of the imaginary axis between $s = -i\omega_0$ and $s = i\omega_0$, where ω_0 is some specified frequency.

EXERCISE 5.11. Show that Assumption 5.1 is satisfied if ω_0 is chosen so that $|q(i\omega)f| \leqslant \theta < 1$ for all $\omega \geqslant \omega_0$, and that this can always be done for given f if $q(s)$ is strictly proper.

When this assumption is satisfied, stability can be investigated by plotting only that part of $\hat{\Gamma}_q$ which corresponds to the segment of the imaginary axis from $\omega = 0$ to $\omega = \omega_0$. It should be noted that the assumption relates to the physical system, not to any mathematical model we may use to represent it. The value of ω_0 must of course be chosen large enough to disclose all crossings by poles which arise in the model, and these crossings must correspond to the behaviour of the physical system if the model is to be useful. No model, however, is valid at arbitrarily high frequencies. Consequently if we are to draw valid conclusions about stability of the physical system, we must explicitly assume that differences between model and system at high frequencies do not affect our conclusions. This will be true if Assumption 5.1 is valid and the model gives $g(i\omega)$ with sufficient accuracy for $0 \leqslant \omega \leqslant \omega_0$.

EXAMPLE 5.4. Let $q(s) = 1/(s+1)^{11}$, so that the part of $\hat{\Gamma}_q$ which maps the upper part of the imaginary axis, winds round the origin and crosses the negative real axis three times. The corresponding frequencies are approximately $\omega = 0 \cdot 29, 1 \cdot 15, 6 \cdot 9$. As the gain is increased, three successive pairs of poles pass into the right half-plane, crossing the imaginary axis at the frequencies given. Usually we shall not be interested in gains higher than the value $1 \cdot 6$ which makes the first such pole pair enter the right half-plane, and it is then sufficient to plot $\hat{\Gamma}_q$ for say $0 \leqslant \omega \leqslant 0 \cdot 5$. We must, however assume that $\hat{\Gamma}_q$ for the actual plant does not cross the negative real axis between 0 and $-1 \cdot 6$ at some much higher frequency, where $1/(s+1)^{11}$ is no longer an adequate description of the plant.

The purpose of stating the assumption explicitly is to emphasize that mathematics alone can never assure us that we have drawn valid conclusions about a physical system. We must first have formulated the mathematical problem so that the conclusions we draw are correct.

As an illustration, suppose that the system consists of an electric motor driving a large inertia. To investigate stability we measure the frequency response for frequencies from zero to ω_0. The choice of ω_0 must then be made in the light of our knowledge about the system. If the drive shaft has significant torsional compliance, we may have to extend the measurements to much higher frequencies than would otherwise be necessary. Alternatively, if a mathematical model is written down from physical principles, the corresponding decision must be made, whether to include structural resonances in the model or to omit them. This is equivalent to a decision about the frequency range over which the stability investigation must be extended.

When the plant is represented by a mathematical model, it is easy to be misled in the following way. From the theory of analytic continuation [Ahlfors, 1966] it is known that two complex functions which take the same values everywhere on the segment $s = 0$ to $s = i\omega_1$ of the imaginary axis, take the same values also at every point in the complex plane to which their analytic continuations can be extended. It is therefore tempting to believe that if the mathematical model agrees sufficiently well on some interval

$0 \leqslant \omega \leqslant \omega_1$, then it agrees with the plant response everywhere, and in particular must have the same stability properties as the plant. However, if ω_1 is less than the appropriate ω_0 defined as above, then no degree of approximation for $0 \leqslant \omega \leqslant \omega_1$, however close it may be short of exact agreement, can ensure that the model faithfully predicts the stability of the plant. This is shown by the following example.

EXAMPLE 5.5.   Consider the closed-loop transfer function

$$h_n(s) = -\sum_{r=1}^{n} \left\{ \frac{2^{r-1}}{[s+1-i(\omega_1+2)]^r} + \frac{2^{r-1}}{[s+1+i(\omega_1+2)]^r} \right\} \quad (5.19)$$

which has poles at $s = -1 \pm i(\omega_1+2)$ and is therefore stable. As $n \to \infty$, the series on the right converges uniformly, for $s = i\omega$ and $0 \leqslant \omega \leqslant \omega_1$, to

$$h(s) = \frac{-2(s-1)}{s^2 - 2s + 1 + (\omega_1+2)^2} \quad (5.20)$$

which has poles at $s = 1 \pm i(\omega_1+2)$ and is therefore unstable. Given any $\varepsilon > 0$, however small, we may therefore find n such that

$$\left| h(i\omega) - h_n(i\omega) \right| < \varepsilon, \qquad 0 \leqslant \omega \leqslant \omega_1 \quad (5.21)$$

This means that no measurement on the interval $0 \leqslant \omega \leqslant \omega_1$ can ever permit us to decide whether the plant should be represented by a $g_n(s)$ giving rise to $h_n(s)$ (which is stable) or by $g(s)$ giving rise to $h(s)$ (which is unstable). Notice that we have called the transfer functions stable or unstable as an abbreviated way of saying that the underlying system, if it has least order, is stable or unstable.

EXERCISE 5.12.   Obtain (5.19) from the equation

$$\frac{1}{s-1 \pm i(\omega_1+2)} = \frac{1}{[s+1 \pm i(\omega_1+2)]-2} \quad (5.22)$$

by expanding the second member in a series.

EXERCISE 5.13.   Sketch $\hat{h}(i\omega)$ from (5.20) and suggest a suitable value of ω_0. Without drawing the curves $\hat{h}_n(i\omega)$, consider qualitatively how they behave on $0 \leqslant \omega \leqslant \omega_1$ and on $\omega > \omega_1$, for $n = 1, 2, \ldots$. [On which side of the origin do the curves $\hat{h}_n(i\omega)$ pass; how do they behave as $\omega \to \infty$; how is the mapping of D completed?]

6. Design of compensators

In this Section, the design of compensators will be considered in terms of the inverse Nyquist diagram. A simple method suitable for computer-aided design will first be described. This will serve for many applications, and it can be modified as necessary in the light of the discussion which follows it. Most of what is said can readily be translated to direct Nyquist plots.

The designer starts with the inverse Nyquist plot $\hat{\Gamma}_g$ which is called up graphically on the computer. It is useful to have values of ω inserted at suitable points on the plot when this is displayed. If the plant is asymptotically stable, and if the inverse plot is as shown in Fig. 2.10, then the closed-

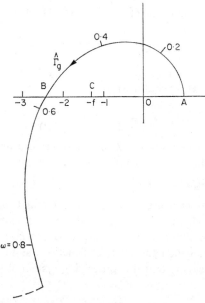

FIG. 2.10.   Inverse Nyquist diagram for $g(s) = 1/(s+1)^6$. The ratio of OA to CA is the offset. The ratio of OB to OC is the gain margin.

loop system is asymptotically stable provided that the critical point is between 0 and B. The frequency of oscillation when the critical point is at B is given by the value of ω corresponding to this point on the plot. This frequency ω_{pc} is called the *phase crossover frequency* of the system. It is an indication of the speed of response which can be expected from the closed-loop system, because as the gain is reduced to its working value the step response usually behaves as in Fig. 2.11. That is to say, the frequency of the damped oscillation decreases slowly and progressively as the gain is decreased, and meanwhile the damping increases. Though ω_{pc} often gives a guide to the speed of response, the connection between the two is a loose one, and too much reliance should not be placed on it.

EXERCISE 6.1.   Relate the frequency of oscillation for $f = 2\cdot4$ in Fig. 2.11 to ω_{pc} in Fig. 2.10.

The amount by which the gain must be reduced in order to give a suitable stability margin can be estimated by rule of thumb. In Fig. 2.10, the *gain margin* is the ratio of the distance *OB* to the distance from 0 to the critical point *C*. A gain margin of 2 usually gives a suitable stability margin for a

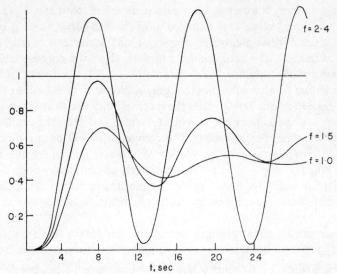

FIG. 2.11.   Step response of closed-loop system with $g(s) = 1/(s+1)^6$ and $f = 2 \cdot 4$, $1 \cdot 5$, $1 \cdot 0$. The gain f has been placed in the forward path.

process control system. A gain margin of 3 to 10 is usually needed for servo systems. A tentative location *C* of the critical point can be decided on this basis.

The offset can then be checked from Fig. 2.10. For a unit step input, $v = U(t)$, the output of the closed-loop system tends as $t \to \infty$ to $y = h(0)$, assuming asymptotic stability [Chapter 1, Theorem 8.4]. In Fig. 2.10, the distance *CA* is $\hat{h}(0)$, while $0A$ is $\hat{h}(0) - f$. The ratio of $0A$ to *CA* is therefore

$$\frac{\hat{h}(0) - f}{\hat{h}(0)} = \frac{f^{-1} - h(0)}{f^{-1}} = 1 - fh(0) \tag{6.1}$$

The second expression is the offset as a proportion of the desired value (which is f^{-1}) when f is actually a gain in the feedback path. The third expression is the offset as a proportion of the desired value (which is 1) when f represents a gain k_2 which has been moved into the feedback path as in Fig. 2.3. In either case the offset is obtained from Fig. 2.10 in the same way.

In process control, offsets as large as 1/10 may be tolerable in some circumstances. Usually, however, offsets must be much smaller, and sometimes no offset can be tolerated. In servomechanisms the offset must almost always be negligibly small.

If at this stage the system seems likely to give sufficient speed of response and sufficiently small offset, the time response to a unit step input is called up graphically from the computer. This will usually not be satisfactory, with the tentative gain margin selected. The gain is therefore treated as a parameter for trimming the design. It is adjusted until the best compromise is reached between speed of response, offset, overshoot, and decrement, as judged from the step response. The compromise will depend on the purpose which the control system has to fulfil.

Either before or after obtaining the time response, it may be clear that the uncompensated system fails to meet the specification. The designer must then, if possible, find a compensator $f(s)$ or $k(s)$ which will allow the compensated system to meet the requirements. The compensator will have a number of adjustable parameters, and the choice of these is guided by the inverse Nyquist plot $\hat{\Gamma}_g$. A new gain is then tentatively chosen, and is regarded as a parameter for final adjustment, guided by the step response. If the design is still unsatisfactory, the compensator is redesigned using inverse Nyquist plots again.

In other words, all parameters except one (the loop gain) are settled by frequency response considerations. The gain is tentatively chosen from the frequency response, but is finally adjusted by considering the step response. The reason for this procedure is that usually the design criteria are most nearly related to the step response. However, the step response fails to give much guidance on the way to choose a suitable compensator. It is therefore desirable to make a preliminary reduction in the number of degrees of freedom.

The design procedure is an iterative one, but in practice it converges very rapidly. Some examples are given later.

6.1 Phase lead

One way in which the uncompensated system may be lacking is in speed of response. To improve this we need to increase the frequency ω_{pc} at which $\hat{\Gamma}_g$ crosses the negative real axis. The usual device for this purpose is the *phase lead* (or *phase advance*) compensator, which we shall suppose at first is in the feedback path. Keeping an adjustable gain f, the compensator is represented by

$$(s) = f \cdot \frac{1+\alpha s\tau}{1+s\tau} \tag{6.2}$$

Here $\tau > 0$ is a time constant and α is a real number greater than 1.

The easiest way to see how the phase lead compensator works is to superimpose a plot of $-f(i\omega)$ on the inverse Nyquist plot, as in Fig. 2.12. The function $-f(i\omega)$ maps the positive half of the imaginary axis into a semi-circle CD, described clockwise. The point C is $(-f, 0)$, while D is $(-\alpha f, 0)$.

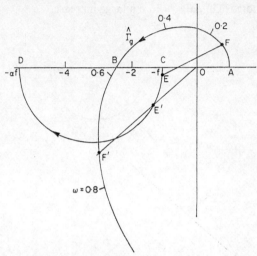

Fig. 2.12.   Inverse Nyquist plot for $g(s) = 1/(s+1)^6$ with superimposed semicircle for phase advance compensator.

Hence the diameter of the semicircle is $(\alpha - 1)f$. Roughly speaking, we may then think of the critical point of $\hat{\Gamma}_g$, not as the fixed point C, but as a point which moves from C to D around the semicircle. The sense in which this is true is defined in the following paragraph.

If we choose a value of ω for which $-f(i\omega)$ is at E and $\hat{g}(i\omega)$ is at F, then EF represents $f(i\omega) + \hat{g}(i\omega)$, which is $\hat{h}(i\omega)$. If this vector makes no net revolutions as s goes round the contour D, the system is stable by Theorem 5.2. Here we are assuming as before that $g(s)$ arises from an asymptotically stable system, and similarly that the compensator (6.2) is implemented by means of an asymptotically stable system. As the implementation of the compensator is in our own hands, the last point offers no difficulty.

Let the vector $E'F'$ be radial from the origin. Then clearly our system is on the verge of instability when f is increased until E' coincides with F'. (Notice that doubling f doubles the diameter of the semicircle and also doubles its distance from the origin.) The frequency of oscillation is then ω'_{pc} corresponding to F', which is higher than the value ω_{pc} corresponding to B. Consequently, phase advance speeds up the response. On the other hand, the gain margin is now the ratio of the distances OF' and OE', which is slightly less than the ratio of OB to OC. Hence, phase advance may force us to reduce the loop gain in order to preserve the original gain margin. This will be true when $\hat{\Gamma}_g$ goes in the general direction from top left to bottom right in the third quadrant, as shown in Fig. 2.12. On the other hand, if $\hat{\Gamma}_g$ goes from top right to bottom left in the third quadrant, as in Fig. 2.13. phase advance may allow an increase in gain—often a large increase.

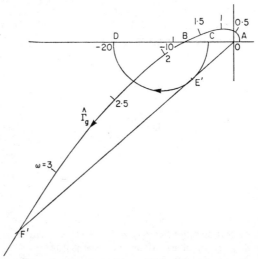

FIG. 2.13.   Inverse Nyquist plot for $g(s) = 1/(s+1)^3$ with superimposed semicircle for phase advance compensator.

In Figs. 2.12 and 2.13, increase of α increases the diameter $(\alpha-1)f$ of the semicircle and allows a further increase of ω_{pc}. However, the gain of the compensator increases by a factor of α as ω goes from 0 to ∞, and if α is too large we shall emphasize high frequency noise in the signal on which the compensator operates. This can lead to nonlinear effects (saturation, etc.) and to excessive wear of mechanical components.

It is therefore usual to make α no greater than 10 or so. On the other hand if $\alpha < 3$, the compensator has a relatively small effect. The maximum phase advance obtainable occurs when OF' is tangential to the semicircle, as in Fig. 2.13. This happens when $\omega\tau = 1/\sqrt{\alpha}$, and the phase advance (the angle COE' in Fig. 2.13) is then determined by

$$\tan\phi = \frac{\alpha-1}{2\sqrt{\alpha}} \tag{6.3}$$

giving $\phi = 30°$ when $\alpha = 3$, and $\phi = 55°$ when $\alpha = 10$. Increasing α beyond 10 brings diminishing returns in the way of phase advance. If more than 55° phase advance is essential, two compensators in series give a better effect. For example two compensators with $\alpha = 3 \cdot 5$ can give $68°$ phase advance for a total amplification at high frequencies of $3 \cdot 5^2 = 12 \cdot 25$. To obtain the same phase advance in one stage would require $\alpha = 26$. Notice that in Figs. 2.12 and 2.13 rather small values of α have been used for graphical convenience.

EXERCISE 6.2.   Verify equation (6.3) and the quoted values of ϕ.

A routine way to design the compensator in the situation illustrated by Fig. 2.13 is to settle on a value of α, according to the expected effects of noise. Then ϕ can be obtained from (6.2), and a ray at this angle can be drawn from the origin. Where this meets $\hat{\Gamma}_g$, at F' in Fig. 2.13, defines ω'_{pc} and τ is obtained from $\tau = 1/\omega'_{pc}\sqrt{\alpha}$. This makes full use of the available phase advance, and because of the form of $\hat{\Gamma}_g$ a suitable gain margin can be obtained without a reduction of the gain f: often with an increased gain. In the situation illustrated by Fig. 2.12, on the other hand, use of the full phase advance may require an excessive reduction in loop gain. In these circumstances a smaller value of τ is chosen, leading to the configuration illustrated. Even in the situation of Fig. 2.13, an adjustment of this type, but smaller, will allow higher loop gain with very little loss of phase advance. Usually the value of τ is not highly critical. A value is estimated on the above lines, and the step response is examined. One or two further values of τ may then be tried: for each value of τ, the loop gain is adjusted to give the most favourable response.

For regulator systems it is usually satisfactory to put the phase advance compensator in the feedback path as suggested above. The control system is intended to respond to disturbances of the output, and for these the response is the same whether the network is in the forward path or the feedback path. If changes of the desired value are put in manually, it can be a positive advantage to have the network in the feedback path. This avoids the large upset to the process which occurs when sudden manual changes of desired value are passed through a phase advance network in the forward path. It is true that most industrial process controllers implement "derivative action" by a phase lead compensator in the forward path, but this is for reasons of manufacturing convenience. In such cases the signal from the "derivative unit" is limited in order to prevent large upsets, but this makes the behaviour nonlinear and therefore difficult to analyse. When a computer is used for process control, the opportunity is often taken of moving the phase advance function (now implemented digitally and discontinuously) into the feedback path.

In many servo systems, on the other hand, inputs are smooth and must be followed with the greatest possible accuracy. The phase advance network is then placed in the forward path. The effect is equivalent, by Fig. 2.3, to putting a phase advance network in the feedback path, and a second phase advance network in front of the servo loop.

The first of these networks has the same effect on the natural frequency of the loop as was explained above. The second has a "forcing" effect on the input: we can write

$$\frac{1+\alpha s\tau}{1+s\tau} = 1 + \frac{(\alpha-1)\,s\tau}{1+s\tau}$$ (6.4)

and the second term on the right is a smoothed (or filtered) derivative. Because of this forcing effect, the gain must be less with a phase advance network in the forward path than with the same network in the feedback path, if equal overshoot is to be maintained. Consequently the same speed of response and overshoot are achieved with higher damping when the network is in the forward path: see Fig. 2.14. Conversely, higher gain can be used for

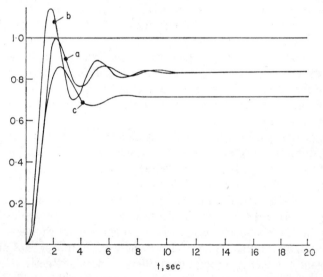

FIG. 2.14. Step response of closed-loop system with $g(s) = 1/(s+1)^3$ and $f(s) = (0 \cdot 625s+1)\,f/(0 \cdot 125s+1)$; (a) $f(s)$ in feedback path, $f = 5$; (b) $f(s)$ in forward path, $f = 5$; (c) $f(s)$ in forward path, $f = 2 \cdot 5$. Responses (a) and (c) have approximately the same proportional overshoot.

the same overshoot (giving smaller offset) if the network is in the feedback path. These remarks apply to desired-value changes: for load disturbances, the response remains the same for either position of the network.

Phase advance has a powerful effect on systems having a small number of effective time constants. It gives much less improvement when there are many significant time constants. This is illustrated in Fig. 2.15 for systems having

$$g(s) = \frac{1}{(1+s\tau/r)^r} \tag{6.5}$$

When $r = 3$ we have the situation of Fig. 2.13. When $r = 6$ we have the situation shown in Fig. 2.12. When $r > 7$, $\hat{\Gamma}_g$ winds round and intersects the negative real axis more than once as s goes from 0 to iR. (It winds back the

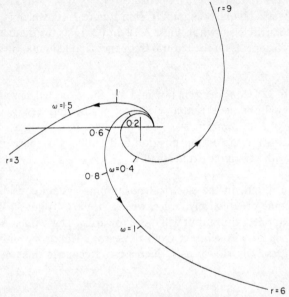

FIG. 2.15. Inverse Nyquist plots for $g(s) = 1/(1+s/r)^r$ with $r = 3, 6, 9$.

same amount as s goes round a quadrant of the semicircle.) As r increases, $g(s)$ tends to $e^{-s\tau}$, and the contour $\hat{\Gamma}_g$ winds round more often and with more nearly constant radius. In this situation there are several rays $E'F'$, $E''F''$, ..., defining possible values ω'_{pc}, ω''_{pc}, ...

The smallest of the ratios OF' to OE', OF'' to OE'', ..., defines the amount by which f can be increased without instability. When r is large or (see Section 10) when $g(s)$ includes a time delay, this may force us to reduce the gain severely when a phase lead compensator is added. Also, because there are several values ω'_{pc}, ω''_{pc}, ..., the simple correlation between phase crossover frequency and speed of response is lost. Phase advance in these circumstances produces little increase in speed of response, while forcing us to reduce f. As a consequence of these remarks, phase advance is widely used in servo systems, which tend to have simple dynamics. In process control, phase advance (that is, "derivative action") tends to be most effective when it is least needed, and is therefore less widely useful.

If we keep $\alpha\tau$ constant and reduce τ, equation (6.4) shows that the effect of the phase advance network approaches $1+(\alpha\tau)\,s$. Such a network cannot be implemented because of its effect on noise. However, the case is different if we can directly measure the signal corresponding to $s\bar{y}$. For example in an electrical positioning servo the speed of rotation can be measured by a tacho-meter: see Fig. 2.4. Then moving k into the feedback path we can consider the effect on the system of a "compensator" $k(1+f_1 s)$. This gives a straight line in the inverse Nyquist diagram, CD in Figure 2.16, which is the limiting case of the semicircle shown in Figs. 2.12 and 2.13 as the diameter becomes very large. The effects on the natural frequency and gain margin are obvious from the Figure.

EXERCISE 6.3. Consider what would be the expected spectrum of the noise in a signal obtained from an electrical positioning servo:
(i) by use of a tachometer
(ii) by measuring the output position and applying a phase advance net-work with very large α and small τ.

EXERCISE 6.4. If, in the electrical positioning system considered above, we let f_1 become progressively larger, we can argue as follows. When a unit step input is applied, the output will move towards a new value. As it does so, the velocity signal will subtract from the error. Hence the movement will become progressively slower as f_1 increases. Reconcile this with what has

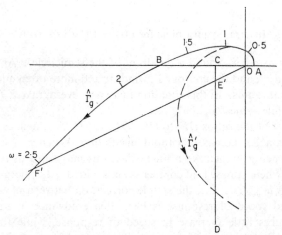

FIG. 2.16. Inverse Nyquist plot for $g(s) = 1/(s+1)^3$ with superimposed line CD for derivative feedback.

been said above. [Note the assumption that stability is maintained as f_1 is progressively increased: this implies the situation shown by $\hat{\Gamma}_g$ in Fig. 2.16, rather than $\hat{\Gamma}'_g$. Increase of f_1 then increases the gain margin. If we increase the loop gain k we can again speed up the response.]

6.2 Phase lag

A second way in which an uncompensated system may be unsatisfactory is that it may give excessive offset. In Fig. 2.10, this means that the ratio of OA to CA is too large. As OA is $\hat{g}(0)$, the remedy is to increase the gain at zero frequency. The scope for increasing gain at all frequencies by using a constant $k > 1$ (hence a constant $\hat{k} < 1$) is severely restricted by the effect on gain margin. What we need is evidently some way of increasing the gain at $s = 0$ while leaving it nearly the same at $s = i\omega_{pc}$, where ω_{pc} is the frequency corresponding to B in Fig. 2.10. A suitable compensator is

$$k(s) = \frac{\alpha + s\tau}{1 + s\tau} \tag{6.6}$$

where $\tau > 0$ is a time constant and α is greater than 1. This is known as a *phase lag* (or *phase retard*) *compensator*. It is always placed in the forward path.

EXERCISE 6.5.   Consider the effect upon offset of placing a phase retard network in the feedback path. [What is the desired value of the output?]

EXERCISE 6.6.   If $k(s)$ is defined by equation (6.6), does its effect upon noise impose any restriction upon the magnitude of α?

Though the phase retard compensator is always placed in the forward path, its effect upon stability and ω_{pc} can be explained by making the transformation shown in Fig. 2.2. Then $k(s)$ in the feedback path is represented by the semicircle CD in Figure 2.17. Setting $f(s)$ in Fig. 2.2 equal to f, we find that the point C is $(-\alpha f, 0)$ and D is $(-f, 0)$. The semicircle is described clockwise as ω goes from 0 to ∞.

By Theorem 5.2, if the open-loop system is asymptotically stable, then so also is the closed-loop system, provided that EF makes no net revolutions as s goes around the contour D. If follows that if E' and F' correspond to the same value of ω (and if there is no other value of ω for which EF is on a ray through the origin) then this is the frequency with which the system will oscillate, when the gain is increased until it is on the verge of instability. This frequency is lower than the frequency corresponding to B. The offset is the ratio of OA to CA, which by (6.1) is also the offset of the system with $k(s)$ in the forward path. If α is large, the offset is therefore very much reduced.

EXERCISE 6.7.   Show that if EF in Fig. 2.17 has rotated clockwise (about half a turn) by the time it reaches $E'F'$, then the closed-loop system is unstable. In this case show that there is another value of ω for which EF is on a ray through the origin.

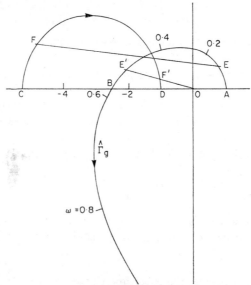

FIG. 2.17.   Inverse Nyquist plot for $g(s) = 1/(s+1)^6$ with superimposed semicircle for phase lag compensator.

The value of α for a phase lag compensator is determined by the reduction in offset which is needed, and by manufacturing convenience. In servo systems the loop gain at $s = 0$ may already be high, and $\alpha = 10$ may give sufficient improvement in offset. In a standard process controller, "integral action" is implemented by the manufacturer as a phase lag compensator with α fixed, and usually in the range 100 to 1000.

The remaining decision left to the designer is the value of the time constant τ. If this is too small, F' in Fig. 2.17 is far from D and the gain (for given gain margin) and the value of ω_{pc} are severely reduced. If τ is too large, elimination of the offset takes place after the initial part of the transient is over, as in Fig. 2.18. In process control, it is usual to make the angle DOF' in Fig. 2.17 about 10°, while in servomechanisms somewhat smaller values may be used, say 5° down to 2°. This is because servomechanisms often have only a small offset before compensation: slow elimination of this small offset is not a disadvantage. As E' is near to B, we may use the frequency ω_{pc} at B in (6.6), which shows, when $\alpha \gg 1$, that the phase lag is 10° at $s = i\omega_{pc}$ if

$$\tau/\alpha \doteqdot 1/\omega_{pc} \tan 10° \doteqdot 5.5/\omega_{pc} \qquad (6.7)$$

This (and corresponding results for different angles DOF') can be used to estimate τ without actually displaying the semicircle in Fig. 2.17.

An important difficulty which arises from phase-lag compensators with large values of α (including "integral action") is *integral saturation*. Suppose, for example, that a temperature controller has proportional action only (that is, a gain k). Let the desired temperature be 55°C, and suppose that the valve

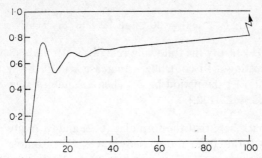

FIG. 2.18. Closed-loop step response for system with phase-lag compensator having too large a time-constant τ.

supplying steam is fully open at 50°C and fully closed at 60°C. Let integral action now be added with $\alpha = 500$: if the gain at high frequencies is left unchanged, then the valve will be fully open after some suitably long time when the temperature is 54·99°C.

Now suppose that the plant is overloaded, so that the temperature falls to 54°C, even though the valve is fully open, and remains there for a considerable time. The integral action unit will accumulate a signal which is much larger than is needed to produce full opening of the valve, and which is limited only by internal effects such as saturation. When the overload is removed, the temperature will rise, but the signal from the integral action unit will continue to hold the valve open: only when the temperature has been above 55°C for a considerable time will the large accumulated signal in the integral action unit be dissipated. This leads to a severe and prolonged overshoot of temperature. Commercial process controllers usually contain a device which prevents the accumulation of excessively large signals in the integral action unit under such conditions, and so mitigates the difficulty.

EXERCISE 6.8. In process control, a PI controller is conventionally assumed to have the transfer function

$$k(s) = k \left(1 + \frac{1}{sT_i}\right) \tag{6.8}$$

where T_i is the integral action time. Show that in the region DF' of Fig. 2.17, this gives substantially the same result as

$$f\frac{\alpha + s\tau}{1 + s\tau} \tag{6.9}$$

if

$$k = f$$

$$T_i = \tau/\alpha \tag{6.10}$$

[Note that at F', $\arg(\alpha + i\omega\tau) \doteq 80°$, and $1 + i\omega\tau$ very nearly equals $i\omega\tau$].

EXERCISE 6.9. Justify the following rule of Ziegler and Nichols [1942] for empirically adjusting a PI controller. Increase k until the system oscillates continuously, and let the period be T. Then a suitable value of T_i is $T/1.2$. [Notice that $5.5 \doteq 2\pi/1.2$.]

We may remark here that the formulae (6.2) and (6.6) are often given in rather different forms from those used above. For example (6.6) is often replaced by

$$\frac{1 + \alpha sT}{1 + sT} \tag{6.11}$$

This keeps the gain unchanged at $s = 0$, and reduces it in the ratio $1/\alpha$ when s is large. Therefore we must increase the gain once more by an amount nearly equal to α in order to give the same gain margin. The compensator actually used is then, within a small adjustment,

$$\alpha\frac{1 + sT}{1 + \alpha sT} \tag{6.12}$$

which is the same as (6.6) if $\alpha T = \tau$. In the same way we have written (6.2) so that the gain is kept approximately the same near ω_{pc}.

6.3 Lead-lag compensation

A system may need both of the preceding types of compensation in order to make its response satisfactory. The procedure then is to design the phase lead compensator first, and incorporate it into the forward path (even if it is to be implemented in the feedback path). This gives a new inverse transfer function $\hat{q}(s)$, for which a phase lag compensator can be designed.

The reason for designing the phase lead compensator first is that its design is insensitive to the presence or absence of a phase lag compensator. That is to say, if we consider the original plant and this plant with a phase lag compensator added, both would demand almost the same phase advance compensator. On the other hand the phase advance compensator may change ω_{pc} and f so greatly that the required phase lag compensator is quite different.

Compensators of greater complexity could be devised by extending the methods given above. For example two phase lead networks could be used with different values of τ. This could be done by designing one, incorporating it into $\hat{q}(s)$ and then designing the other. Alternatively the response $f(s)$ of the two compensators together could be plotted to replace the semicircle CD in Fig. 2.12 or 2.13. In such a case the effect of the compensators on noise in the system would probably force us to accept a relatively small value of α for each.

Frequency response methods are seldom used for the design of anything more complicated than a lead-lag compensator. There are several reasons for this. Where the plant is complicated (as in process control) and frequency response methods are preferred, a phase lag compensator and perhaps some restricted phase advance are all that can usually be justified. Where a complete change in the dynamic behaviour is possible (as in some servomechanisms) the plant dynamics are usually simple and root locus methods can be used [see Section 7]. These provide an insight into the effect of complicated compensators on simple plants which cannot easily be obtained by frequency response methods.

6.4 Further criteria

The methods given above are easy to apply, and usually give an acceptable answer. They should not be used without thought, however, because there are a number of aspects of the problem which they ignore. For example, nothing that has been said so far would indicate that a system having the $\hat{\Gamma}_g$ shown in Fig. 2.19 is unsatisfactory with $f = 1.7$. It has a gain margin of 4, but its time response is quite unsatisfactory, as is shown in Fig. 2.20.

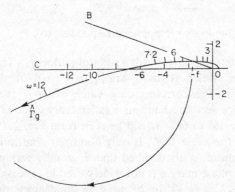

FIG. 2.19. Inverse Nyquist plot for a system having small phase margin:

$$g(s) = \frac{1000 - 10s}{s^3 + 101s^2 + 145 \cdot 25s + 525}$$

With the design method suggested, the unsatisfactory nature of the system would become apparent when the step response was inspected. We need to know why the system behaves in this way, however, in order to see what must be done to improve it.

To give warning of unsatisfactory situations such as the one described, two further quantities are introduced which correlate rather better than the gain

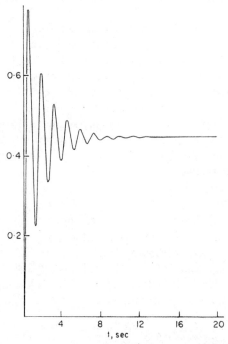

FIG. 2.20.   Closed-loop step response corresponding to Fig. 2.19 with $f = 1 \cdot 7$.

margin with the step response (though still not perfectly). The first of these is the *phase margin*, which is $180° - \arg [\hat{q}(i\omega)/f(i\omega)]$ at the point where $|\hat{q}(i\omega)| = |f(i\omega)|$. The corresponding value of ω is the *gain crossover frequency*, ω_{gc}. For servomechanisms a satisfactory value of phase margin is often found to be 45° to 60°. It will be seen from Fig. 2.19 that the phase margin, which is the angle *BOC*, is only about 20°, indicating that the step response will be more lightly damped than is usually permitted for a servo-mechanism. The phase margin is not widely used in process control, but if it is used a value as low as 30° or 20° may be satisfactory, depending on the problem: here 20° would be too small.

The second quantity is the *M*-value, which is defined by $M(\omega) = |f(i\omega)/\hat{h}(i\omega)|$. For a satisfactory step response, the maximum value

M_m of M for a servomechanism should not greatly exceed 1.2. In Fig. 2.19 it can be seen that M_m, which is f times the reciprocal of the least distance between $\hat{\Gamma}_g$ and the critical point, is about 3. M-values also are not much used in process control: if they are used, values as high as 2 or 3 may be satisfactory.

EXERCISE 6.10. Show that the phase margin and the value of M_m are invariant under transfer of gain from the forward path to the feedback path. [Use $h(i\omega) = 1/[f(i\omega)+\hat{q}(i\omega)]$.]

The phase margin and M-value both indicate that $\hat{\Gamma}_g$ must not be allowed to pass so close to the critical point as it does in Fig. 2.19. Alternatively we may reach the same conclusion by noting that approach of the critical point to $\hat{\Gamma}_g$ represents the approach of a pole to some point on the segment of the imaginary axis included in the contour D. The remedy is to use phase advance, as is shown by the (incomplete) semicircle in Fig. 2.19. Roughly speaking, this increases the distance from $\hat{\Gamma}_g$ to the critical point, which now moves around the semicircle. The new phase margin and M_m are most easily found by plotting $\hat{\Gamma}_q$ for the compensated plant. However, this may not be necessary: enough guidance may be available from Fig. 2.19 to allow a satisfactory compensator to be found. This can be checked by displaying the time response.

EXERCISE 6.11. Show how the phase margin and M_m may be obtained for the compensated plant directly from Fig. 2.19. [Notice that the phase margin is easily obtained. To find the maximum M_m of $M(\omega)$ is less easy: as $f(i\omega)$ now depends on ω, we are no longer concerned simply with the least distance from a fixed point to a curve.]

Yet another criterion which may have to be considered in the design is *bandwidth*. This is particularly important in communication amplifiers. If ω_b is the frequency at which $|\hat{h}(i\omega)/f(i\omega)| = 1.414$, then ω_b defines the bandwidth. Since the closed-loop gain in decibels is $20\log_{10}|h(i\omega)|$, this is the same, when f is independent of s, as saying that ω_b is the frequency at which the gain has fallen 3 dB below the desired value $1/f$. If more than one value of ω satisfies the definition, the lowest is taken as ω_b.

In the inverse Nyquist plot, it is easy to locate ω_b when f is constant. A circle of radius $1.414f$ is drawn around the critical point and the appropriate intersection with $\hat{\Gamma}_g$ defines ω_b. If $f(s)$ depends on s and is actually implemented in the feedback path, the definition is not very meaningful. If however $f(s)$ represents a compensator which will be implemented in the forward path, the definition gives the correct result. This is to say, ω_b as defined is invariant under transfer of $f(s)$ from the forward path to the feedback path.

F

6.5 Stabilization

The examples given previously in this Section have illustrated the simplest and commonest situation. More complicated situations usually offer no real increase in difficulty. If the plant is open-loop unstable, Theorem 5.2 shows that p_0 net counterclockwise encirclements must be acquired as the critical point goes from the origin to its design point, if the system is to be stabilized. The loss of clockwise encirclements counts equally with the gain of counterclockwise encirclements to produce the net change, as in Fig. 2.21. If $\hat{q}(0) = 0$, care must be taken to represent correctly in $\hat{\Gamma}_q$ the map of the indentation.

Figure 2.22 illustrates one type of problem which can arise. The open-loop system has a simple pole at the origin, and so is unstable: all other poles are in the open left half-plane. The contour D is indented to include the pole at the

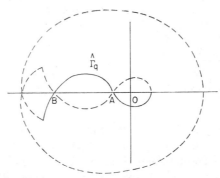

FIG. 2.21. Stabilization of an open-loop unstable system. The origin is encircled twice clockwise, whereas points between A and B are not encircled. If $p_0 = 2$, the closed-loop system is stable when the critical point is between A and B.

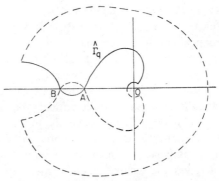

FIG. 2.22. Stabilization of an open-loop unstable system with $p_0 = 1$. The closed-loop system is stable when the critical point is between 0 and A, or to the left of B.

origin, and the indentation maps as shown. When f is increased from zero, the critical point crosses $\hat{\Gamma}_q$ if the indentation of D is small enough, and the system becomes asymptotically stable. When the critical point reaches A the system again goes unstable, becoming stable again after B. In all cases such as this, where $\hat{\Gamma}_q$ indicates stability for arbitrarily large gains, the limitations of the plant model should be borne in mind.

As another example, Fig. 2.23 shows the conditional stability of an open-loop stable system. When the critical point is between A and B the system is

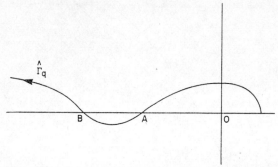

FIG. 2.23.   Inverse Nyquist plot for a conditionally stable system having $p_0 = 0$.

unstable. For all other (positive) loop gains it is stable. Again the limitations of the model at high frequencies should be borne in mind: for any practical system the phase lag will ultimately exceed 180°, giving a further unstable range of positive gain.

EXERCISE 6.12.   Interpret Figs. 2.21, 2.22 and 2.23 as in Section 5.2. [Notice that $q(s)$ is strictly proper if and only if we can make $|\hat{q}(s)|$ as large as we please, everywhere on the semicircular arc of D, by suitably large choice of R. Interpret the crossings of $\hat{\Gamma}_q$ by the critical point as in Section 5.1.]

When the shape of $\hat{\Gamma}_g$ does not allow any suitable choice of critical point which will give stability, it is necessary to change the shape of $\hat{\Gamma}_g$ by means of a compensator. Usually a phase lead compensator is required, and the situation can be analysed by superimposing the semicircular locus for the compensator on the plot of $\hat{\Gamma}_g$. As an example, Fig. 2.24 shows the stabilization of a system by phase advance. Here the uncompensated system is unstable for all $k > 0$. By adding phase advance as shown, the phase lag of the compensated plant can be made less than 180° for $0 < \omega < 0.92$ approximately. The gain margin is then OF'/OE' which is about 2·8. The phase margin is obtained by finding the value of ω for which the distances from the origin to the compensator locus and to $\hat{g}(i\omega)$ are equal. The angle between the corresponding rays is the phase margin. Notice that the maximum phase advance is now placed well below the phase crossover frequency.

No general rules can be given for such problems because of the great variety in which they may arise. The general principles which apply will,

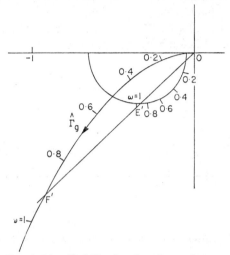

FIG. 2.24. Stabilization by phase advance:
$$g(s) = 1/s^2(s+1), \quad k(s) = 0 \cdot 054(1+12s)/(1+s).$$

however, be clear from what has been said already. Usually the designer will have no difficulty in seeing what must be done to improve the system, provided that phase-lead or phase-lag compensation will suffice. Only when the required compensator is itself complicated do the methods of the following Section become necessary.

EXERCISE 6.13. When $\hat{q}(s)$ is rational it maps the complex plane conformally into itself. Hence the map of a square grid is a curvilinear grid

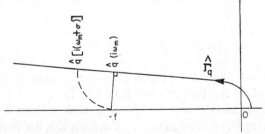

FIG. 2.25. Relation between inverse Nyquist plot and pole location.

preserving the right angles of the original intersections. Suppose that $\hat{\Gamma}_q$ passes close to the critical point and is substantially straight in the vicinity of this point: see Fig. 2.25. Let M take its maximum value M_m where $\omega = \omega_m$, and let the change in ω in a distance $1/M_m$ along $\hat{\Gamma}_q$ be σ, as in Fig. 2.25. Show that the closed-loop system has poles at approximately

$$s = -\sigma \pm i\omega_m \qquad (6.13)$$

where the approximation improves as M_m increases. Relate (6.13) to the height and breadth of the resonance peak (the peak in M) at ω_m. [Note that at the point $\hat{q}(i(\omega_m + \sigma))]$ in Fig. 2.25, $M = 0.707 M_m$ if $\hat{\Gamma}_q$ is straight over the appropriate segment.]

EXERCISE 6.14.   What does equation (6.13) suggest about the use of M_m as a criterion for relative damping of a servomechanism? [We should expect the damping to depend not only on M_m but also on the rate at which $\hat{\Gamma}_q$ is traversed: what could affect this rate?.]

7. Root loci

For a closed-loop system with $f(s) = f$ and $g(s) k(s) = q(s)$, we have from equation (4.27)

$$h(s) = \frac{q(s)}{1 + fq(s)} \qquad (7.1)$$

We assume that $q(s)$ can be written, in the notation of Chapter 1, Section 4.1,

$$q(s) = \frac{\varepsilon(s)}{\psi(s)} \qquad (7.2)$$

where $\psi(s)$ and $\varepsilon(s)$ are relatively prime polynomials, respectively of degree a and z, and are monic. To satisfy this last condition we assume $q(s)$ to have been divided by an appropriate constant, which we regard as a gain k_2 transferred from the forward path to the feedback path. Notice that the underlying system need not have least order: if it does not, then decoupling zeros will cancel when we form $q(s)$, and we shall have $a < n$. On using (7.2) in (7.1) we obtain

$$h(s) = \frac{\varepsilon(s)}{\psi(s) + f\varepsilon(s)} \qquad (7.3)$$

From Section 3.1 of Chapter 1, we know that the decoupling zeros of the open-loop system are the same as those of the closed-loop system. Consequently no cancellation can occur between numerator and denominator of (7.3), for if it did the same factor would cancel in (7.2) and so $\varepsilon(s)$ and $\psi(s)$

could not be relatively prime. This shows that if $q(s)$ is strictly proper, $h(s)$ has the same finite and infinite zeros as $q(s)$. That is to say, any zero of $\varepsilon(s)$ is a zero of $q(s)$ and of $h(s)$, and both $q(s)$ and $h(s)$ have a zero at $s = \infty$, the multiplicity being the same for both.

When f is large we may write

$$h(s) = \frac{\varepsilon(s)}{f\left[\varepsilon(s) + \dfrac{\psi(s)}{f}\right]} \tag{7.4}$$

The poles of $h(s)$ are the a zeros of $\varepsilon(s) + \psi(s)/f$, and as $f \to \infty$ it follows that any finite zero of this expression tends to a zero of $\varepsilon(s)$; that is, to a zero of $q(s)$. Furthermore, let C be a circular contour of radius R centred on the origin and enclosing all zeros of $\varepsilon(s)$. By choosing f sufficiently large we may ensure that $|\psi(s)/f| < |\varepsilon(s)|$ everywhere on C. Then by Rouché's theorem [Chapter 1, Section 8] the functions $\varepsilon(s)$ and $\varepsilon(s) + \psi(s)/f$ have the same number of zeros within C. This is true however large the initial choice of R, whence it follows that as $f \to \infty$, z poles of $h(s)$ tend to the finite zeros of $q(s)$; while $a-z$ poles tend to infinity, and so tend to the remaining zeros of $q(s)$.

Therefore if we plot the poles of $h(s)$ in the complex plane as functions of f as f goes from 0 to ∞, we shall obtain continuous curves, a in number, called *root loci*. For $f = 0$, (7.3) shows that each root locus will start at a zero of $\psi(s)$, which is a pole of $q(s)$. As $f \to \infty$, z of the root loci will tend to the z finite zeros of $q(s)$, while $a-z$ of the root loci will go off to infinity. By calibrating the root loci with the value of f, we may read off at once from such a diagram the poles and zeros of $h(s)$ for any f.

It will be noticed that the root loci show the behaviour of the poles of $h(s)$. If the underlying open-loop system does not have least order, then its de-coupling zeros are poles of the open-loop system, as in Section 4.1, but they do not appear as poles of $q(s)$ or $h(s)$. These poles, which do not move when feedback is applied, are usually omitted, but if desired they may be shown by poles with superimposed zeros.

Traditionally, root loci were used for three purposes. First, the positions of the closed-loop poles in the complex plane indicated the stability and stability margin of the system. Secondly, by summing the contributions of the poles to the step response, the latter could be obtained with relatively little work. Thirdly, the form of the root loci was used to suggest how further poles and zeros (a compensator $k(s)$) could be added to those of $g(s)$ to improve the performance. These three objectives were attainable because the root loci could be constructed by simple graphical procedures, at least when $q(s)$ had no more than say 4 or 6 poles.

Our viewpoint is different, being directed towards the graphical display of computer output. We assume that the poles of $h(s)$ are computed as functions of f by suitable numerical methods, and are displayed on a cathode-ray tube. Also we assume that time responses can be called up on the display as needed. There remain two useful functions of the root loci: to show stability margins and to suggest the form of a suitable compensator.

Nevertheless, the simple rules for constructing root loci which were used in pencil-and-paper work retain some value. They give insight into the behaviour of the root loci which is helpful when designing compensators. We therefore state some of the simpler rules, leaving most of the proofs as exercises.

(i) The root loci start (when $f = 0$) at the poles of $q(s)$.

(ii) The root loci terminate (as $f \to \infty$) on the finite and infinite zeros of $q(s)$. Both (i) and (ii) were established above.

(iii) Let s be a point in the complex plane and let rays be drawn to s from each of the poles and each of the finite zeros of $q(s)$. Let the angles of the rays from the poles, measured counterclockwise from the direction of the positive real axis be θ_1, θ_2, ..., θ_a, and let the angles of the rays from the zeros similarly be ϕ_1, ϕ_2, ..., ϕ_z. Then s lies on a root locus for some $f > 0$ if and only if

$$\phi_1 + \phi_2 + \ ... \ + \phi_z - \theta_1 - \theta_2 - \ ... \ - \theta_a = (2p+1)\,\pi \qquad (7.5)$$

for some integer p. The corresponding value of f is $f = -1/q(s)$, which is real and positive. Notice that multiple poles or zeros of $q(s)$ are counted according to their multiplicity in evaluating (7.5).

(iv) A point on the real axis lies on the locus of some root, for $f > 0$, if and only if there is an odd number of poles and zeros of $q(s)$, taken together, on the real axis to the right of it.

(v) Two poles (not separated by a zero) which approach each other along the real axis break away from it when they meet, the two branches of the locus at this point being at right-angles to the real axis. Conversely two complex poles which approach a common point (not a zero) on the real axis do so along a path which meets the real axis at right-angles. After meeting they move apart on the real axis.

(vi) The angles, from the origin to the a–z poles which go off to infinity, tend as $f \to \infty$ to

$$\frac{\pi}{a-z}, \quad \frac{3\pi}{a-z}, \quad ..., \quad \frac{(2a-2z-1)\,\pi}{a-z} \qquad (7.6)$$

EXAMPLE 7.1.   Let $q(s) = g(s) = (s+1)/(s+2)(s+3)$. The zero of $g(s)$ is marked by a circle in Fig. 2.26, and the poles by crosses. By (iv) the two segments $(-\infty, -3)$ and $(-2, -1)$ of the real axis are parts of root loci. The loci of the poles are as shown: the pole at -2 moves to the right and approaches -1 as $f \to \infty$, while the pole at -3 moves off to infinity at the left.

EXAMPLE 7.2. Let $q(s) = g(s) = (s+3)/(s+1)(s+2)$. In Fig. 2.27, the two segments $(-\infty, -3)$ and $(-2, -1)$ are again parts of root loci. Now however, the two poles move together, then separate from the real axis and travel round until they unite again on the negative real axis. One then goes to the zero at -3, while the other goes off to infinity at the left.

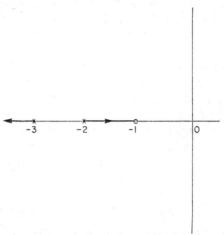

FIG. 2.26. Root loci for $g(s) = (s+1)/(s+2)(s+3)$.

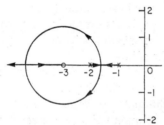

FIG. 2.27. Root loci for $g(s) = (s+3)/(s+1)(s+2)$.

EXERCISE 7.1. Prove rule (iii) above. [Let

$$q(s) = \frac{(s-\zeta_1)(s-\zeta_2)\ldots(s-\zeta_z)}{(s-\alpha_1)(s-\alpha_2)\ldots(s-\alpha_a)} \tag{7.7}$$

and find the condition for $1+fq(s) = 0$].

EXERCISE 7.2. Prove rule (iv) above. [Use (iii)].

EXERCISE 7.3. Prove rule (v) above. [The loci of the two poles cannot terminate except at zeros, whether finite or infinite. Let $\phi(f, s) = 1+fq(s)$ have a double root s_0 when $f = f_0$, so that $\partial\phi/\partial s = 0$ at $f = f_0, s = s_0$. Then consider the implications of $\phi(f, s) \equiv 0$, which gives

$$\frac{\partial \phi}{\partial f}\, \delta f + \frac{\partial \phi}{\partial s}\, \delta s + \frac{1}{2}\frac{\partial^2 \phi}{\partial s^2}\, (\delta s)^2 + \ldots = 0 \qquad (7.8)$$

Use this to evaluate δs at $s = s_0$ for positive and negative δf.]

EXERCISE 7.4. Prove rule (vi) above. [Write equation (7.3) in the form

$$h(s) = \cfrac{1}{\cfrac{\psi(s)}{\varepsilon(s)} + f} \qquad (7.9)$$

and notice that $\psi(s)/\varepsilon(s) = s^{a-z}\{1 + 0(s^{-1})\}$.]

EXERCISE 7.5. If s_0 is a triple pole of $h(s)$, how do the root loci depart from s_0? [Take the Taylor series (7.8) to the term in $(\delta s)^3$.]

The poles α_k' of $h(s)$ which are shown by the root loci all contribute to the step response. Usually $h(s)$ is strictly proper and the poles are distinct and nonzero: the step response can then be written

$$h(0) + \sum_{k=1}^{a} \rho_k\, e^{\sigma_k t}\, [\cos \omega_k t + i \sin \omega_k t] \qquad (7.10)$$

where $\alpha_k' = \sigma_k + i\omega_k$. The complex coefficients ρ_k can be obtained when $z \geqslant 1$ from the equation

$$\rho_k = \prod_{j=1}^{z} (\alpha_k' - \zeta_j) \Big/ \alpha_k' \prod_{\substack{j=1 \\ j \neq k}}^{a} (\alpha_k' - \alpha_j') \qquad (7.11)$$

where ζ_j are the zeros of $h(s)$. Since complex poles and zeros occur in conjugate pairs, the response (7.10) is real.

EXERCISE 7.6. Write

$$\frac{h(s)}{s} = \prod_{j=1}^{z} (s - \zeta_i) \Big/ s \prod_{j=1}^{a} (s - \alpha_j') \qquad (7.12)$$

and expand this in partial fractions to obtain (7.11). [Use the fact that the α_j' are distinct.]

EXERCISE 7.7. Show that if $h(s)$ has no zero, the numerator in (7.11) is 1. [The general formula for the numerator is $\varepsilon(\alpha_k')$.]

Equation (7.11) shows that $|\rho_k|$ can be obtained in the following way. Multiply together the distances from α_k' to each of the ζ_j. Also multiply together the distances from α_k' to the origin and to each of the other poles. The ratio of the first product to the second is $|\rho_k|$. It often happens, when this calculation is made, that there is one pole pair which provides the major

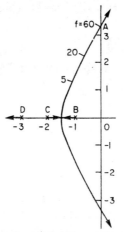

FIG. 2.28.   Root loci for $g(s) = 1/(s+1)(s+2)(s+3)$.

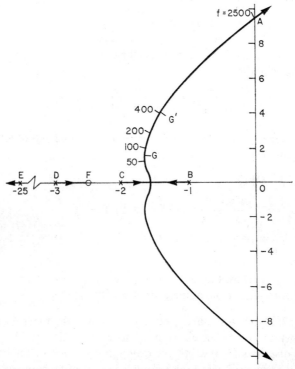

FIG. 2.29.   Effect of adding a phase lead compensator to the system of Fig. 2.28; $k(s) = (1+0\cdot4s)/(1+0\cdot04s)$. Note the difference in scales of the two axes.

contribution to (7.10). This is usually the pole pair nearest to the origin, and is called the dominant pole pair. In such circumstances the frequency and damping of the transient can be obtained at once from the location of the dominant poles. This relationship is useful as a guide in selecting the gain f. Final adjustment of f, however, is usually best made by displaying the step response.

EXAMPLE 7.3.   The root loci for $g(s) = 1/(s+1)(s+2)(s+3)$ are shown in Fig. 2.28. The frequency ω_{pc} with which the system oscillates when it is on the verge of instability is defined by the point A on the imaginary axis. Notice that the sum of the three angles OBA, OCA, ODA is π, which can be used to fix A in pencil-and-paper work. If we wish to increase this frequency we may use a phase lead compensator

$$k(s) = \frac{s+1/\alpha\tau}{s+1/\tau} \tag{7.13}$$

in the forward path. That is, we add a zero at $s = -1/\alpha\tau$ and a pole at

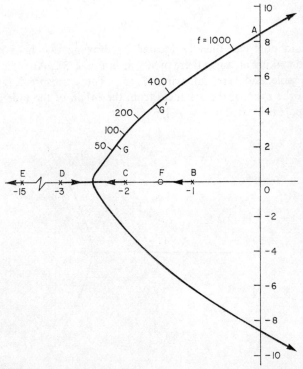

FIG. 2.30.   Effect of an alternative phase lead compensator on the system of Fig. 2.28, $k(s) = (1+0\cdot67s)/(1+0\cdot067s)$.

$s = -1/\tau$, as in Fig. 2.29. To agree with (7.2) the numerator and denominator have been made monic while a gain α has been moved into the
feedback path. The root loci now depend on the locations of the new pole and
zero: Figs. 2.29 and 2.30 show two possibilities. In each Figure the sum of
the angles OBA, OCA and OEA, less the angle OFA, is π. This shows that the
frequency corresponding to A has been increased. The appropriate gain for a
given degree of stability can be read off the root locus as at G or G'.

EXAMPLE 7.4.   Suppose that we wish to choose α and τ in Example 7.3
so that the root locus for the compensated system passes through the point
$-2+i2$ in Fig. 2.28. On evaluating the sum of the angles corresponding to
the three existing poles, we find for the left-hand side of (7.5) when $s = -2$
$+i2$,

$$\theta_1 + \theta_2 + \theta_3 = 116.6° + 90° + 63.4° = 270° \qquad (7.14)$$

When the new pole and zero are added, we shall require

$$\theta_1 + \theta_2 + \theta_3 + \theta_4 - \phi_1 = 180° \qquad (7.15)$$

which gives

$$\phi_1 - \theta_4 = 90° \qquad (7.16)$$

The zero and pole can then be located by drawing two lines meeting at
$-2+i2$ and making an angle there of 90°, as in Fig. 2.31. Any two such lines
will give a pole and zero satisfying (7.15). The corresponding α can be
obtained as the ratio of the distances from the origin of the pole and of the
zero. The pole is located at $s = -1/\tau$.

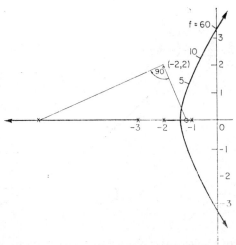

FIG. 2.31.   Choice of a compensator to place a pair of poles at $s = 2 \pm i2$.

EXERCISE 7.8. Sketch the lines of constant $\phi - \theta$ for a phase advance compensator as in (7.13) with $\alpha = 10$. Suggest how τ might be chosen.

EXERCISE 7.9. From equation (6.3) we know that the maximum phase advance obtainable from $k(s)$ in (7.13), for $\alpha = 10$ and s imaginary, is $55°$. Obtain this result from the sketch in Exercise 7.8.

When the compensator (7.13) does not give enough improvement, two zeros and two poles may be used, due account being taken of the limitations imposed by noise. This was illustrated in Section 6.1, where real poles and zeros were assumed to be chosen. It is also possible to use complex poles and zeros, and an example is shown in Fig. 2.32.

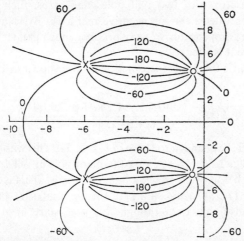

FIG. 2.32.   Phase angle contributed to the sum in equation (7.5) by a compensator having zeros at $s = 0·75 \pm i4·5$ and poles at $s = -6 \pm i5$.

In this Figure there are shown the lines, on which the contribution $\phi_1 + \phi_2 - \theta_1 - \theta_2$ to the sum in (7.5) takes given constant values. Notice that for $s = i\omega$, this contribution is the phase advance considered in Section 6.1: it is zero for $\omega = 0$, becomes negative as ω increases, then is zero again for $\omega = 3·9$ and finally becomes positive. This phase angle can be uniquely defined everywhere on the imaginary axis by continuity. On the other hand it is clear from Fig. 2.32 that the angle cannot be continuous everywhere in the complex plane (consider for example a path going around a pole). This offers no difficulty in equation (7.5), because the sum need only be defined within multiples of 2π. In Fig. 2.32 we have chosen to locate the discontinuity in the angle at $\pm \pi$.

It will be seen that above and to the right of the zero at $-0.75 + i4.5$ the contribution to (7.5) is beneficial. Below and to the left of this zero, however, the contribution has an adverse effect. By suitably locating the poles and zeros, we can ensure that the beneficial effect of the compensator is concentrated in the region where it will give most improvement in the plant loci. In doing this we must ensure that the region of adverse effect is placed where it will not cause difficulties.

EXAMPLE 7.5.   Suppose that

$$g(s) = \frac{1}{(s+1)(s+1-i5)(s+1+i5)} \qquad (7.17)$$

which has a pair of complex poles giving a lightly damped response. If we used a compensator with two real poles and zeros, then beneficial effect would be concentrated near the negative real axis. By using complex poles and zeros in the compensator we may produce much greater improvement in the region where it is needed.

The root loci for the uncompensated plant are shown in Fig. 2.33. When the compensator

$$k(s) = \frac{(s+0 \cdot 75 - i4 \cdot 5)(s+0 \cdot 75 + i4 \cdot 5)}{(s+6-i5)(s+6+i5)} \qquad (7.18)$$

is added, the loci are changed to those in Fig. 2.34. This was the compensator considered in Fig. 2.32. Notice that the plant pole at $-1+i5$ is now drawn back to the left before it crosses the imaginary axis. This is the result of the contribution by (7.18) to the sum (7.5) in the region traversed by the new locus. Notice also that even though this pole starts near to the zero at

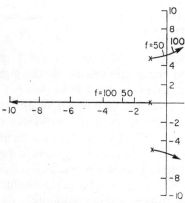

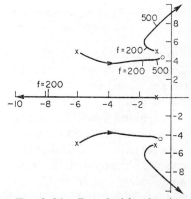

FIG. 2.33.   Root loci for
$g(s) = 1/(s+1)(s^2+2s+26)$.

FIG. 2.34.   Root loci for the plant of Fig. 2.33 when the compensator of Fig. 2.32 is added.

$-0.75+i4.5$, it does not end on it: often poles do go to a nearby zero, but this is by no means invariable. The step response with $f = 200$ is shown in Fig. 2.35, where f has been placed in the forward path.

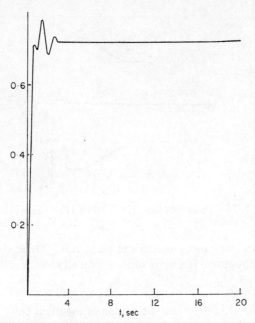

FIG. 2.35.   Step response corresponding to Fig. 2.34 when a gain $f = 200$ is placed in the forward path.

An inappropriate choice of compensator is illustrated by Fig. 2.36, which is for

$$k(s) = \frac{(s+1-i6)(s+1+i6)}{(s+6+i5)(s+6+i5)} \qquad (7.19)$$

The plant pole at $-1+i5$ is now in a region where the compensator produces an adverse effect, and its locus is therefore drawn somewhat downward.

EXERCISE 7.10.   It appears from a comparison between Figs. 2.33 and 2.36 that the compensator (7.19), though inappropriate, has nevertheless allowed a higher gain f without instability. Explain this apparent anomaly. [Find the value of $k(s)$ at $s = 0$, $s = i\omega_{pc}$. Note that the compensator produces phase lag for small imaginary values of s.]

An alternative way of choosing the compensator is to place its zeros where they will cancel some of the plant poles. The resulting system then has an i.d. zero, assuming that the compensator is placed in the usual position, preceding the plant. The cancelled pole will still exist physically, and the corresponding mode may be excited by disturbances entering by paths other than the one from the plant input. The mode will also be excited from the plant input if the

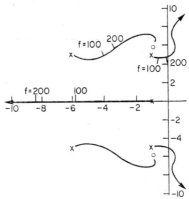

FIG. 2.36. Root loci for $g(s) = 1/(s+1)(s^2+2s+26)$ and
$k(s) = (s^2+2s+37)/(s^2+12s+61)$.

added zero does not exactly cancel the plant role. These contingencies are easily assessed, but there is a more serious difficulty which is illustrated by the following example.

EXAMPLE 7.6.   Let the transfer function of the plant be

$$g(s) = \frac{1}{(s+1)(s+1-i6)(s+1+i6)} \tag{7.20}$$

The compensator

$$k(s) = \frac{(s+1-i6)(s+1+i6)}{(s+6-i5)(s+6+i5)} \tag{7.21}$$

cancels the original complex poles and replaces them by others further to the left. The corresponding root loci are shown in Fig. 2.37. With $f = 200$ the response will be satisfactory.

Suppose, however, that the plant characteristics change, until it is represented by (7.17) rather than (7.20). The root loci are now those shown in Fig. 2.36, and the compensator has become quite inappropriate, exerting an adverse effect on the loci. Changes in the plant can always produce such an effect if they are large enough, but by placing the compensator zeros over the assumed plant poles we clearly provide less margin than if we had placed the zeros nearer to the origin (compare Fig. 2.34).

The sensitivity of the compensated system to likely changes in the plant is one of the matters which must be considered in the design procedure. It may force us to compromise by accepting a worse performance (in the design condition) for the sake of a reduced sensitivity to plant changes. Changes in the compensator would have similar effects, but usually the compensator can be constructed of elements which change very little.

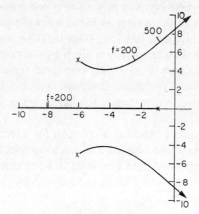

FIG. 2.37. Root loci for $g(s) = 1/(s+1)(s^2+2s+37)$ and
$$k(s) = (s^2+2s+37)/(s^2+12s+61).$$

EXERCISE 7.11. What is the difference between cancelling a lightly-damped pole by a zero in $k(s)$ at the input of the plant, and cancelling the same pole by a zero in $l(s)$ at the output, where $q(s) = l(s) g(s) k(s)$? [Consider the effect of an input on the corresponding mode. Notice that we are not often able to make $l(s) \neq 1$: to do so is to change the output of the system, that is, to measure a different output variable or to alter the measuring instrument].

7.1 Design procedure

When the root locus technique is used for design, the basic approach is similar to that explained in Section 6. The root locus diagram for $g(s)$ is computed numerically and is displayed graphically. It may be obvious at this stage that compensation is required, in which case $k(s)$ is specified in terms of its poles and zeros, and the root loci are displayed for $q(s) = g(s) k(s)$. When the root loci indicate that the system may be satisfactory, a tentative gain f is selected. Notice that we are still considering the gain to be in the feedback path, in order to conform with previous notation and with equation (7.2).

Having chosen a tentative gain, we display the step response (with the gain now in the correct position) and make suitable changes in the gain if needed. If no adjustment of the gain can be found which gives satisfactory response, the compensation is adjusted, using the root locus plot again for guidance.

G

By this iterative technique the design requirements are satisfied as well as possible.

In judging whether a given root locus diagram is likely to represent a satisfactory design, most of the same information can be obtained as was obtained from the inverse Nyquist plot. The phase crossover frequency ω_{pc} is the frequency at which the system oscillates when the gain is increased until the system is on the verge of instability. (Our language assumes the system to be open-loop stable.) This frequency is given by the point at which the root locus crosses the imaginary axis, if only one (or a symmetric pair) does so. If more than one locus (or more than one symmetric pair) crosses the imaginary axis, then ω_{pc} corresponds to that crossing which occurs at the lowest gain.

The gain margin could be used as a criterion for selecting a tentative loop gain. However, the root locus diagram allows us to select the gain in a direct way so as to give any desired (and available) stability margin. This margin is measured for a pole at $s = -\sigma + i\omega$, as in Section 2, by the angle θ defined by

$$\theta = \tan^{-1}\frac{\sigma}{\omega} \tag{7.22}$$

By drawing a ray from the origin at the chosen angle θ, the value of gain f can be found which just makes the most lightly-damped complex pair of poles lie on the ray.

The ease with which a specified stability margin can be obtained is an important advantage of the root locus technique. For pencil-and-paper work, the correlation between pole locations and step response was equally important. With computer graphic facilities available, this correlation becomes less essential: the time response can be displayed and the gain finally adjusted to give satisfactory response. This final adjustment is particularly necessary when more than two poles contribute significantly to the step response, as it then becomes more difficult to correlate the response with the information contained in the root loci.

The steady-state offset can be obtained from the root loci, though less easily than from the inverse Nyquist plot. It is readily shown that the proportional offset, assuming asymptotic stability of the closed-loop system, is

$$\frac{1}{1+q(0)f} \tag{7.23}$$

and this is true however the gain f is distributed between the forward path and the feedback path. By (7.7),

$$q(0) = \frac{(-\zeta_1)(-\zeta_2)\dots(-\zeta_z)}{(-\alpha_1)(-\alpha_2)\dots(-\alpha_a)} \tag{7.24}$$

and this is a real number, ordinarily positive. Therefore we obtain $q(0)$ by multiplying together the distances from the origin of the zeros, and dividing by the distances from the origin of the poles, of $q(s)$. If $q(0)f$ is large, we may approximate (7.23) by $1/q(0)f$.

The method just given for evaluating the offset is useful in suggesting a suitable compensator. For example it shows that to reduce offset we may add a pole near the origin and a zero further away: compare this with the phase-lag compensator, Section 6.2. However, it is probably worth while having the computer evaluate (7.23), once f has been chosen, rather than attempt to find it from the graphical display.

EXERCISE 7.12. Obtain equation (7.23). [Let the forward path have transfer function $q(s)f_1$ and the feedback path have gain f_2. The desired output for a unit step input is then $1/f_2$. Compare this with the actual output: write $f = f_1 f_2$ and use Theorem 8.4 of Chapter 1. Notice that the result is valid if $q(s)$ has a pole in the closed right half-plane; in particular at the origin. Examine the details of the proof in this last case.]

In concluding this Section we reiterate a point made earlier, which needs to be kept in mind when comparing the root locus diagram with the inverse Nyquist diagram. In the latter we transfer gain from the forward path to the feedback path and back again as convenient. In the former, however, we always represent $q(s)$ as in (7.2). This expression has monic polynomials in numerator and denominator, showing that some fixed gain has been transferred to the feedback path. Thereafter we may modify the gain in the feedback path, but we refrain from transferring gain into the forward path until after the design is completed (or until we simulate a tentative design).

7.2 Comparison of techniques

To some extent, the suitability of a design method depends on the problem in hand. For example, the root locus technique has never been popular in process control, because complicated transfer functions (often with time delays) are the rule, and the method does not cope well with these. There are also personal and national preferences—the root locus approach has never become so popular in Britain as in the U.S.A.

In general terms, however, the root locus technique has the advantage of giving direct information about stability margin, easy visualization of step response, and guidance on complicated compensators. These advantages are clearest when the plant dynamics are simple.

The inverse Nyquist method can be used with measured plant responses, and is insensitive to increase in complexity of the plant. It gives good guidance for simple compensators, but less guidance for more complicated compensators. It also generalizes to nonlinear and time-dependent systems as in Section 11, and to multivariable systems as in Chapter 3: no corresponding generalizations of the root locus method have yet been found. Direct Nyquist plots share the same advantages and disadvantages as inverse Nyquist plots, except that they are generally less appropriate for multivariable systems.

When computer-aided design facilities are available, the need to find time responses by indirect methods disappears. The most important advantage of the root locus method is then the guidance which it gives in designing compensators beyond the simple lead-lag compensator. It can do this for systems with one input and one output, provided that the plant is not too complicated.

In view of these remarks it seems best to have both methods available; to work preferentially with the inverse Nyquist method; but to use the root locus method when circumstances are appropriate.

EXERCISE 7.13. Attempt to design a phase-lead compensator for a plant having $g(s) = 1/(1+s/12)^{12}$ by the root locus technique. [Even if computer facilities are available, it is difficult to obtain the information which comes easily from the inverse Nyquist method.]

EXERCISE 7.14. Attempt to design a compensator with a pair of complex zeros and two poles, for a plant having the transfer function given in equation (7.17), using the inverse Nyquist method. [Again the method shows up badly, even with computer-aided design facilities.]

8. Sensitivity

If a small perturbation is made in a control system, the signals throughout the system will generally change. A *sensitivity coefficient* relates the change in a signal to the perturbation, often by reference to some datum case.

In a control system we are interested in two types of sensitivity. The first is the change in the output signal $\bar{y}$ when a disturbance $\bar{d}$ enters the system, with the input $\bar{v}$ held constant. The response of the system to disturbance signals is, of course, linear. The second type of sensitivity in which we are interested is the change in the output $\bar{y}$ when the coefficients in the forward transfer function $q(s)$ are changed, the input again remaining constant. The response of the output to such changes is nonlinear. The sensitivity of the

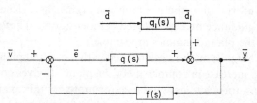

FIG. 2.38. Control system with injected disturbance.

output to changes in $f(s)$ is not usually of equal interest: it is generally high, and only elements of high stability are therefore placed in the feedback path.

To consider the first kind of sensitivity we take the situation shown in Fig. 2.38. We assume, here and in what follows, that $q(s) \not\equiv 0$ and that the open-loop and closed-loop systems are asymptotically stable. The disturbance $\bar{d}$ enters the system at some point, where the transfer function between $\bar{d}$ and the output $\bar{y}$ is $q_1(s)$. The "disturbance referred to the output" is then $\bar{d}_1 = q_1(s)\,\bar{d}$, which is combined additively with the signal $q(s)\,\bar{e}$. We thus have

$$\bar{y} = \bar{d}_1 + q\bar{e} \tag{8.1}$$

$$= \bar{d}_1 + q(\bar{v} - f\bar{y}) \tag{8.2}$$

$$\bar{y} = \frac{q}{1+qf}\,\bar{v} + \frac{1}{1+qf}\,\bar{d}_1 \tag{8.3}$$

The change $\delta\bar{y}$ due to the presence of $\bar{d}$ is therefore $\bar{d}_1/(1+qf)$, whereas if the feedback path were opened it would be just $\bar{d}_1$. Consequently the effect of feedback is to change the sensitivity to load disturbances in the ratio

$$S(s) = \frac{1}{1+q(s)f(s)} = \frac{h(s)}{q(s)} = \frac{\hat{q}(s)}{\hat{h}(s)} \tag{8.4}$$

so that $S(s)$ is the reciprocal of the return difference. The last expression shows how $S(i\omega)$ can be obtained from the inverse Nyquist diagram. Notice that $S(0)$ is also equal to the offset for a unit step input as defined in Section 6.

To consider the second kind of perturbation, let q_0 and h_0 be the datum values of $q = q_0 + \delta q$ and $h = h_0 + \delta h$. Then δh is related to δq in the following way,

$$\hat{h} = f + \hat{q} \tag{8.5}$$

$$\delta\hat{h} = \delta\hat{q} \tag{8.6}$$

that is, to the first order,

$$\delta\left(\frac{1}{h}\right) = -\frac{1}{h_0{}^2}\,\delta h = -\frac{1}{q_0{}^2}\,\delta q = \delta\left(\frac{1}{q}\right) \tag{8.7}$$

$$\frac{\delta h(s)}{h_0(s)} = S(s)\frac{\delta q(s)}{q_0(s)} \tag{8.8}$$

where $S(s)$ is defined by (8.4) and is evaluated at the datum value q_0. Equation (8.8) expresses the proportional change $\delta h/h_0$ in terms of the proportional change $\delta q/q_0$.

As an alternative way of showing the effect of feedback on the sensitivity of the output to changes δq, we may compare two systems, one with and one without feedback. In order to make the outputs comparable let the two systems be

(i) an open-loop system with transfer function

$$\frac{h_0(s)}{q_0(s)} q(s) \qquad (8.9)$$

(ii) a closed-loop system with transfer function

$$h(s) = \frac{q(s)}{1 + q(s) f(s)} \qquad (8.10)$$

For a given input $\bar{v}$, and perturbation δq, the change in the output of the first is

$$\frac{h_0}{q_0} \delta q \, \bar{v} \qquad (8.11)$$

while the change in the output of the second is to the first order

$$\delta h \, \bar{v} = \frac{h_0{}^2}{q_0{}^2} \delta q \, \bar{v} \qquad (8.12)$$

by (8.7). Hence the sensitivity of the closed-loop system is related to that of the open-loop system in the ratio

$$S(s) = \frac{h_0(s)}{q_0(s)} \qquad (8.13)$$

which is the same as (8.4)

We have to recognize in using these results that δq arises from a change in the underlying system, and not simply from a change in q. For example, if the system has a decoupling zero when in its datum state, it may lose this decoupling zero after it is perturbed. Since the decoupling zero cancels when we form q_0, we cannot see the result of such a perturbation from q_0 alone. However, if we use

$$q(s) = |P_q(s)| \div |T_q(s)| \qquad (8.14)$$

as in Chapter 1, Section 2, the difficulty disappears. Changes in the underlying system change P_q and T_q, and we obtain, to the first order,

$$q(s) = \frac{|T_q(s)| \{\delta |P_q(s)|\} - |P_q(s)| \{\delta |T_q(s)|\}}{|T_q(s)|^2} \qquad (8.15)$$

EXAMPLE 8.1.   Let q arise from the system matrix

$$P_q(s) = \begin{bmatrix} 1 & 0 & | & 0 \\ 0 & (s+1)(s+\alpha) & | & s+2 \\ \underline{} & \underline{} & | & \underline{} \\ 0 & -1 & | & 0 \end{bmatrix} \qquad (8.16)$$

with $\alpha = 2$ in the datum case, so that $s = -2$ is an i.d. zero and

$$q_0(s) = \frac{1}{s+1} \qquad (8.17)$$

If α is perturbed to $2+\varepsilon$, we obtain

$$q_0(s) + \delta q(s) = \frac{s+2}{(s+1)(s+2+\varepsilon)} \qquad (8.18)$$

whence

$$\delta q(s) = \frac{-\varepsilon}{(s+1)(s+2+\varepsilon)} \qquad (8.19)$$

This result could not be obtained from (8.17).

The above results show that the effect of feedback in reducing several kinds of disturbance is measured by $1(1+qf)$ or, what is the same thing, by $\hat{q}/\hat{h}$. It is instructive to consider this ratio for $s = i\omega$ as ω increases from zero: we assume in doing so that $f(s) = f$, a constant. In practice, the phase of $q(i\omega)$ must always exceed π at high enough frequencies. Then it is clear from the inverse Nyquist diagram that although $\hat{q}/\hat{h}$ can be made small at low frequencies, it must exceed 1 at the frequency ω_{pc} at which $\arg \hat{q} = \pi$. The beneficial effects of feedback on sensitivity are then restricted to some low-frequency band, and the aim of the designer must be to make this wide enough to cover the likely disturbances. If a disturbance has most of its energy at frequencies near ω_{pc}, feedback increases rather than reduces its effect on the output.

EXERCISE 8.1.   Using the inverse Nyquist diagram, consider the effect of a phase lead compensator on S for the situations illustrated by Figs. 2.12 and 2.13. Consider also the effect of a phase lag compensator.

EXERCISE 8.2.   Show that if $f(s) = f$, a constant, then $|S(i\omega)| < 1$ for all points on $\hat{\Gamma}_q$ to the right of a line through $(-f/2, 0)$ parallel to the imaginary axis. For all points to the left of this line, $|S(i\omega)| > 1$.

EXERCISE 8.3.   How does the assumption of open-loop and closed-loop stability enter into the preceding discussion of sensitivity? [Note that the output in general depends on the initial conditions, as well as the input.]

9. Design criteria

We now take up again the subject of Section 3. Having considered the design methods which will be used, we can express the design criteria in a more quantitative way. The criteria can be divided into three groups, according as they relate to step response, frequency response, or pole location.

9.1 Step response

It should be stressed that although control systems are sometimes required to respond to step inputs when operating, this is not very common. Step inputs are used for test purposes, not because they represent the typical input, but because the response to them is informative and easily obtained. The following quantities (when they apply) are easily measured.

(i) *Overshoot.* This is measured as a percentage overshoot beyond the final value. It is sometimes of direct interest, and sometimes an indication of the stability margin.

(ii) *Speed of response.* This can be measured, provided that the response overshoots, by the time taken to reach the final value for the first time.

(iii) *Time to maximum overshoot.* This is usually up to 50% longer than the time in (ii), but may be up to 100% longer if the system is lightly damped. If two or more pairs of complex poles contribute significantly to the step response, the first local maximum may not be the greatest, in which case the maximum overshoot may be further delayed: compare Fig. 2.35.

(iv) *Transient frequency.* Often the first overshoot is followed by a distinct damped oscillation with a clearly-defined frequency and decrement.

(v) *Decrement.* This is measured, in the situation described in (iv), by the decrease in amplitude in one period. The decrement is chiefly useful to the extent that it correlates with the stability margin, (xvi). If more than one pair of complex poles contributes significantly to the step response, (iv) and (v) may not be well defined.

(vi) *Settling time.* This is defined as the least time after which the step response is always within some band (say $\pm 5\%$) centred on the final value.

(vii) *Offset.* Measured as a proportion of the desired value.

(viii) *Position* (or *displacement*) *error coefficient.* This is defined as the ratio of steady-state to offset: it is very nearly the reciprocal of the offset when this is small.

9.2 Frequency response

Some of the preceding quantities can be obtained exactly from the frequency response, in which case they are listed under the same number. Other quantities obtained from the frequency response correlate more or less well with those given previously, and may replace them as design criteria or be used for guidance in design. Still others have a direct significance as design criteria, without regard to the step response. The definitions are usually given for $f(s) = f$, independent of s. They are given here for the general case because their values are unaffected by transfer of $f(s)$ from the forward path to the feedback path. The physical meaning of the criteria may, however, become unclear when $f(s)$ varies with s.

(vii) *Offset.* This can be obtained, as the ratio $\hat{q}(0)/\hat{h}(0)$, from the inverse Nyquist diagram.

(viii) *Position error coefficient.* This is obtained from the inverse Nyquist diagram as $f(0)/\hat{q}(0)$.

(ix) *Phase crossover frequency,* ω_{pc}. Defined as the least value of ω for which $\arg \hat{q}(i\omega) - \arg f(i\omega) = \pi$.

(x) *Gain crossover frequency,* ω_{gc}. Defined as the least value of ω for which $|\hat{q}(i\omega)| = |f(i\omega)|$. Both ω_{pc} and ω_{gc} are useful chiefly to the extent that they correlate with the speed of response and the transient frequency.

(xi) *Gain margin.* Defined as $-\hat{q}(i\omega_{pc})/f(i\omega_{pc})$, which is real and positive, and normally greater than 1.

(xii) *Phase margin.* Defined as $\arg \hat{q}(i\omega_{gc}) - \arg f(i\omega_{gc})$.

(xiii) M_m. Defined by $M_m = \max_\omega |f(i\omega)/\hat{h}(i\omega)|$. This, as well as the gain margin and phase margin, are useful chiefly to the extent that they correlate with overshoot, decrement, and stability margin.

(xiv) *Sensitivity crossover frequency,* ω_{sc}. This is not a standard term. We define it as the least value of ω for which $|S(i\omega)| = 1$, where $S(s)$ is defined in (8.4). Normally the sensitivity of the system is reduced by feedback at frequencies less than ω_s and increased at frequencies above ω_s.

(xv) *Bandwidth,* ω_b. Defined as the least value of ω for which

$$|\hat{h}(i\omega)| = 1.414|f(i\omega)|.$$

9.3 Pole locations

The pole locations are again partly used as indicators of other criteria, and partly in their own right.

(iv) *Transient frequency.* When there is only one pair of closed-loop poles $-\sigma \pm i\omega$ near to the imaginary axis, the transient frequency is usually well-defined and is equal to ω.

(v) *Decrement.* In the circumstances just described, the decrement is $e^{-2\pi\sigma/\omega}$.

(vii) *Offset.* This can be obtained from the root locus diagram in the following way. Any dynamics in the feedback path are moved into the forward path. In the root locus diagram for $q(s)$, which is the transfer function now in the forward path, find $q(0)$ in the following way. Multiply together the distances from the origin of all zeros, and divide by the distances from the origin of all open-loop poles. Then the offset is $1/[1 + q(0)f]$. Here f is the gain in the feedback path, determined in such a way that the numerator and denominator of $q(s)$ are both monic.

(viii) *Position error coefficient.* This is $fq(0)$, where f and $q(0)$ are found as in (vii).

(ix) *Phase crossover frequency*, ω_{pc}. Locate the points on the imaginary axis, where root loci cross it, and choose the crossing corresponding to the lowest value f_0 of f. The crossing-point on the imaginary axis gives ω_{pc}.

(xvi) *Stability margin*. For each closed-loop pole $s = -\sigma+i\omega$, take the principal value of the angle θ defined by $\tan \theta = \sigma/\omega$. The smallest of these angles defines the stability margin.

9.4 Selection of criteria

The more directly meaningful the criteria used, the more closely will they be defined by the problem in hand. For example in the pen servo for a high-speed recorder, very little overshoot may be tolerable, and it is not difficult to settle on an allowable figure. For the same example a restriction on M_m may be meaningful in an equally direct way. On the other hand criteria such as gain margin, which are chiefly used as indicators of other quantities, can often be specified only in a tentative way.

10. Irrational transfer functions

We have assumed so far in this chapter that the transfer functions $g(s)$, $k(s)$ and $f(s)$ are rational, when it follows that $h(s)$ is also rational. For $k(s)$ and $f(s)$ the assumption is usually satisfied, but we often have to deal with systems for which $g(s)$ contains exponentials, $e^{-s\tau}$. These represent pure time delays, which are particularly common in process control. In addition, theoretical studies of distributed systems (heat conduction in bars, electrical transmission lines, etc.) can give rise to other types of irrational function $g(s)$. Such transfer functions are considered in this Section, in which we do not aim at the same completeness as elsewhere.

Irrational transfer functions offer a number of new mathematical difficulties. First, though we know that the transfer function $g(s)$ exists, because it is given, we have no general proof that the closed-loop system has a transfer function. When $q(s)$ [and also $k(s)$, $f(s)$] is rational, the closed-loop system is described by a set of ordinary differential equations and it is easily shown [compare Rosenbrock and Storey, 1970, Chapter 8, Section 5.2] that $h(s)$ exists. Though much more general theorems are available which guarantee the existence of a transfer function [see Rosenbrock and Storey, 1970, Chapter 8, Section 8] they rely on information about the corresponding step response or impulse response. It is just such information which we wish to obtain for the closed-loop system from the transfer function $h(s)$, if it exists.

Secondly, our definitions of stability in Section 7 of Chapter 1 were given only for systems having rational transfer functions. Fortunately, the definition of input–output stability generalizes without much difficulty.

Thirdly, for the systems which we considered earlier, stability could be examined by studying the location of the poles. For the more general systems giving irrational transfer functions, stability is no longer a simple and universal consequence of analyticity in the closed right half-plane.

The control engineer may adopt one of several attitudes to these difficulties. Conceptually, the simplest approach is to acknowledge that any mathematical formulation of an engineering problem is only an approximation. We are at liberty to choose another approximation if this offers mathematical advantages. So if a plant has been described by an irrational $g(s)$, it can equally well be described by a rational $g(s)$.

An appropriate rational $g(s)$ can be obtained, for example, by finite-differencing (lumping) of distributed systems. Alternatively, if the frequency response of a plant has been measured, we may use curve-fitting techniques to fit a rational $g(s)$. Then the analytical difficulties disappear: but unfortunately the rational $g(s)$ may sometimes be complicated and may give rise to numerical problems.

A second approach is to argue that since the plant is equally well described by an irrational $g(s)$, or by a rational $g(s)$ which "agrees closely with it", we may apply to the irrational $g(s)$ those theorems such as the Nyquist stability theorem which would be true for the rational $g(s)$. If this ever led to false conclusions, then the irrational $g(s)$ would fall under suspicion equally with the rational. For no physical test can ever allow us to decide whether a transfer function is "really" rational or not: the question is as meaningless as asking whether the length of a given bar of metal, expressed in millimetres, is rational or irrational. Though the meaning of "agrees closely with it" cannot be defined except by a circular argument, we know of no case where this procedure has led to error.

A third, and intellectually more satisfactory approach, is to develop the necessary theorems which allow us to deal directly with irrational transfer functions. Theorems of this kind which justify the use of the Nyquist criterion have been given by Desoer and Wu [1968; see also Willems, 1970, Chapter 3, Section 7.2]. Some slightly less general forms of these, sufficient for applications, will be given below. For further details the reader is referred to the original paper.

Before giving the theorems we need some preliminary notation. A function f is said to belong to the class D_R^1 [Rosenbrock and Storey, 1970, Chapter 4, Section 9] if it can be written, on any open interval J,

$$f(t) = \sum_{i=1}^{p} p_i\, U(t-p_i) + \sum_{i=1}^{q} (t-q_i)\, \phi_i\, U(t-q_i) + \psi(t) \qquad (10.1)$$

where the $p_i \in J$, $q_i \in J$ and ϕ_i are constants, and ψ is continuous and bounded on J, and has continuous and bounded derivatives $D\psi$ on J. The symbol

$U(t)$ in (10.1) represents the unit step defined by

$$U(t) = \begin{cases} 0, & t \leqslant 0 \\ 1, & t > 0 \end{cases}$$

The numbers p and q defining the range of the sums in (10.1) depend in general on J; they may tend to infinity as J is enlarged provided that on any finite interval p and q are finite. The class $D_R{}^1$ is a subset of the piecewise differentiable functions.

The zero initial condition of a linear time-invariant system containing time delays is that condition in which all internal variables are zero. (We use the informal word "condition" instead of the formal "state" because we do not intend to give a precise definition.) In general, for systems with time delays, it is necessary to specify one or more functions to define the zero condition rather than just a finite set of values as in the systems considered previously.

EXAMPLE 10.1.   A system consists of two electrical delay lines in parallel, one with a delay of 0.1 μs and one with a delay of $0 \cdot 25$ μs. The input u is applied to both of them and the output of the first is subtracted from that of the second to give the system output y. To specify the zero initial condition it is necessary to specify the functions stored in the two delay lines at $t = 0$.

EXERCISE 10.1.   For the system in Example 10.1, can the condition at $t = 0$ be deduced from observations of the output y on $[0, 0 \cdot 25]$?

The zero condition of such a system is said to be input–output stable if for any positive M_1 there exists a positive M_2 such that $|u(t)| < M_1$ for all $t \geqslant 0$ implies $|y(t)| < M_2$ for all $t \geqslant 0$. Here $y(t)$ is the output resulting from the input $u(t)$ applied at $t = 0$ to the system in the zero condition. Notice that input–output stability of the zero condition is a weaker condition than input–output stability of a system. The latter would replace the zero condition in our definition by an arbitrarily chosen initial condition [compare Chapter 1, Section 7]. By restricting attention in what follows to input–output stability of the zero condition, we are making the same sort of restriction as if we had previously considered only the stability of least-order representations.

Let the plant which we wish to control satisfy the following requirements when it is initially in the zero condition.
(i) It is linear.
(ii) It is non-anticipative.
(iii) If the input u satisfies $u(t) = 0$, $t \leqslant 0$, and $|u(t)| < M_1(T)$, $0 < t \leqslant T$, then the output y satisfies $|y(t)| < M_2(M_1, T)$, $0 < t \leqslant T$.

(iv) If $\gamma(t)$ is the output corresponding to an input $U(t)$, then $\gamma(t-\tau)$ is the output corresponding to the input $U(t-\tau)$, $\tau > 0$.

(v) The response $\gamma(t)$ to the input $U(t)$ is in $D_R{}^1$.

(vi) The variation of $\gamma(t)$ on $[0, \theta]$ is less than $Ne^{\beta\theta}$ for some fixed N and $\beta \geqslant 0$ and for all $\theta \geqslant 0$. [For the definition of variation, see Rosenbrock and Storey, 1970, Chapter 4, Section 9.1.]

Then it has been shown [Rosenbrock and Storey, 1970, Chapter 8, Section 8] that the output y of the plant can be expressed by the Riemann–Stieltjes integral

$$y(t) = \int_0^t \gamma(t-\tau)\, du(\tau) \tag{10.2}$$

and that the plant has a transfer function

$$g(s) = s\bar{y}(s) \tag{10.3}$$

where $\bar{y}(s)$ is the Laplace transform of the step response $\gamma(t)$ and is exponentially convergent for $\mathrm{Re}\, s > \beta$. We are now able to state the desired theorems.

THEOREM 10.1. Let the open-loop system (that is, the plant) satisfy conditions (i) to (vi) above, and in (vi) let $\beta = 0$. Then the closed-loop system with gain $f > 0$ in the feedback path has a transfer function $h(s)$ given by $h(s) = g(s)/(1+fg(s))$. Also the zero condition of this closed-loop system is input–output stable if

$$\inf_{\mathrm{Re}\, s \geqslant 0} |1+fg(s)| > 0 \tag{10.4}$$

Proof. We show that the conditions stated imply those assumed by Desoer and Wu [1968]. By condition (v), the step response $\gamma(t)$ can be written on any open interval J

$$\gamma(t) = \sum_{i=1}^p \gamma_i\, U(t-p_i) + \sum_{i=1}^q (t-q_i)\, \phi_i\, U(t-q_i) + \psi(t) \tag{10.5}$$

$$= \sum_{i=1}^p \gamma_i\, U(t-p_i) + \chi(t) \tag{10.6}$$

The impulse response $\zeta(t)$ of the plant is defined on J by

$$\zeta(t) = D\gamma(t) \tag{10.7}$$

$$= \sum_{i=1}^p \gamma_i\, \delta(t-p_i) + \sum_{i=1}^q \phi_i\, U(t-q_i) + D\psi(t) \tag{10.8}$$

$$= \sum_{i=1}^p \gamma_i\, \delta(t-p_i) + \omega(t) \tag{10.9}$$

where $\omega(t) = D\chi(t)$ and $\delta(t)$ is the Dirac delta function [Rosenbrock and Storey, 1970, Chapter 5, Sections 8, 9]. The variation of $\gamma(t)$ on $[0, \theta]$ is readily shown to be

$$\sum_i |\gamma_i| + \int_0^\theta |\omega(t)| \, dt \qquad (10.10)$$

where $\omega(t)$ is defined by (10.9) and the sum over i is taken appropriately for the interval $[0, \theta]$. By condition (vi) we certainly have

$$\sum_i |\gamma_i| < N \qquad (10.11)$$

$$\int_0^\theta |\omega(t)| \, dt < N \qquad (10.12)$$

for all $\theta > 0$. These are the conditions assumed by Desoer and Wu.

THEOREM 10.2. Let conditions (i) to (vi) above be satisfied, with $\beta = 0$ in (iv), and let $g(s)$ be strictly proper. Let D be a closed contour consisting of the imaginary axis from $s = -iR$ to $s = iR$, completed by a semicircle of radius R in the right half-plane, where R is chosen so that $|fg(s)| \leqslant \alpha < 1$ for all $|s| \geqslant R$. Let $g(s)$ be analytic inside and on D. Then (10.4) is true if and only if the map Γ of D by g does not encircle the critical point $(-1/f, 0)$.

Proof. Since $g(s)$ is strictly proper, R can be chosen as specified. Then $|1+fg(s)| \geqslant 1-\alpha$ for all $|s| \geqslant R$, and in particular $|1+fg(s)| \neq 0$ on D. The "principle of the argument" shows that if Γ does not encircle the critical point, $1+fg(s)$ $[=f(f^{-1}+g(s))]$ has as many zeros inside D as it has poles. But as $g(s)$ is analytic inside D, so is $1+fg(s)$, which therefore has no pole inside D. As D is compact, (10.4) is satisfied inside D (Rosenbrock and Storey, 1970, p. 140) and by what was proved earlier it is satisfied everywhere else in the closed right half-plane.

Conversely, if Γ encircles the critical point (necessarily clockwise) then $1+fg(s)$ has a zero inside D and (10.4) is not satisfied.

The assumption that $g(s)$ is strictly proper is a simple way of ensuring that $1+fg(s)$ does not tend to zero as $|s|$ is increased. Less stringent conditions would serve the same purpose, but physical arguments make the assumption a reasonable one to use [compare Section 5.2].

The conditions of Theorem 10.1 can be relaxed to allow a pole at the origin [Desoer and Wu, 1968]. On the other hand, if the conditions of Theorem 10.1 are strengthened by requiring that the variation of $\gamma(t) \, e^{\beta t}$ is less than N on $[0, \theta]$ for some fixed N and $\beta > 0$ and all $\theta \geqslant 0$, it can be shown that $g(s)$ certainly satisfies the analyticity condition in Theorem 10.2.

For a wide class of process plants involving heat and material transfer, even when nonlinear, it can be shown that the step response is monotonic [Rosenbrock, 1962, Theorem 7: the result follows if the input has the same sign in each differential equation where it occurs]. The proof applies to systems described by ordinary differential equations, but can be expected to hold for more general systems. When this is true it becomes particularly easy to check condition (vi) above.

EXERCISE 10.2. Derive a generalized inverse Nyquist criterion from Theorems 10.1 and 10.2.

10.1 Non-minimum phase response

This is a convenient point to mention a difficulty which may arise in systems having either rational or irrational transfer functions. A rational transfer function $g(s)$ having all its poles in the open left half-plane is called *minimum phase* if it has no zero in the open right half-plane. The reason for the name is that if $g(s)$ has certain of its zeros, $\alpha_1, \alpha_2, ..., \alpha_p$ in the open right half-plane we may write it

$$g(s) = \frac{(\alpha_1 - s)(\alpha_2 - s) \ldots (\alpha_p - s)}{(\alpha_1 + s)(\alpha_2 + s) \ldots (\alpha_p + s)} g_1(s) \tag{10.13}$$

where $g_1(s)$ is minimum phase. If α_1 is real, we find that

$$\frac{\alpha_1 - i\omega}{\alpha_1 + i\omega} = e^{-2i\theta(\omega)} \tag{10.14}$$

where

$$\theta(\omega) = \tan^{-1} \frac{\omega}{\alpha_1} \tag{10.15}$$

Similarly if α_1 is complex there is another zero, say α_2, equal to the complex conjugate $\bar{\alpha}_1$. Then

$$\frac{(\alpha_1 - i\omega)(\bar{\alpha}_1 - i\omega)}{(\alpha_1 + i\omega)(\bar{\alpha} + i\omega)} = e^{-2i[\theta_1(\omega) + \theta_2(\omega)]} \tag{10.16}$$

where if $\alpha_1 = \sigma_1 + i\omega_1$,

$$\theta_1(\omega) = \tan^{-1} \frac{\omega - \omega_1}{\sigma_1} \tag{10.17}$$

$$\theta_2(\omega) = \tan^{-1} \frac{\omega + \omega_1}{\sigma_1} \tag{10.18}$$

It is easily verified that $\theta_1(\omega)$ in (10.15) is positive when $\omega > 0$, and $\theta_1(\omega) + \theta_2(\omega)$ in (10.16) is also positive if $\omega > 0$. Hence it follows that $g(i\omega)$ has the same modulus as $g_1(i\omega)$, but has greater phase lag, when as usual we consider $\omega > 0$.

EXERCISE 10.3. Obtain the result just stated by examining the rational functions in (10.14) and (10.16), using the methods of the root locus diagram to evaluate gain and phase.

A rational function having all its poles in the open left half-plane, but one or more zeros in the open right half-plane is called *non-minimum phase*. The condition on the poles should be noted: if poles in the open right half-plane are allowed, the phase lag may be less than that associated with a minimum phase transfer function having the same modulus.

EXERCISE 10.4. Show that

$$g(s) = \frac{s-2}{(s+1)(s-1)} \tag{10.19}$$

has the same gain as the minimum phase transfer function

$$g_1(s) = \frac{s+2}{(s+1)^2} \tag{10.20}$$

but has smaller phase lag.

In the same way a transfer function

$$g(s)\, e^{-s\tau} \tag{10.21}$$

where $g(s)$ is rational and has its poles in the open left half-plane is also called non-minimum phase.

For our purposes, the restriction above to rational functions having all their poles in the open left half-plane (which is needed to justify the nomenclature) is not essential. The important point is that if zeros of a transfer function $g(s)$ are moved from the left half-plane to the right half-plane by reflection in the imaginary axis, then the gain is unchanged but the phase lag is increased. Consideration of the Nyquist diagram (or the inverse Nyquist diagram) shows at once that the closed-loop natural frequency will be reduced. Similar remarks apply to transfer functions with time delays, such as (10.21).

When the time-constants associated with the right half-plane zeros, or with the time delay, are short, the effect will be relatively small. When the time constants are long, the extra phase lag will be relatively large. This extra phase lag is associated with a gain which is independent of frequency. Compensation therefore becomes difficult, because stable compensators which produce phase advance also produce a gain increasing with frequency.

EXERCISE 10.5. Sketch the Nyquist or inverse Nyquist plot for

$$g(s) = \frac{(1-s)}{(1+s)(2+s)^3} \tag{10.22}$$

and consider the effect of a phase advance compensator. [Notice that we have chosen the sign so that $g(0) > 0$. This ensures that feedback gains $f > 0$ correspond to negative feedback when the usual sign change is inserted in the loop.]

EXERCISE 10.6.   Examine the phase lead or phase lag contributed near the phase crossover frequency ω_{pc} by the zero in

$$g(s) = \frac{\alpha - s}{\alpha(1+s)^3} \qquad (10.23)$$

as α goes from $-\infty$ through zero to $+\infty$. [Notice that we have ensured that $g(0) = +1$ for all α.]

EXERCISE 10.7.   If

$$g(s) = \frac{1-s}{(1+s)^2} \qquad (10.24)$$

show that the open-loop step response is

$$y(t) = [1 - e^{-t} - 2te^{-t}]\, U(t) \qquad (10.25)$$

Show that $y(t)$ first goes negative before finally approaching $+1$. Comment qualitatively on the difficulty which this implies for feedback control.

EXERCISE 10.8.   Given that $g(s)$ has no pole in the closed right half-plane, and that when $U(t)$ is a unit step at $t = 0$ then

$$\left. \begin{array}{l} \lim\limits_{t \to \infty} y(t) = \lim\limits_{s \to 0} g(s) > 0 \\[2mm] \lim\limits_{t \to 0} \dot{y}(t) = \lim\limits_{s \to \infty} sg(s) < 0 \end{array} \right\} \qquad (10.26)$$

show that $g(s)$ has at least one zero in the open right half-plane. [The complete characterization of non-minimum phase responses in the time domain appears to be an unsolved problem.]

When a system gives a non-minimum phase response, control is often poor and compensation can give little improvement. The only solution to the difficulty is then to change the structure of the system if possible, by measuring or manipulating some other variable.

EXERCISE 10.9.   The power in the jet of water striking the buckets of a Pelton wheel is controlled by varying the diameter of the jet. If the load on the Pelton wheel is suddenly reduced, the power in the jet will have to be reduced quickly in order to prevent overspeeding. An attempt to do this by

H

reducing the diameter of the jet will cause the water in the supply pipe, usually several miles long, to slow down. This will increase the pressure at the nozzle and may in fact temporarily increase the power in the jet (compare Exercise 10.8). Suggest how a further manipulated variable (a jet deflector) can be used to overcome this difficulty. How should the system operate in order to avoid a loss of efficiency in normal conditions? Is there any way of overcoming the difficulty in control when the load suddenly increases?

EXERCISE 10.10.   In a large steam-generating boiler, the water level in the drum has to be measured and controlled within narrow limits by manipulation of feed-water flow. If feed-water supply is kept constant while steam flow is suddenly increased, the pressure in the drum is reduced. Bubbles in the water expand, causing the measured level to rise (this is called "swell") before settling to a steady rate of decrease. Sketch the water level response to a step change in steam flow, and discuss the effect on level control in a system which uses measured level to manipulate feed-water flow. Devise a cascade system (Section 2) to overcome the difficulty, using a measurement of steam flow. [This cascade system is called "two element feed-water control".]

EXERCISE 10.11.   In Exercise 10.9 the difficulty was overcome by introducing a new manipulated variable, while in Exercise 10.10 a new measured variable was used. Examine the reasons for this difference. [Note the distinction between non-minimum phase response to a manipulated variable and to a disturbance variable.]

11. The circle criterion

Section 10 removed one limitation of the treatment in earlier Sections. Another limitation which we should like to remove is the exclusion of non-linear and time-dependent systems. This is a more troublesome problem than the one considered in Section 10. There we could argue that the difficulties associated with irrational transfer functions were mathematical, rather than physical, and could be avoided by taking a different and equally valid mathematical description of the physical system. The behaviour of non-linear or time-dependent systems, however, is essentially more complicated than that of linear systems.

It is therefore not surprising that in spite of prolonged efforts by mathematicians, the results available are fragmentary. What we shall do in this Section is to give without proof one important generalization of the earlier results which has a very similar form to those obtained before. This generalization is known as the *circle criterion* and it grew out of a control problem studied by Lur'e [1951]. The subsequent history of work on this problem is sketched in the Appendix: the form of the result quoted here can be found most easily by specializing the results in Section 10 of Chapter 3.

The system which we study is shown in Fig. 2.39. The forward path con-

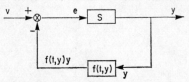

FIG. 2.39. System with nonlinear, time-dependent feedback; S is a linear, time-invariant system with strictly proper transfer function $q(s)$.

tains a linear time-invariant system with proper transfer function $q(s) = g(s) k(s)$. This we suppose to arise from the system

$$
\left.
\begin{aligned}
T_q(s)\, \bar{\xi}_q &= U_q(s)\, \bar{e} \\[2mm]
\bar{y} &= V_q(s)\, \bar{\xi}_q + W(s)\, \bar{e}
\end{aligned}
\right\}
\tag{11.1}
$$

which need not have least order. If we wish, the system (11.1) can be decomposed, as in Section 4, into two subsystems giving $g(s)$ and $k(s)$ respectively.

The feedback path contains a nonlinear, time-dependent gain $f(t, y)$ satisfying, for all t and y,

$$
0 < \alpha \leqslant f(t, y) \leqslant \beta, \qquad \alpha < \beta
\tag{11.2}
$$

This gain multiplies the signal in the feedback path, so that

$$
v - e = f(t, y)\, y
\tag{11.3}
$$

By rearranging the loop as in Section 2 the following analysis can be applied whenever there is a single nonlinear time-dependent gain in the loop satisfying (11.2). We are interested in what follows in stability, so that v in (11.3) can be made zero, and rearrangement of the loop then does not affect any of our conclusions.

In the circle criterion we replace the critical point by a *critical disc*. This has as diameter the segment of the negative real axis between $s = -1/\beta$ and $s = -1/\alpha$, as in Fig. 2.40. We suppose that the open-loop system (11.1) has p_0 poles in the closed right half-plane: that is, $|T_q(s)|$ has p_0 zeros there. Notice that if we write separate subsystems giving $g(s)$ and $k(s)$, as in (4.1) and (4.12), then

$$
|T_q(s)| = |T_g(s)| |T_k(s)|
\tag{11.4}
$$

[compare Exercise 5.6].

A contour D is defined, consisting of the imaginary axis from $s = -iR$ to

$s = iR$, together with a semicircle of radius R in the right half-plane. The contour D is suitably indented and the radius R is chosen large enough to ensure that every finite pole of $q(s)$ which lies in the closed right half-plane is inside D. With this notation we have the following theorem.

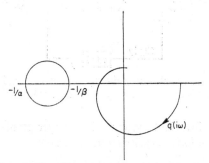

FIG. 2.40.   Illustrating the circle criterion.

THEOREM 11.1.   Let the least distance, between the critical disc and the mapping of D by q, be $\varepsilon > 0$. Let this be true for all contours D' satisfying the condition for D and having $R' \geqslant R$. Let the mapping of D by q encircle the critical disc N_q times clockwise as s goes once clockwise around D. Then if

$$N_q = -p_0 \qquad\qquad (11.5)$$

the closed-loop system defined by (11.1) and (11.3) is uniformly asymptotically stable in the large [Chapter 1, Section 7].

In this result, (11.5) is only a sufficient condition, subject to the remaining conditions of the theorem. In other respects it clearly generalizes Theorem 5.1. If f is constant we may allow α and β to tend to f, when the critical disc tends to the critical point $(-1/f, 0)$.

The corresponding theorem for the inverse Nyquist plot follows very similar lines, though now a little more care is needed to ensure that as $\hat{q}(s) \to \infty$, the distance between the Nyquist plot and the critical disc remains

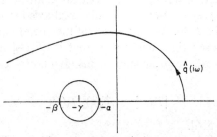

FIG. 2.41.   Illustrating the circle criterion for the inverse Nyquist plot.

adequate. The critical disc has as diameter the segment of the negative real axis from $s = -\alpha$ to $s = -\beta$. Its centre is therefore at

$$s = -\tfrac{1}{2}(\alpha+\beta) = -\gamma \qquad (11.6)$$

as illustrated by Fig. 2.41. The contour D is suitably indented and the radius R of the semicircular arc is chosen large enough to ensure that every finite pole of $\hat{q}(s)$ which lies in the closed right half-plane is inside D.

THEOREM 11.2. Let the least distance, between the critical disc and the point $\hat{q}(s)$, where s is on D, be greater than $\varepsilon|\gamma+\hat{q}(s)| > 0$. Let this be true for all s on D', where D' is any contour satisfying the conditions for D and with $R' \geqslant R$. Let the mapping $\hat{\Gamma}_q$ of D by $\hat{q}$ encircle the origin $\hat{N}_q$ times clockwise, and let it encircle the critical disc $\hat{N}_c$ times clockwise, as s goes once clockwise round D. Then if

$$\hat{N}_q - \hat{N}_c = p_0 \qquad (11.7)$$

the closed-loop system defined by (11.1), (11.3) is uniformly asymptotically stable in the large.

This again bears a very close relationship with Theorem 5.2. We have used the notation $\hat{N}_c$ instead of $\hat{N}_h$ in order to avoid suggesting that the closed-loop system has a transfer function. Theorems 11.1 and 11.2 can be applied directly to some physical systems. Sometimes, however, they are too conservative to be useful.

Apart from their possible utility in applications the theorems have a considerable theoretical importance. No practical system is linear or time-invariant, and it is important that our design methods should not depend critically on these assumptions. For the particular nonlinear, time-dependent systems defined by (11.1) and (11.3), Theorems 11.1 and 11.2 provide a valuable reassurance. Small departures from linearity and time-invariance (in a sense which we may define exactly) will not invalidate a design based on a linear time-invariant model. Experience shows that this conclusion holds, in a qualitative sense, for a much wider class of nonlinearity and time-dependence than we have considered here.

11.1 Connection with the describing function

As was said above, the circle criterion may be too conservative in some applications. Consequently many systems are designed by means of the "describing function", which deals with nonlinear, but not time-dependent, systems. Only a brief sketch of the method will be given here, in order to compare it with the circle criterion. The describing function, in its usual form, does not lead to precisely formulated mathematical theorems. Rather it gives an indication of what to expect, which experience shows to be highly useful.

As no physical system ever obeys exactly the assumptions of any mathematical theorem which the designer applies, this lack of mathematical rigour
is not an insuperable disadvantage for the engineer. However, it must be
admitted that more than the usual amount of experience is needed to use the
describing function reliably. The reader is referred to extensive standard
works [see the Appendix].

The scope of the describing function is quite wide, but we shall apply it
only to the system defined by (11.1) and (11.3), with f now a function of y
alone. We ask the question, can this system support a periodic solution?
If such a periodic solution (a *limit cycle*) can exist then the system is not
stable. If the linearized system is asymptotically stable and no limit cycle can
exist, it is often assumed that the nonlinear system will be globally asymptotically stable, though this does not follow when the order of the system
exceeds 2.

The basic assumption underlying the describing function is that the plant
acts as a very effective low-pass filter. If the signal e is periodic it can be
expressed as a Fourier series

$$e(t) = \sum_{k=1}^{\infty} e_k \exp(ik\omega t) \qquad (11.8)$$

where as usual the real part represents the physical variable, and we have
assumed that the mean value of e is zero. Then if the plant is a sufficiently
good low-pass filter, the harmonics will be negligible at the output, and we
shall have

$$y(t) = q(i\omega) e_1 \exp(i\omega t) \qquad (11.9)$$

This will give rise to

$$e(t) = -f[y(t)] y(t) \qquad (11.10)$$

and the fundamental component of e must be $e_1 \exp(i\omega t)$ as in (11.8). If
a is a real number, and we define the *describing function* by

$$N(a) = \frac{1}{\pi} \int_0^{2\pi} f[a \cos \theta] \cos^2 \theta \, d\theta \qquad (11.11)$$

then this condition is

$$q(i\omega) = -\frac{1}{N(a)} \qquad (11.12)$$

EXERCISE 11.1.   Obtain (11.12) from (11.8) and (11.10). [Put $e_1 = aq^{-1}(i\omega)$].

If f is independent of y, (11.11) gives simply $N(a) = f$, and (11.12) is the condition for a continuing oscillation of the resulting linear system. In general N will depend on a, and we may plot $-1/N(a)$ on the Nyquist diagram as in Fig. 2.42. If the Nyquist diagram intersects the plot of

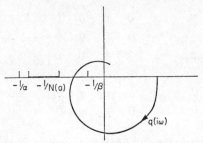

FIG. 2.42. Illustrating the describing function. A system with the Nyquist plot shown would not satisfy the circle criterion, but the describing function indicates that a limit cycle is unlikely.

$-1/N(a)$, the intersection defines a value of a and a value of ω. Then for this a and ω,

$$y = a \cos \omega t \qquad (11.13)$$

satisfies (11.12) which, subject to the assumption that q acts as a highly effective low-pass filter, is a necessary condition for the existence of a limit cycle. The condition (11.12) is only a necessary condition, and then only when q has the assumed properties. Nevertheless the condition is often quite an accurate guide to the existence of limit cycles.

It is clear from the definition (11.11) and from (11.2) that

$$\alpha \leqslant N(a) \leqslant \beta \qquad (11.14)$$

Hence the plot of $-1/N(a)$ must lie in the diameter of the critical disc which was used in Theorem 11.1. If asymptotic stability of the linearized system and absence of a limit cycle can be equated with global asymptotic stability, this shows a satisfactory degree of agreement between the circle criterion, which is known to be often conservative, and the describing function (compare Fig. 2.42).

If the nonlinear gain f has memory, for example if it represents hysteresis, the circle criterion remains valid. The describing function $N(a)$ when suitably defined becomes complex, but Cook [1973a] has shown that $-1/N(a)$ still remains within the critical disc. If the describing function could be made into a rigorous criterion, while retaining its simplicity and sharpness, it would have very great practical value [Lighthill and Mees, 1973].

12. Problems

(1) Let $p(s) = p_0 + p_1 s + \ldots + p_{n-1} s^{n-1} + s^n$ and $q(s) = q_0 + q_1 s + \ldots + q_{n-1} s^{n-1}$ be two polynomials with real coefficients. Then it is known that $p(s), q(s)$ are relatively prime if and only if the $2n \times 2n$ matrix

$$
R = \begin{bmatrix}
1 & 0 & \cdots & 0 & 0 & 0 & 0 & \cdots & 0 & 0 \\
p_{n-1} & 1 & \cdots & 0 & 0 & 0 & 0 & \cdots & 0 & q_{n-1} \\
p_{n-2} & p_{n-1} & \cdots & 0 & 0 & 0 & 0 & \cdots & q_{n-1} & q_{n-2} \\
\vdots & \vdots & & \vdots & \vdots & \vdots & \vdots & & \vdots & \vdots \\
0 & 0 & \cdots & p_0 & p_1 & q_1 & q_0 & \cdots & 0 & 0 \\
0 & 0 & \cdots & 0 & p_0 & q_0 & 0 & \cdots & 0 & 0
\end{bmatrix}
\tag{12.1}
$$

has rank $2n$. [See for example SSMVT, Chapter 1, Section 3.] Let $\phi(s)$ be any given monic polynomial of degree $2n-1$. Show that if $p(s)$, $q(s)$ are relatively prime, the equation

$$p(s)\, a(s) + q(s)\, b(s) = \phi(s) \tag{12.2}$$

can be satisfied by polynomials $a(s)$, $b(s)$ of degree $n-1$, $\beta \leqslant n-1$ respectively, and with $a(s)$ monic. [Equate coefficients of powers of s in (12.2) and examine the coefficient matrix.]

(2) From the result of Problem 1 deduce the following. Let $g(s)$ be a rational, strictly proper transfer function with its denominator monic of degree n and with its numerator and denominator relatively prime. Then there exists a rational matrix $k(s)$, with its denominator of degree $n-1$ and its numerator of degree $\beta \leqslant n-1$, such that the $2n-1$ zeros of $1 + g(s) k(s)$ are in any specified locations (subject to the usual condition that complex zeros occur in conjugate pairs). [Write $g(s) = q(s)/p(s)$, $k(s) = b(s)/a(s)$ and let $\phi(s)$ have its zeros in the required locations.]

(3) In equation (4.19) let $f(s) = 1$, $|T_f(s)| = 1$. Show that by choice of $k(s)$ the poles of the closed-loop system can be moved to any desired locations (subject to the usual condition on conjugate complex pairs) provided that the system (4.1) has least order. If (4.1) does not have least order, which poles can be arbitrarily located and which cannot? [When (4.1) has least order, $|T_g(s)|$ will be the denominator of $g(s)$. When (4.1) does not have least order, cancellation will occur in forming $g(s)$, and then $\phi(s)$ in (4.19) must contain the cancelled factor. We can arrange to implement $k(s)$ by a least-order system.]

(4) Let $g(s) = (s+1)/(s-1)(s+2)$ arise from a least-order system. Find $k(s)$ which will make the closed-loop system with $f = 1$ asymptotically stable. [Choose suitable locations for the three closed-loop poles.]

(5) For the $g(s)$ in Problem 4, find $k(s)$ which moves all three closed-loop poles to $s = -100$. Comment on the phase advance produced by $k(s)$ and on its stability.

(6) In the light of Problems 2 to 5, re-invent the method of "pole assignment" for designing control systems. Comment on its advantages and disadvantages. [This method is usually presented in a state-space framework, as in Problem 7, which tends to conceal the unwelcome properties that $k(s)$ may possess].

(7) Show that if

$$A = \begin{bmatrix} 0 & 1 & 0 & \cdots & 0 & 0 \\ 0 & 0 & 1 & \cdots & 0 & 0 \\ \vdots & \vdots & \ddots & & \vdots & \vdots \\ 0 & 0 & 0 & \cdots & 0 & 1 \\ -p_0 & -p_1 & -p_2 & \cdots & p_{n-2} & -p_{n-1} \end{bmatrix} \quad (12.3)$$

$$B = \begin{bmatrix} 0 \\ 0 \\ \vdots \\ 0 \\ 1 \end{bmatrix}, \quad C = (q_0 \quad q_1 \quad q_2 \cdots q_{n-2} \quad q_{n-1}) \quad (12.4)$$

then $\bar{y} = g\bar{u}$ where

$$g(s) = C(sI_n - A)^{-1} B$$

$$= \frac{q_{n-1} s^{n-1} + q_{n-2} s^{n-2} + \ldots + q_0}{s^n + p_{n-1} s^{n-1} + \ldots + p_0} \quad (12.5)$$

If feedback is applied according to

$$u = v - Kx \quad (12.6)$$

show that the equations of the closed-loop system are

$$\left. \begin{array}{l} \dot{x} = (A - BK)\, x + Bv \\ y = Cx \end{array} \right\} \quad (12.7)$$

Hence show that the row vector K may be chosen so that the eigenvalues of $A - BK$ have any desired locations. Deduce that access to x allows us to dispense with the compensator $k(s)$ so far as pole assignment is concerned. Comment on the practical implications. [Since it is usually too expensive to measure all the elements of the state vector, a *state observer* is usually suggested: see SSMVT, Chapter 5, Section 5. This gives precisely the same effect as the procedure in Problem 6.]

(8) In Problem 7, it was not assumed that the system (12.3), (12.4) has least order. Contrast this with Problem 3, and explain the apparent discrepancy. If the system (12.3), (12.4) does not have least order, can (12.7) have least order? [The system (12.3), (12.4) has no i.d. zero. In (12.6), C does not enter, but K appears in its place, and K is subject to choice in order to achieve the desired pole locations.]

(9) Equation (4.19) reduces the stability problem for a closed-loop system to the problem of finding how many zeros of a polynomial $\phi(s)$ lie in the closed right half-plane. As in Section 5, this problem can be solved by using the "principle of the argument." It can also be solved by the algebraic criteria of Hermite, Routh, Hurwitz and others [see for example Gantmacher, 1959]. The following result is a step in Routh's argument [Routh, 1877]. Let

$$\phi(s) = \phi_0 + \phi_1 s + \ldots + \phi_r s^r \qquad (12.8)$$

and let D be the usual contour consisting of the imaginary axis from $s = -iR$ to $s = iR$ and a semicircle of radius R in the right half-plane. Let (12.8) have no imaginary zero, and suppose that r is even. Show that if R is large enough, the point $\phi(s)$ crosses the imaginary axis r times as s goes once clockwise round the semicircular arc of D. For $s = i\omega$, write $\phi(s) = x(\omega) + iy(\omega)$. Show that a necessary and sufficient condition for $\phi(s)$ to have no zero in the closed right half-plane is that x/y changes sign from positive to negative exactly r times as ω goes from $-\infty$ to $+\infty$. [Consider the contour Γ_ϕ defined in Section 5, use the "principle of the argument," relate encirclements of the origin to crossings of the imaginary axis and hence to the sign changes of x/y. Note from the degrees of $x(\omega)$ and $y(\omega)$ that x/y cannot have more than $2r-1$ sign changes.]

(10) If r is odd in Problem 10, show that the necessary and sufficient condition for $\phi(s)$ to have no zero in the closed right half-plane is that $x(\omega)/y(\omega)$ changes sign from positive to negative exactly $r-1$ times as ω goes from $-\infty$ to ∞. [Note that one of the r zeros of x/y is at infinity, and does not contribute a sign change.]

(11) Show that the conditions in Problems 9 and 10 can be restated in the following way. Let r be even [resp. odd]. Then $\phi(s)$ has no zero in the closed right half-plane if and only if $x(\omega)$, $y(\omega)$ have their coefficients of highest degree of the same sign, have all their zeros real, and in addition the zeros of $y(\omega)$ separate those of $x(\omega)$ [resp. the zeros of $x(\omega)$ separate those of $y(\omega)$]. Here, when we say that the zeros of one polynomial separate those of a second polynomial, we mean that the second polynomial has simple zeros, and between any two of these which are adjacent, there is one zero of the

first polynomial. Note that whether $\phi(s)$ is even or odd, the zeros of the polynomial of lower degree have to separate those of the polynomial of higher degree.

(12) Show that

$$\phi(s) = s^3 + s^2 + 4s + 1 \qquad (12.9)$$

has no zero in the closed right half-plane. [Examine the zeros of $x(\omega)$, $y(\omega)$ as in Problem 11.]

(13) Change the sign of $x(\omega)$ in Problem 9, if necessary, to make the coefficient of highest degree positive, and make the corresponding change in $y(\omega)$. Call the polynomial of higher degree thus obtained $f_1(\omega)$, and the other $f_2(\omega)$. Define successive remainders $f_3(\omega), f_4(\omega), \ldots$, by

$$\left.\begin{aligned} f_1(\omega) &= \alpha_1(\omega) f_2(\omega) - f_3(\omega) \\ f_2(\omega) &= \alpha_2(\omega) f_3(\omega) - f_4(\omega) \\ &\cdots \\ f_{q-1}(\omega) &= \alpha_{q-1}(\omega) f_q(\omega) - f_{q+1}(\omega) \end{aligned}\right\} \qquad (12.10)$$

Here we know from Problem 11 that $f_1(\omega)$ has degree r, $f_2(\omega)$ has degree $r-1$, and consequently $f_3(\omega)$ has degree $r-2$ or less, $\ldots, f_{q+1}(\omega)$ has degree zero. Show that if $f_p(\omega_1) = 0$ for some p satisfying $1 < p < q-1$, then $f_{p-1}(\omega_1)$ and $f_{p+1}(\omega_1)$ have opposite signs provided they are not both zero. If they are both zero, show that $f_1(\omega_1) = f_2(\omega_1) = 0$ and so $\phi(i\omega_1) = 0$: we exclude this possibility as in Problem 9. Hence show that the number of changes of sign in the sequence $f_1, f_2, \ldots, f_{q+1}$ can only vary when f_1 passes through zero. Such a sequence is called a Sturm sequence.

(14) Show that if $q = r$ in (12.10), and each of the polynomials $f_1, f_2, \ldots, f_{r+1}$ has a positive coefficient for the term of highest degree, then all zeros of f_1 and f_2 are real, and those of the latter separate those of the former. [When ω is large and positive, there are no sign changes in the sequence $f_1, f_2, \ldots, f_{r+1}$. When ω is large and negative there are r sign changes. Hence r sign changes are gained as ω goes from ∞ to $-\infty$: but this can only happen if $f_1(\omega)$ passes through zero r times. Use a similar argument to show that $f_2(\omega)$ passes through zero $r-1$ times. Then consider how changes of sign propagate along the sequence $f_1, f_2, \ldots, f_{r+1}$].

(15) Given the polynomial (12.8), with $\phi_r > 0$, write down the following array

$$\left.\begin{array}{llll} \phi_r & \phi_{r-2} & \phi_{r-4} & \cdots \\ \phi_{r-1} & \phi_{r-3} & \phi_{r-5} & \cdots \\ \phi_{r-2}^{(1)} & \phi_{r-4}^{(1)} & \phi_{r-6}^{(1)} & \cdots \\ \phi_{r-3}^{(2)} & \phi_{r-5}^{(2)} & \phi_{r-7}^{(2)} & \cdots \\ \cdots & & & \\ \phi_0^{(r-1)} & & & \end{array}\right\} \qquad (12.11)$$

where

$$\left.\begin{aligned}
\phi^{(1)}_{r-2} &= \phi_{r-1}\,\phi_{r-2} - \phi_r\,\phi_{r-3} \\[4pt]
\phi^{(1)}_{r-4} &= \phi_{r-1}\,\phi_{r-4} - \phi_r\,\phi_{r-5} \\
&\cdots
\end{aligned}\right\} \tag{12.12}$$

and successive rows are formed in a similar way from the two preceding rows: (12.11) is called the Routh array. Often the table is modified by dividing the entries in rows 3, 4, ..., $r+1$ by certain factors. This allows the number of roots in the right half-plane to be found [Gantmacher, 1959] but is unnecessary if we wish to know simply whether or not this number is zero. Show that if $\phi_{r-1}, \phi^{(1)}_{r-2}, \phi^{(2)}_{r-3}, ..., \phi^{(r-1)}_0$ are all positive, then $\phi(s)$ has no zero in the closed right half-plane. [The successive rows in (12.11) give the coefficients in the polynomials, $f_1, f_2, ..., f_{r+1}$, apart from certain sign changes which do not affect the first column, and apart from multiplication of rows 3, 4, ..., $r+1$ by $\phi_{r-1}, \phi_{r-1}\,\phi^{(1)}_{r-2}, ..., \phi_{r-1}\,\phi^{(1)}_{r-2} ... \phi^{(r-2)}_1$ respectively.]

(16) Write down the Routh array for (12.9).

(17) If $g(s) = 1/(s+1)(s+2)(s+3)$ arises from a least-order system, show that the feedback system with gain f is asymptotically stable for $-6 < f < 60$. Compare Fig. 2.28. [Write down the Routh array for $\phi(s)$ with f left indefinite.]

(18) Problem 17 shows that if we wish to find the range of f for which a closed-loop system is stable, then when $g(s)$ is sufficiently simple the Routh array is very convenient. Would this form a good general method for designing control systems? [Examine the various criteria in Section 9: compare with frequency response and root locus methods: consider the problem of compensation.]

(19) The Hurwitz matrix associated with (12.8) is the $r \times r$ matrix

$$h = \begin{bmatrix}
\phi_{r-1} & \phi_{r-3} & \phi_{r-5} & \cdots & 0 \\
\phi_r & \phi_{r-2} & \phi_{r-4} & \cdots & 0 \\
0 & \phi_{r-1} & \phi_{r-3} & \cdots & 0 \\
0 & \phi_r & \phi_{r-2} & \cdots & 0 \\
0 & 0 & \phi_{r-1} & \cdots & 0 \\
\vdots & \vdots & \vdots & & \vdots \\
0 & 0 & 0 & \cdots & \phi_0
\end{bmatrix} \tag{12.13}$$

Show that by elementary operations this can be brought to the form

$$\begin{bmatrix}
\phi_{r-1} & \phi_{r-3} & \phi_{r-5} & \cdots & 0 \\
0 & \phi^{(1)}_{r-2} & \phi^{(1)}_{r-4} & \cdots & 0 \\
0 & 0 & \phi^{(2)}_{r-3} & \cdots & 0 \\
\vdots & \vdots & \vdots & & \vdots \\
0 & 0 & 0 & \cdots & \phi^{(r-1)}_0
\end{bmatrix} \tag{12.14}$$

where the notation is defined by (12.11) and (12.12). In the elementary operations used, no row is added to an earlier row. Deduce the *Hurwitz criterion*: $\phi(s)$ has no zero in the closed right half-plane if ϕ_r and every principal minor of H is positive.

(20) Let $g(s)$ be a rational transfer function with real coefficients which is strictly proper and has no pole or zero in the closed right half-plane, and write $\log g(s) = a(s) + ib(s)$ where a and b are real. Let D be a contour consisting of the imaginary axis from $s = -iR$ to $s = iR$, and a semicircle of radius R in the right half-plane. Let D be indented into the right half-plane to avoid the points $s = \pm i\omega_0$. Prove the following

(i) The contour integral around D of

$$z(s) = \frac{a(s) + ib(s) - a(i\omega_0)}{s - i\omega_0} - \frac{a(s) + ib(s) - a(i\omega_0)}{s + i\omega_0} \tag{12.15}$$

$$= 2i\omega_0 \left[\frac{a(s) + ib(s) - a(i\omega_0)}{s^2 + \omega_0^2} \right] \tag{12.16}$$

is zero. [Use Cauchy's theorem: see for example Rosenbrock and Storey, 1970, Chapter 7, Section 3.2.]

(ii) As $R \to \infty$, the contribution from the large semicircle to the integral in (i) tends to zero. [Note that $R|z(Re^{i\theta})| \to 0$ as $R \to \infty$.]

(iii) The contribution to the contour integral in (i) from the indentation around $s = i\omega_0$ tends, as the radius r of the indentation tends to zero, to $-\pi b(i\omega_0)$. The same contribution arises from the indentation at $s = -i\omega_0$. [Write $s - i\omega_0 = re^{i\theta}$ in (11.15) and use the continuity of $g(s)$ at $s = i\omega_0$.]

(iv) The contribution from $b(s)$ to the integral along the imaginary axis in (i) is zero. [Use the fact that $b(i\omega)$ is an odd function of ω.]

(21) From Problem 20, conclude that

$$b(i\omega_0) = \frac{\omega_0}{\pi} \int_{-\infty}^{\infty} \frac{a(i\omega) - a(i\omega_0)}{\omega^2 - \omega_0^2} \, d\omega \tag{12.17}$$

$$= \frac{2\omega_0}{\pi} \int_{0}^{\infty} \frac{a(i\omega) - a(i\omega_0)}{\omega^2 - \omega_0^2} \, d\omega \tag{12.18}$$

The integrand in (12.18) becomes infinite as $\omega \to \omega_0$, and the Cauchy principal value is implied [see Rosenbrock and Storey, 1970, Chapter 5, Section 6]. Change the variable in (12.18) to $u = \log(\omega/\omega_0)$ and integrate by parts to give.

$$b(i\omega_0) = \frac{1}{\pi} \int_{-\infty}^{\infty} \frac{da}{du} \log \coth \frac{|u|}{2} \, du \tag{12.19}$$

[Compare Bode, 1945, p. 313.]

(22) Sketch the function log coth $|u|/2$ as a function of $u = \log(\omega/\omega_0)$. What do you conclude about the way in which the phase $b(i\omega_0)$ is determined by the gain $a(i\omega)$?

(23) Given that

$$\int_{-\infty}^{\infty} \log \coth \frac{|u|}{2}\, du = \frac{\pi^2}{2} \tag{12.20}$$

find approximately the phase shift at $s = i\omega_0$ if $da/du \doteq -p$ for all u in some interval $|u| < \alpha$, where α is large. Deduce that if the denominator of $g(s)$ has degree q, and the numerator has degree $q-p$, then the phase lag at high frequencies is approximately $p\pi/2$.

(24) Why does the result in Problem 23 fail to hold for the transfer functions

$$g(s) = \frac{1-s}{(1+s)^2}, \quad g(s) = \frac{e^{-st}}{1+s}? \tag{12.21}$$

(25) Let $g(s)$ be a rational transfer function with real coefficients, such that $s^2 g(s)$ remains finite as $s \to \infty$. Let $g(s)$ and $h(s) = g(s)/[1+fg(s)]$ have no pole in the closed right half-plane. Integrate the function

$$z(s) = \log g(s) - \log h(s) = \log [1+fg(s)] \tag{12.22}$$

around a suitable contour D (compare Problem 20) and show that

$$\int_0^{\infty} \log |h(i\omega)|\, d\omega = \int_0^{\infty} \log |g(i\omega)|\, d\omega \tag{12.23}$$

Compare with the remarks on sensitivity as a function of ω in Section 8. Show from the inverse Nyquist diagram that (12.23) is not true for $g(s) = 1/(s+1)$. [Compare Westcott, 1952.]

(26) If the system

$$\dot{x} = Ax + bu \tag{12.24}$$

is controllable (p.s.) and if the symmetric $n \times n$ matrix Q is positive definite, it is known that the *steady-state matrix Riccati equation*

$$A^T P + PA - Pbb^T P + Q = 0 \tag{12.25}$$

has a unique, symmetric, positive definite solution P.
Show that

$$\int_0^{\theta} [x^T Q x + u^T u]\, dt$$

$$= \int_0^{\theta} \left[x^T Q x + u^T u + \frac{d}{dt} x^T P x \right] dt - x^T(\theta) P x(\theta) + x^T(0) P x(0) \qquad (12.26)$$

$$= \int_0^{\theta} (u^T + x^T P b)(u + b^T P x) \, dt - x^T(\theta) P x(\theta) + x^T(0) P x(0) \qquad (12.27)$$

Deduce that the control law

$$u = -b^T P x \qquad (12.28)$$

minimizes the integral $\int_0^{\infty} [x^T Q x + u^T u] \, dt$ for any $x(0)$ provided that (12.28) makes (12.24) asymptotically stable. By considering the Liapunov function $x^T P x$ show that this last condition is satisfied. [See Brockett, 1970, Sections 21, 23.]

(27) The optimal system in Problem 26 gives

$$g(s) = b^T P(sI - A)^{-1} b \qquad (12.29)$$

Show from equation (2.7) of Chapter 1 that

$$\lim_{s \to \infty} s g(s) = b^T P b > 0 \qquad (12.30)$$

If we are given $g_1(s)$ such that $s^q g_1(s)$ tends to a finite nonzero limit as $s \to \infty$, and if we choose a compensator $k(s)$ which converts $g_1(s)$ into the optimal $g(s) = g_1(s) k(s)$, show that $k(s)/s^{q-1}$ remains finite as $s \to \infty$. Comment on the engineering implications.

(28) For a plant having $g(s) = 1/(s+1)^6$, design a phase advance compensator with $\alpha = 10$ to give as fast a response as possible with a gain margin of 4.

(29) Examine the effect of a phase advance compensator on a plant having $g(s) = e^{-s}$. [Look at the inverse Nyquist diagram and the step response.]

(30) For $g(s) = 1/(s+1)^6$ design a lead-lag compensator to give an offset of 1 % or better, an overshoot of less than 10 %, and a fast rise time subject to $\propto \leqslant 10$ in the phase-advance compensator.

(31) From the inverse Nyquist diagram it is clear that phase advance is least useful when the phase lag of the plant increases without a corresponding attenuation (compare Figs. 2.12 and 2.13). How can this effect be recognized in the root locus diagram?

(32) Find the step response corresponding to Fig. 2.24. If this response is considered too oscillatory, how can it be improved?

(33) Suppose that a plant has the inverse frequency response shown in

Fig. 2.19, but with the origin shifted to $(-2, 0)$. That is, the plant gives

$$\hat{g} = \frac{s^3 + 101s^2 + 145 \cdot 25s + 525}{1000 - 10s} + 2 = \frac{(s^2 + s + 25 \cdot 25)(100 + s)}{10(100 - s)} \quad \ldots \quad (12.31)$$

Use the result in Exercise 6.13 to estimate the damping when gains $f = 0, 1, 2$ are applied to this plant. Deduce that the phase margin and M_m are not reliable guides when the frequency response has the features illustrated by (12.31). How can these features be recognized in the inverse Nyquist plot?

Chapter 3

Multivariable systems

In this chapter we pass to a more complicated situation than was considered previously. The plant is still supposed to be described by linear, time-invariant differential equations, and our methods are still based largely upon the response to sinusoidal inputs. Now, however, the plant has more than one input or more than one output, so that we have a multivariable control problem. In general there will be l inputs and m outputs, but as we are interested in feedback control we usually have $l = m$.

1. Notation

Because they may have a complicated structure, multivariable control systems pose a difficulty of notation. We wish to refer to transfer functions between different inputs and outputs, with different compensators, and with various loops either open or closed. It is necessary first to have an unambiguous way of describing the transfer function in question.

The most general situation which we shall need to discuss is shown in Fig. 3.1. The plant is described by the $m \times l$ transfer function matrix $G(s)$.

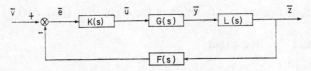

Fig. 3.1.   The general multivariable closed-loop system.

The *input compensator* is described by the $l \times k$ matrix $K(s)$ and the *output compensator* by the $k \times m$ matrix $L(s)$. A *feedback matrix* $F(s)$ is inserted in the return path, and is $k \times k$. In most applications we have $k = l = m$, and we shall then use m as the common symbol.

For the system shown in Fig. 3.1, we define $H(s)$ to be the transfer function

117

matrix relating outputs $\bar{z}(s)$ to inputs $\bar{v}(s)$. Then we have

$$\bar{z} = LGK\bar{e} = LGK(\bar{v} - F\bar{z}) \tag{1.1}$$

whence if $|I_k + LGKF|$ is not identically zero,

$$\bar{z} = [I_k + LGKF]^{-1} LGK\bar{v} = H\bar{v} \tag{1.2}$$

Alternatively we have

$$\bar{e} = \bar{v} - F\bar{z} = \bar{v} - FLGK\bar{e} \tag{1.3}$$

whence if $|I_k + FLGK| \not\equiv 0$,

$$\bar{z} = LGK\bar{e} = LGK[I_k + FLGK]^{-1} \bar{v} = H\bar{v} \tag{1.4}$$

If we define

$$LGK = Q \tag{1.5}$$

it follows that H can be written in the alternative forms

$$H = [I_k + QF]^{-1} Q \tag{1.6}$$

$$= Q[I_k + FQ]^{-1} \tag{1.7}$$

EXERCISE 1.1. Obtain (1.7) from (1.6) without assuming that $|Q(s)| \not\equiv 0$. [First show that $\begin{vmatrix} I_k & F \\ -Q & I_k \end{vmatrix} = |I_k + QF| = |I_k + FQ|$ as in Chapter 1, Section 9, so that $(I_k + FQ)^{-1}$ exists if $(I_k + QF)^{-1}$ exists. Then write down $H(I_k + FQ)$ from (1.6) and use $Q(I_k + FQ) = (I_k + QF) Q]$.

From (1.6) or (1.7), H depends only on Q and F, so that if we write

$$H(s) = H[Q(s), F(s)] \tag{1.8}$$

or more briefly

$$H = H[Q, F] \tag{1.9}$$

then H is fully defined as a function of the arguments $Q(s)$, $F(s)$.

EXERCISE 1.2. Show that

$$h_{12}\left[\begin{pmatrix} \dfrac{1}{s+1} & \dfrac{2}{s+2} \\ \dfrac{3}{s+3} & \dfrac{4}{s+4} \end{pmatrix}, \begin{pmatrix} 1 & 0 \\ 0 & 3 \end{pmatrix}\right] = \dfrac{2(s+1)(s+3)(s+4)}{s^4 + 23s^3 + 110s^2 + 178s + 120} \tag{1.10}$$

If we put $F = 0$ in (1.6) or (1.7) we obtain

$$H[Q, 0] = Q \tag{1.11}$$

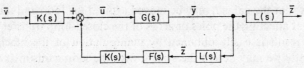

FIG. 3.2.   The block diagram shown in Fig. 3.1 can be manipulated into this form.

as is otherwise obvious. Also if we manipulate the block diagram in Fig. 3.1 into the form shown in Fig. 3.2 we obtain

$$H[LGK, F] = L\{H[G, KFL]\}\, K \tag{1.12}$$

EXERCISE 1.3.   Obtain (1.12) by matrix manipulation without assuming $k = l = m$ or $|K(s)| \not\equiv 0$ or $|L(s)| \not\equiv 0$. [Show first that

$$\begin{vmatrix} I_k & L \\ -GKF & I_m \end{vmatrix} = |I_m + GKFL| = |I_k + LGKF|$$

so that if $(I_m + GKFL)^{-1}$ or $(I_k + LGKF)^{-1}$ exists, then so does the other. Then manipulate the identity

$$LGK = L[I_m + GKFL]^{-1}\, [GK + GKFLGK]$$

to obtain (1.12)].

Up to this point, the results given in this Section are true whether or not the $k \times k$ matrix $Q(s)$ has an inverse. We shall assume in everything that follows (unless stated otherwise) that $|Q(s)| \not\equiv 0$, as if this were not true the system would not be controllable (f) [Chapter 1, Section 6]. The results given above are also true whether or not $k = l = m$. In Section 7 of this chapter, and a few other places where stated, we shall assume that $k = l = m$, which is the most usual case. Then the assumption $|Q(s)| \not\equiv 0$ implies $|G(s)| \not\equiv 0$, $|K(s)| \not\equiv 0$ and $|L(s)| \not\equiv 0$.

In any practical system we shall almost always have $L = I$. It is convenient to leave this matrix more general, however, as we thus obtain some extra freedom in design. For example if L and F are independent of s, $L = \text{diag}\,(l_i)$, $F = \text{diag}\,(f_i)$, $|L| \neq 0$, we find from (1.12)

$$H[LGK, F] = LH[GK, FL] \tag{1.13}$$

and by a second application

$$H[GKL, F] = H[GK, LF]\, L \tag{1.14}$$

Because L and F are diagonal, $FL = LF$, and as we have assumed L non-singular, we obtain from (1.13) and (1.14)

$$H[LGK, F] = L\{H[GKL, F]\}\, L^{-1} \tag{1.15}$$

This shows that the gains l_i may be moved around the loop and incorporated in K without affecting the poles or zeros of the closed-loop transfer function.* The same result is easily obtained by manipulation of the block diagram. Consequently we may design the system with the loop gains in L, but implement it with the gains in K. The advantages to be obtained in this way will become clear later.

The $l \times k$ matrix K may conveniently be written

$$K(s) = K_1(s) K_2(s) \qquad (1.16)$$

where

$$K_2(s) = \text{diag}(k_i(s)), \quad k \times k \qquad (1.17)$$

and the $k_i(s)$ are thought of as single-loop controllers. Similarly we may write

$$L(s) = L_2(s) L_1(s) \qquad (1.18)$$

with

$$L_2(s) = \text{diag}(l_i(s)), \quad k \times k \qquad (1.19)$$

Our design procedure will show how a suitable choice of K_1 (or L_1) may allow K_2 (or L_2) to be designed by the methods of Chapter 2. We shall also see, in Section 2, how (1.16) allows us to follow the effects of transducer failures, while (1.18) reveals the effects of actuator failures.

The matrix F is zero when all loops are open. In most practical systems we shall have $F = I$ in the closed-loop system. When some loops are open and some closed, F has 1 on the principal diagonal for each loop that is closed, and zeros everywhere else. It is very convenient for design and simulation purposes to make use of (1.12) and (1.16) with K_2 diagonal and independent of s to obtain

$$H[QK_2, F] = \{H[Q, K_2 F]\} K_2 \qquad (1.20)$$

where $Q = LGK_1$. Then for most purposes we may deal with $H[Q, K_2 F]$ rather than $H[QK_2, F]$. In an analogue simulation this allows us to change loop gains or to open any of the loops by adjusting the single matrix $K_2 F$. For example we may open a particular loop by putting the appropriate element in the diagonal matrix $K_2 F$ equal to zero. The corresponding device was used in Chapter 2 for single-loop systems. A similar treatment can be applied to (1.18).

EXERCISE 1.4. Draw the block diagrams corresponding to $H[QK_2, F]$ and $H[Q, K_2 F]$ and show that they differ only in the point at which the inputs $\bar{v}$ are injected.

The rather general comments of this Section will take on a greater signifi-

* Nor indeed of the closed-loop system, as can be shown by the methods used in Section 3.1.

cance in the light of what is said later. For the moment, the important point is that manipulation of the block diagram (or of the matrix equations) can produce a number of equivalent systems. Some of these may be more convenient for design purposes than the original system.

1.1 Inverse relationships

Provided that Q^{-1} exists, the formulae given above can be presented in a much simpler form. We shall wish to refer to the elements of matrices such as H^{-1} and Q^{-1}, and we therefore introduce the notation $H^{-1} = \hat{H}$, $Q^{-1} = \hat{Q}$ and similarly for other matrices. Then, for example, $\hat{h}_{12}$ is the element of H^{-1} in position $(1, 2)$. On the other hand h_{12}^{-1} is the inverse of the element in position $(1, 2)$ of H. Notice that

$$\hat{h}_{12} \neq h_{12}^{-1} \qquad (1.21)$$

in general.

EXAMPLE 1.1. If we have

$$H(s) = \begin{bmatrix} \dfrac{1}{s+1} & \dfrac{1}{s+2} \\ \dfrac{1}{s+3} & \dfrac{1}{s+4} \end{bmatrix} \qquad (1.22)$$

then

$$\hat{H}(s) = H^{-1}(s) = \frac{1}{2}\begin{bmatrix} (s+1)(s+2)(s+3) & -(s+1)(s+3)(s+4) \\ -(s+1)(s+2)(s+4) & (s+2)(s+3)(s+4) \end{bmatrix} \qquad (1.23)$$

so that

$$\hat{h}_{11}(s) = \frac{1}{2}(s+1)(s+2)(s+3) \qquad (1.24)$$

whereas

$$h_{11}^{-1}(s) = s+1 \qquad (1.25)$$

With this notation, (1.6) and (1.7) both lead to the same formula

$$\hat{H} = F + \hat{Q} \qquad (1.26)$$

which is considerably easier to deal with, and which shows that $\hat{H}$ exists if and only if $\hat{Q}$ exists. Equation (1.12) translates to

$$\hat{H}[\hat{K}\hat{G}\hat{L}, F] = \hat{K}\{\hat{H}[\hat{G}, KFL]\}\hat{L} \qquad (1.27)$$

which merely expresses the relation

$$F + \hat{K}\hat{G}\hat{L} = \hat{K}\{KFL + \hat{G}\}\hat{L} \qquad (1.28)$$

2. The gain space

Consider now the system shown in Fig. 3.1, in which

$$K(s) = K_1(s)\, K_2 \qquad (2.1)$$

Here K_2 is a nonsingular, constant, diagonal matrix of loop gains, while we assume that F is a diagonal matrix having 1 on its principal diagonal for each loop which is closed, and zero elsewhere. We wish to study the stability of the system with various combinations of loops closed, and with various loop gains.

The system can be rearranged as in Fig. 3.3, which corresponds to equation

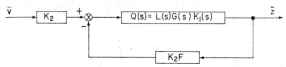

FIG. 3.3.   If we write $K(s) = K_1(s)\, K_2$, with K_2 a diagonal matrix independent of s, then the block diagram in Fig. 3.1 can be rearranged as shown.

(1.20). Stability is unaffected by the matrix K_2 outside the loop, so we may ignore this. Then for convenience we rename the matrix $K_2\, F$ as F, which is now a diagonal matrix, independent of s, $F = \mathrm{diag}\,(f_i)$. All combinations of gains and of open or closed loops are obtained by suitable choice of the elements of F on the principal diagonal. It will be noticed that our system can now be represented again by Fig. 3.1, with F suitably defined.

The elements f_i of $F = \mathrm{diag}\,(f_i)$ can be represented by points in a k-dimensional space, which following MacFarlane [1970b] we call the *gain space*. That region of the gain space in which $f_i > 0$, $i = 1, 2, ..., k$ corresponds to negative feedback in all loops, and is the region of most practical interest. Usually the system will be stable for some values of $f_1, f_2, ..., f_k$, and unstable for others. The gain space is therefore divided into stable and unstable regions. To avoid ambiguity, we shall adopt the following definitions: the point $(f_1, f_2, ..., f_k)$ belongs to the *asymptotically stable region* [resp. *stable region*] in the gain space if the system is asymptotically stable [resp. stable] with $F = \mathrm{diag}\,(f_i)$. The stable region therefore includes the asymptotically stable region. We say that $(f_1, f_2, ..., f_k)$ belongs to the *unstable region* in the gain space if the system is unstable with $F = \mathrm{diag}\,(f_i)$.

EXAMPLE 2.1.   If the open-loop system has least order and gives

$$Q(s) = \begin{bmatrix} \dfrac{1}{1+s} & \dfrac{2}{3+s} \\[2ex] \dfrac{1}{1+s} & \dfrac{1}{1+s} \end{bmatrix} \qquad (2.2)$$

Then (50, 0) lies in the asymptotically stable region of the gain space, because

$$H[Q, F] = Q[I_2 + FQ]^{-1} \tag{2.3}$$

$$= \begin{bmatrix} \dfrac{1}{1+s} & \dfrac{2}{3+s} \\[2ex] \dfrac{1}{1+s} & \dfrac{1}{1+s} \end{bmatrix} \begin{bmatrix} \dfrac{1+s}{51+s} & -\dfrac{100(1+s)}{(3+s)(51+s)} \\[2ex] 0 & 1 \end{bmatrix} \tag{2.4}$$

The closed-loop system is also least-order (Chapter 1, Section 3) and because H has all its poles in the open left half-plane the system is asymptotically stable.

EXERCISE 2.1.   Show that for the system in Example 2.1, the point (10, 10) is in the unstable region of the gain space.

EXAMPLE 2.2.   For the system described in Example 2.1, the stable region has been computed and is shown in Fig. 3.4. If either loop alone is closed,

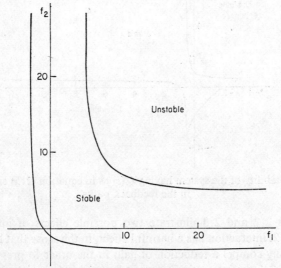

FIG. 3.4.   Stability of the system having $Q(s)$ as in equation (2.2) and gains f_1, f_2 in the feedback paths.

indefinitely high gain can be used (in the usual negative feedback sense) without instability. Increase of gain from zero in one loop reduces the permissible gain in the other. The stable region extends a little way into the positive feedback region.

EXAMPLE 2.3.   For a least-order system having

$$
Q(s) = \begin{bmatrix} \dfrac{s-1}{(s+1)^2} & \dfrac{5s+1}{(s+1)^2} \\[3mm] \dfrac{-1}{(s+1)^2} & \dfrac{s-1}{(s+1)^2} \end{bmatrix}
\tag{2.5}
$$

the stable region is shown in Fig. 3.5. Increase of one gain from zero now allows increase of the other without instability. Notice that $q_{11}(0) = q_{22}(0) = -1$, so that the loop gains have the opposite sign to what would usually be regarded as normal.

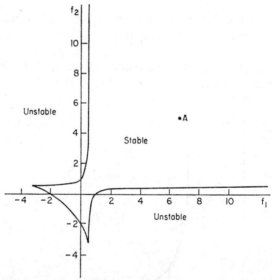

FIG. 3.5.   Stability of the system having $Q(s)$ as in equation (2.5) and gains f_1, f_2 in the feedback paths.

Examples 2.2 and 2.3 illustrate two possible effects of interaction. In Example 2.2, interaction has a harmful effect, in the sense that higher gain in one loop may compel a reduction of gain in the other to preserve stability. In Example 2.3 the interaction seems at first sight beneficial—increased gain in one loop can allow an increased gain in the other. Consider, however, what may happen if this possibility is exploited by operating the system at the point marked A. If one of the two transducers fails, the gain of its loop is reduced to zero, and the system is then unstable. A similar result is obtained if one of the two actuators fails. Such a system is *conditionally stable* in a new sense, and often this possibility will be unacceptable.

More complicated situations than those shown in Fig. 3.4 and 3.5 may arise even in two dimensions: one possibility is shown in Fig. 3.6. In three or more dimensions the possible complications are further increased. This is a

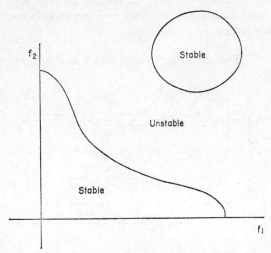

FIG. 3.6.   Possible stability regions for a plant with two inputs and two outputs and with gains f_1, f_2 in the feedback paths.

central difficulty of multivariable control systems, and one which must be faced in their design. In many applications it will be essential to guarantee that the system is asymptotically stable, and (in an appropriate sense) has sufficient stability margin, at least for all gains f_i satisfying $0 \leqslant f_i \leqslant f_{i0}$, $i = 1, 2, \ldots, k$, where f_{i0} represents the designed operating value in loop i. Notice that if $Q(s)$ were diagonal, this is exactly the information which could be obtained from an application of the single-loop theory.

2.1 Definition of loops

In equation (2.1) we supposed that $K(s)$ could be written $K_1(s) K_2$ with K_2 diagonal and independent of s. We associated K_2 with F as in Fig. 3.3, and could then study all combinations of loop gains (expressed by the elements of K_2) and loop closures (expressed by the elements 0 or 1 on the principal diagonal of F).

It is important to notice that if we had assumed

$$K(s) = K_2 K_1(s) \tag{2.6}$$

with K_2 again diagonal and independent of s, we should have had an essentially different situation. It would not then be possible to associate K_2 with F, because $K_1(s)$ intervenes between them: indeed K_2 is in general $l \times l$ whereas

F is $k \times k$. Putting the leading element of K_2 equal to zero then leaves a system which in general is different from the one obtained by putting the leading element of F equal to zero. We can in fact distinguish one set of loops passing through F, and a different set passing through K_2. Any diagonal matrix in the block diagram, or any vector connection between blocks can be used in this way to define a set of loops.

EXAMPLE 2.4.   The least-order system shown in Fig. 3.7 is asymptotically

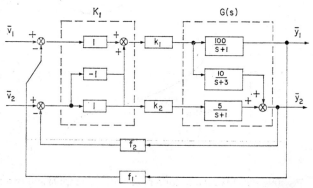

FIG. 3.7.   A multivariable system illustrating the different gain spaces defined by the gains k_1, k_2 and the gains f_1, f_2.

stable when $k_1 = k_2 = f_1 = f_2 = 1$ [see Exercise 3.3 below]. On changing k_1 from 1 to 0, a single loop remains with return difference

$$1 + \frac{5}{s+1} = \frac{s+6}{s+1} \tag{2.7}$$

so that asymptotic stability is maintained [Chapter 2, Theorem 4.1]. On changing f_1 in the original system from 1 to 0, however, a different single loop remains with return difference

$$1 + \frac{5}{s+1} - \frac{10}{s+3} = \frac{s^2 - s + 8}{(s+1)(s+3)} \tag{2.8}$$

so that the system then becomes unstable.

In Example 2.4, putting $k_1 = 0$ shows the effect of an actuator failure at the first input of G. Putting $f_1 = 0$ shows the effect of a transducer failure at the first output of G. When the controller $K(s)$ is not diagonal these types of failure can have quite different effects. The same is true when a non-diagonal $L(s)$ is used.

In later Sections of this chapter we shall wish to take account of the effects of actuator, or transducer, or sometimes other failures. When transducer failures are most important we shall put $L(s) = I$ and write $K(s) = K_1(s) K_2$ as in (2.1), and shall then assimilate K_2 with F as in Fig. 3.3. Then putting any elements of the diagonal matrix $K_2 F$ equal to zero shows the effects of the corresponding transducer failures. These effects can easily be followed as the design progresses. Failure of actuators in this case gives effects which are not obvious during the design procedure, and may have to be checked subsequently.

If on the other hand actuator failures are most important, we shall put $K(s) = I$, and write $L(s) = L_2 L_1(s)$, where L_2 is diagonal. Then assimilating L_2 with F, we can readily take account of actuator failures during the design procedure. After the design is completed, we shall usually move $L(s)$ round the loop. This leads to certain other difficulties which will be considered later [see Chapter 4, Section 4].

In general, when other types of failure (for example failure of amplifier elements in $K(s)$) are most important, we shall arrange if possible that the elements subject to failure are assimilated into F. Therefore when loops are referred to they will always be those defined by a diagonal matrix F unless something is said to the contrary.

EXERCISE 2.2. In Fig. 3.7, find the effect when $k_1 = k_2 = 1$ of opening the second feedback loop by putting $f_1 = 1, f_2 = 0$. Find also the effect of putting $k_2 = 0$ (with $k_1 = f_1 = f_2 = 1$) and redraw the Figure to emphasize that this corresponds to opening a different loop.

When single-loop compensators are used they will be incorporated generally into $K_1(s)$ or $L_1(s)$, and so assimilated into $Q(s)$. Generally we shall drop the suffix on K_1 and L_1, and shall replace $K_2 F$ or FL_2 by F, so returning to the notation of Fig. 3.1, but with F diagonal and independent of s. This corresponds with what was done for single-loop systems, but it is now more important to keep in mind the implicit transformation which has been made.

3. Stability

As was seen earlier for single-input single-output systems, cancellation of decoupling zeros can occur when forming the transfer function. Consequently the transfer function can give no information about the location of the cancelled poles, which may be stable or unstable. A similar cancellation can occur in multivariable systems, though now we have to take account of the non-commutativity of matrix multiplication.

EXAMPLE 3.1. The system

$$\dot{x} = Ax + Bu \qquad (3.1)$$
$$y = Cx \qquad (3.2)$$

with

$$A = \begin{bmatrix} 0 & -1 & 0 \\ -1 & 0 & 0 \\ 0 & -2 & -3 \end{bmatrix} \tag{3.3}$$

$$B = \begin{bmatrix} 1 & 0 \\ 1 & 0 \\ 0 & 1 \end{bmatrix} \tag{3.4}$$

$$C = \begin{bmatrix} 1 & 0 & 0 \\ 0 & 0 & 1 \end{bmatrix} \tag{3.5}$$

gives

$$G(s) = C(sI_3 - A)^{-1}B \tag{3.6}$$

$$= \begin{bmatrix} \dfrac{1}{s+1} & 0 \\ \dfrac{-2}{(s+1)(s+3)} & \dfrac{1}{s+3} \end{bmatrix} \tag{3.7}$$

But we have

$$(sI_3 - A) = \begin{bmatrix} s & 1 & 0 \\ 1 & s & 0 \\ 0 & 2 & s+3 \end{bmatrix} = \begin{bmatrix} s & 1 & 0 \\ 1 & 1 & 0 \\ 0 & 0 & 1 \end{bmatrix} \begin{bmatrix} 1 & -1 & 0 \\ 0 & s+1 & 0 \\ 0 & 2 & s+3 \end{bmatrix} \tag{3.8}$$

$$B = \begin{bmatrix} 1 & 0 \\ 1 & 0 \\ 0 & 1 \end{bmatrix} = \begin{bmatrix} s & 1 & 0 \\ 1 & 1 & 0 \\ 0 & 0 & 1 \end{bmatrix} \begin{bmatrix} 0 & 0 \\ 1 & 0 \\ 0 & 1 \end{bmatrix} \tag{3.9}$$

so that when we form the product $(sI - A)^{-1} B$, the common left factor

$$\begin{bmatrix} s & 1 & 0 \\ 1 & 1 & 0 \\ 0 & 0 & 1 \end{bmatrix} \tag{3.10}$$

cancels. This factor has determinant $s-1$, and the corresponding pole at

$s = 1$ does not appear in $G(s)$, though it clearly makes the system (3.1) unstable. We say that the system matrix

$$P(s) = \begin{bmatrix} sI_3 - A & B \\ -C & 0 \end{bmatrix} \tag{3.11}$$

with A, B, C as in (3.3) has an input decoupling (i.d.) zero $s = 1$. Alternatively we may say [Chapter 1, Section 6] that the system (3.1) is not controllable (p.s.), though this statement carries implications which should be resisted. Controllability (p.s.)—the ability to take the state to any desired point—is in itself of no direct interest to us in the problem we are considering: it is controllability (f) which we need [compare Chapter 2, Section 4.1].

EXAMPLE 3.2.   After Laplace transformation with zero initial conditions, we may write the equations of the system

$$\left. \begin{aligned} \dot{\xi}_1 &= \xi_1 + u_1 \\ 2\dot{\xi}_1 + \dot{\xi}_2 &= 2\xi_1 - 3\xi_2 + u_2 \end{aligned} \right\} \tag{3.12}$$

$$\left. \begin{aligned} y_1 &= \dot{\xi}_1 - \xi_1 \\ y_2 &= \xi_2 \end{aligned} \right\} \tag{3.13}$$

in the form

$$T(s)\,\xi = U(s)\,\bar{u} \tag{3.14}$$

$$\bar{y} = V(s)\,\xi \tag{3.15}$$

with

$$T(s) = \begin{bmatrix} s^2 - 1 & 0 \\ 2(s-1) & s+3 \end{bmatrix} = \begin{bmatrix} s+1 & 0 \\ 2 & s+3 \end{bmatrix} \begin{bmatrix} s-1 & 0 \\ 0 & 1 \end{bmatrix} \tag{3.16}$$

$$U(s) = I_2 \tag{3.17}$$

$$V(s) = \begin{bmatrix} s-1 & 0 \\ 0 & 1 \end{bmatrix} = \begin{bmatrix} 1 & 0 \\ 0 & 1 \end{bmatrix} \begin{bmatrix} s-1 & 0 \\ 0 & 1 \end{bmatrix} \tag{3.18}$$

The polynomial matrices $T(s)$, $V(s)$ have the common right factor

$$\begin{bmatrix} s-1 & 0 \\ 0 & 1 \end{bmatrix} \tag{3.19}$$

with determinant $s-1$. This factor cancels when we form the transfer function matrix

$$G(s) = V(s)\, T^{-1}(s)\, U(s) = \begin{bmatrix} \dfrac{1}{s+1} & 0 \\[2ex] \dfrac{-2}{(s+1)(s+3)} & \dfrac{1}{s+3} \end{bmatrix} \tag{3.20}$$

The corresponding system matrix

$$P(s) = \begin{bmatrix} 1 & 0 & \vline & 0 \\ 0 & T(s) & \vline & U(s) \\ \hline 0 & -V(s) & \vline & 0 \end{bmatrix} \tag{3.21}$$

with $T(s)$, $U(s)$, $V(s)$ given by (3.16), (3.17), (3.18) has an output decoupling (o.d.) zero $s = 1$.

If a system has no i.d. zero and no o.d. zero, it has least order. Only in this case can stability be investigated with no other information than is contained in the transfer function matrix. In Fig. 3.1 it is very natural to assume that $K(s)$, $L(s)$ and $F(s)$ arise from subsystems of least order, since we have to implement these matrices in order to control the plant, and usually there is no reason to use an implementation of higher order than necessary. On the other hand $G(s)$ arises from the given plant and from our choice if inputs $\bar{u}$ and outputs $\bar{y}$. It can easily happen that cancellation occurs in forming $G(s)$. An example of this was given for a single-input single-output system in Section 4 of Chapter 2. For generality, we shall not require any of the subsystems to have least order when we investigate stability. Nor shall we require $G(s)$ to be square and invertible except where stated.

When designing the matrices $K(s)$, $L(s)$ and $F(s)$, we shall usually try to ensure that the least-order systems giving rise to them are asymptotically stable. We shall also try to ensure that these matrices have no zero in the closed right half-plane, where the zeros of a rational matrix have been defined in Section 4.1 of Chapter 1. This last requirement ensures that the subsystems giving rise to $K(s)$, $L(s)$ and $F(s)$ are controllable (l), and therefore do not contribute new difficulties of nonminimum phase behaviour [see Chapter 1, Section 6; Chapter 2, Section 10.1; also the Appendix].

EXERCISE 3.1. Show that if $k = l = m$ and $K(s)$ [resp. $L(s)$, $F(s)$] has no pole in the closed right half-plane, while $|K(s)|$ [resp. $|L(s)|$, $|F(s)|$] has no zero there, then $K(s)$ [resp. $L(s) F(s)$] has no zero in the closed right half-plane. [The zeros of $K(s)$ are by definition the zeros of the numerator polynomials in its McMillan form. These are the same as the zeros of $|K(s)|$ if no cancellation can occur with zeros of the denominator polynomials: see the end of Section 4.1, Chapter 1.]

3.1 A stability theorem

Let $G(s)$ arise from the system, not necessarily of least order,

$$\left.\begin{aligned} T_G(s)\, \xi_G &= U_G(s)\, \bar{u} \\ \bar{y} &= V_G(s)\, \xi_G + W_G(s)\, \bar{u} \end{aligned}\right\} \tag{3.22}$$

with corresponding system matrix

$$P_G(s) = \begin{bmatrix} T_G(s) & U_G(s) \\ -V_G(s) & W_G(s) \end{bmatrix} \tag{3.23}$$

Let $K(s)$, $L(s)$, $F(s)$ arise respectively from the systems, not necessarily of least order,

$$\left.\begin{aligned} T_K(s)\, \xi_K &= U_K(s)\, \bar{e} \\ \bar{u} &= V_K(s)\, \xi_K + W_K(s)\, \bar{e} \end{aligned}\right\} \tag{3.24}$$

$$\left.\begin{aligned} T_L(s)\, \xi_L &= U_L(s)\, \bar{y} \\ \bar{z} &= V_L(s)\, \xi_L + W_L(s)\, \bar{y} \end{aligned}\right\} \tag{3.25}$$

$$\left.\begin{aligned} T_F(s)\, \xi_F &= U_F(s)\, \bar{z} \\ \bar{v} - \bar{e} &= V_F(s)\, \xi_F + W_F(s)\, \bar{z} \end{aligned}\right\} \tag{3.26}$$

where the inputs and outputs of these systems have been chosen to conform with Fig. 3.1. The dimensions of the vectors $\bar{u}$, $\bar{y}$, $\bar{e}$, $\bar{z}$, $\bar{v}$ are respectively l, m, k, k, k, as in Section 1. Corresponding to (3.24), (3.25), (3.26) are system matrices $P_K(s)$, $P_L(s)$, $P_F(s)$. The form of these equations includes the case where one or more of K, L, F is independent of s. For example, if $T_F = I$, $U_F = I$, $V_F = F$, $W_F = 0$, equations (3.26) give $\bar{v} - \bar{e} = F\bar{z}$.

The entire set of closed-loop equations can be written

$$
\begin{bmatrix}
T_K & U_K & 0 & 0 & 0 & 0 & 0 & 0 & \vline & 0 \\
-V_K & W_K & 0 & -I_l & 0 & 0 & 0 & 0 & \vline & 0 \\
0 & 0 & T_G & U_G & 0 & 0 & 0 & 0 & \vline & 0 \\
0 & 0 & -V_G & W_G & 0 & -I_m & 0 & 0 & \vline & 0 \\
0 & 0 & 0 & 0 & T_L & U_L & 0 & 0 & \vline & 0 \\
0 & 0 & 0 & 0 & -V_L & W_L & 0 & -I_k & \vline & 0 \\
0 & 0 & 0 & 0 & 0 & 0 & T_F & U_F & \vline & 0 \\
0 & I_k & 0 & 0 & 0 & 0 & -V_F & W_F & \vline & -I_k \\
\hline
0 & 0 & 0 & 0 & 0 & 0 & 0 & I_k & \vline & 0
\end{bmatrix}
\begin{bmatrix}
\xi_k \\
-\bar{e} \\
\xi_G \\
-\bar{u} \\
\xi_L \\
-\bar{y} \\
\xi_F \\
-\bar{z} \\
\hline
-\bar{v}
\end{bmatrix}
=
\begin{bmatrix}
0 \\
0 \\
0 \\
0 \\
0 \\
0 \\
0 \\
0 \\
\hline
-\bar{z}
\end{bmatrix}
$$

$$(3.27)$$

Because the two vectors in (3.27) have the appropriate form [Chapter 1, Section 2.1] the matrix is a system matrix for the closed-loop system, and we write it

$$
P_H(s) =
\begin{bmatrix}
T_H(s) & U_H(s) \\
-V_H(s) & W_H(s)
\end{bmatrix}
$$

$$(3.28)$$

The matrix P_H is square, and in accordance with the definition of a system matrix we require that $|T_H(s)| \not\equiv 0$ and that the degree of $|T_H(s)|$ does not exceed its dimension. As a preliminary to the investigation of closed-loop stability we prove the following lemma.

LEMMA 3.1. With the above notation,

$$|T_H| = \pm |I_k + LGKF| |T_L| |T_G| |T_K| |T_F| \qquad (3.29)$$

where if $k = l = m$ the sign is positive.

Proof. By Theorem 9.2 of Chapter 1 we obtain from (3.27), on making an appropriate subdivision of T_H,

$$
|T_H| = |T_K|
\begin{bmatrix}
V_K T_K^{-1} U_K + W_K & 0 & -I & 0 & 0 & 0 & 0 \\
0 & T_G & U_G & 0 & 0 & 0 & 0 \\
0 & -V_G & W_G & 0 & -I & 0 & 0 \\
0 & 0 & 0 & T_L & U_L & 0 & 0 \\
0 & 0 & 0 & -V_L & W_L & 0 & -I \\
0 & 0 & 0 & 0 & 0 & T_F & U_F \\
I & 0 & 0 & 0 & 0 & -V_F & W_F
\end{bmatrix}
\qquad (3.30)
$$

Then inserting

$$K = V_K T_K^{-1} U_K + W_K \tag{3.31}$$

and by row and column interchanges

$$|T_H| = (-1)^{p_1}|T_K|
\begin{bmatrix}
T_G & U_G & 0 & 0 & 0 & 0 & 0 \\
-V_G & W_G & 0 & -I & 0 & 0 & 0 \\
0 & 0 & T_L & U_L & 0 & 0 & 0 \\
0 & 0 & -V_L & W_L & 0 & -I & 0 \\
0 & 0 & 0 & 0 & T_F & U_F & 0 \\
0 & 0 & 0 & 0 & -V_F & W_F & I \\
0 & -I & 0 & 0 & 0 & 0 & K
\end{bmatrix} \tag{3.32}$$

By repetition of the same procedure we obtain

$$|T_H| = (-1)^{p_2}|T_K||T_G|
\begin{bmatrix}
T_L & U_L & 0 & 0 & 0 & 0 \\
-V_L & W_L & 0 & -I & 0 & 0 \\
0 & 0 & T_F & U_F & 0 & 0 \\
0 & 0 & -V_F & W_F & I & 0 \\
0 & 0 & 0 & 0 & K & -I \\
0 & -I & 0 & 0 & 0 & G
\end{bmatrix} \tag{3.33}$$

$$= (-1)^{p_3}|T_K||T_G||T_L|
\begin{bmatrix}
T_F & U_F & 0 & 0 & 0 \\
-V_F & W_F & I & 0 & 0 \\
0 & 0 & K & -I & -0 \\
0 & 0 & 0 & G & -I \\
0 & -I & 0 & 0 & L
\end{bmatrix} \tag{3.34}$$

$$= (-1)^{p_4}|T_K||T_G||T_L||T_F|
\begin{bmatrix}
F & I_k & 0 & 0 \\
0 & K & -I_l & 0 \\
0 & 0 & G & -I_m \\
-I_k & 0 & 0 & L
\end{bmatrix} \tag{3.35}$$

Now in the last determinant in (3.35), subtract K times the first block row from the second, and proceed similarly to obtain

$$(-1)^{p_4}
\begin{bmatrix}
F & I & 0 & 0 \\
-KF & 0 & -I & 0 \\
0 & 0 & G & -I \\
-I & 0 & 0 & L
\end{bmatrix}
= (-1)^{p_4}
\begin{bmatrix}
F & I & 0 & 0 \\
-KF & 0 & -I & 0 \\
-GKF & 0 & 0 & -I \\
-I & 0 & 0 & L
\end{bmatrix} \tag{3.36}$$

$$= (-1)^{p_4} \begin{bmatrix} F & I & 0 & 0 \\ -KF & 0 & -I & 0 \\ -GKF & 0 & 0 & -I \\ -I-LGKF & 0 & 0 & 0 \end{bmatrix}$$

(3.37)

$$= (-1)^{p_5} \begin{bmatrix} I & 0 & 0 & 0 \\ 0 & I & 0 & 0 \\ 0 & 0 & I & 0 \\ 0 & 0 & 0 & I+LGKF \end{bmatrix}$$

(3.38)

where (3.38) is obtained by column operations and changes of sign. Equations (3.35) and (3.38) give (3.29). A count of row and column interchanges and of changes of sign shows that when $k = l = m$, p_5 is even, so that the positive sign then holds in (3.29).

COROLLARY 1. The determinant of the return difference matrix $I_k + LGKF$ in (3.29) can be evaluated in the following equivalent ways

$$|I_k+LGKF| = |I_k+FLGK| \tag{3.39}$$
$$= |I_l+KFLG| \tag{3.40}$$
$$= |I_m+GKFL| \tag{3.41}$$

Proof. These results arise from different ways of evaluating the last determinant in (3.35). For example (3.41) is obtained thus

$$\begin{vmatrix} F & I & 0 & 0 \\ 0 & K & -I & 0 \\ 0 & 0 & G & -I \\ -I & 0 & 0 & L \end{vmatrix} = \begin{vmatrix} 0 & I & 0 & FL \\ 0 & K & -I & 0 \\ 0 & 0 & G & -I \\ -I & 0 & 0 & L \end{vmatrix}$$

(3.42)

$$= \begin{vmatrix} 0 & I & 0 & FL \\ 0 & 0 & -I & -KFL \\ 0 & 0 & G & -I \\ -I & 0 & 0 & L \end{vmatrix}$$

(3.43)

$$= \begin{vmatrix} 0 & I & 0 & FL \\ 0 & 0 & -I & KFL \\ 0 & 0 & 0 & -I-GKFL \\ -I & 0 & 0 & L \end{vmatrix}$$

(3.44)

This can readily be brought by elementary operations to a form corresponding to (3.38), and requires the same number $(k+1)(k+l+m)$ of sign changes in the process. The other results are obtained in a similar way.

COROLLARY 2.   If $|Q(s)| \not\equiv 0$, then $|H(s)| \not\equiv 0$, and

$$|I_k+LGKF| = \frac{|LGK|}{|H|} = \frac{|Q|}{|H|} \qquad (3.45)$$

$$= \frac{|\hat{H}|}{|\hat{Q}|} \qquad (3.46)$$

where $\hat{H} = H^{-1}$, $\hat{Q} = Q^{-1}$.

Proof.   By our assumption that $|T_H(s)| \not\equiv 0$, it follows from (3.29) that $|I_k+LGKF| \not\equiv 0$. Then $|H(s)| \not\equiv 0$ by (1.6), (3.45) follows from (1.2), and (3.46) from the definitions of $\hat{H}$, $\hat{Q}$.

EXERCISE 3.2.   Verify the number of sign changes needed in bringing (3.37) to (3.38), and (3.44) to the corresponding form. (Do not forget sign changes due to row or column interchanges.)

EXERCISE 3.3.   Explain physically why the matrices L, G, K, F are conformable for the products $LGKF$, $FLGK$, $KFLG$, $GKFL$, and why these product matrices are square.

The zeros of $|T_H|$ are the poles of the closed-loop system. Similarly the zeros of $|T_L|$, $|T_G|$, $|T_K|$, $|T_F|$ are the poles of the subsystems from which the closed-loop system was constructed. The possible negative sign in (3.29) obviously does not affect this relationship between the poles. We therefore see that the determinant of the return difference matrix $I+LGKF$ (or any of the other equal expressions given in the Corollaries) relates the closed-loop poles to the open-loop poles. We also have immediately the following stability theorem.

THEOREM 3.1.   The system shown in Fig. 3.1 and described by equations (3.22) to (3.26) is asymptotically stable if and only if all the zeros of the polynomial $\phi(s) = |I+LGKF||T_L||T_G||T_K||T_F|$ are in the open left half-plane.

So far we have made no special assumptions about the systems (3.22) to (3.26). We now assume, what is always true in practice, that $LGKF$ is strictly proper: that is, $LGKF \rightarrow 0$ as $s \rightarrow \infty$. It follows then that $|I+LGKF| \rightarrow 1$ as $s \rightarrow \infty$, whence the degree of $|T_H|$ is the sum of the degrees of $|T_L|$, $|T_G|$,

$|T_K|$ and $|T_F|$. It also follows, after dividing top and bottom on the right-hand side by the coefficient of the highest power of s, that

$$|I+LGKF| = \frac{\prod\limits_{i=1}^{n} (s-\alpha_i')}{\prod\limits_{i=1}^{n} (s-\alpha_i)} \qquad (3.47)$$

Here the α_i' are the closed-loop poles, n in number, while α_i are the open-loop poles arising from $|T_L|$, $|T_G|$, $|T_K|$ and $|T_F|$ all together.

It is important to notice that two different kinds of cancellation can occur on the right-hand side of (3.47). First suppose that one or more of L, G, K, F arises from a system which does not have least order. Then certain of the α_i (namely the decoupling zeros) will not appear as poles on the left-hand side of (3.47), while on the right-hand side they will cancel. Secondly it may happen fortuitously than an α_i is equal to an α_i': then cancellation will occur on both sides of (3.47).

EXAMPLE 3.3.   Suppose that $L = K = F = I_2$, while G arises from (3.1) to (3.5). Then for the left-hand side of (3.47) we have

$$|I+LGKF| = \begin{vmatrix} \dfrac{s+2}{s+1} & 0 \\ \dfrac{-2}{(s+1)(s+3)} & \dfrac{s+4}{s+3} \end{vmatrix} = \frac{(s+2)(s+4)}{(s+1)(s+3)} \qquad (3.48)$$

while on putting $\bar{u} = \bar{v} - \bar{y}$ in (3.1) we readily find that $T_H(s) = sI_3 - A + BC$. We therefore have

$$\frac{\prod\limits_{i=1}^{3} (s-\alpha_i')}{\prod\limits_{i=1}^{3} (s-\alpha_i)} = \frac{|T_H|}{|T_G|} = \frac{|sI_3 - A + BC|}{|sI_3 - A|} \qquad (3.49)$$

$$= \frac{(s-1)(s+2)(s+4)}{(s-1)(s+1)(s+3)} \qquad (3.50)$$

on using (3.3) to (3.5). This illustrates the first kind of cancellation.

EXERCISE 3.4.   Obtain the result $T_H(s) = sI_3 - A + BC$ in Example 3.3 by direct evaluation from (3.27). Show that $s = 1$ is an i.d. zero of the closed-loop (as well as the open-loop) system.

EXAMPLE 3.4.   Suppose that $L = K = F = I_2$, while G arises from the system matrix

$$P(s) = \begin{bmatrix} sI-A & B \\ -C & 0 \end{bmatrix} = \left[\begin{array}{cc|cc} s+1 & 0 & 1 & 0 \\ 0 & s+2 & 0 & 1 \\ \hline -1 & 0 & 0 & 0 \\ 0 & -1 & 0 & 0 \end{array}\right] \tag{3.51}$$

which has least order. Then

$$G(s) = \begin{bmatrix} \dfrac{1}{s+1} & 0 \\ 0 & \dfrac{1}{s+2} \end{bmatrix} \tag{3.52}$$

and

$$|I_2+LGKF| = \begin{vmatrix} \dfrac{s+2}{s+1} & 0 \\ 0 & \dfrac{s+3}{s+2} \end{vmatrix} = \frac{(s+2)(s+3)}{(s+1)(s+2)} \tag{3.53}$$

while

$$\frac{\prod\limits_{i=1}^{2}(s-\alpha_i')}{\prod\limits_{i=1}^{2}(s-\alpha_i)} = \frac{|sI_2-A+BC|}{|sI_2-A|} = \frac{(s+2)(s+3)}{(s+1)(s+2)} \tag{3.54}$$

This illustrates the second way in which poles may be lost, which clearly depends on the particular values of L, K and F. For example if $L = K = I_2$, $F = 2I_2$, then

$$|I_2+LGKF| = \frac{(s+3)(s+4)}{(s+1)(s+2)} \tag{3.55}$$

and there is no cancellation. The first type of cancellation (of decoupling zeros) can occur in single-input single-output systems, but the second type can occur only in multivariable systems.

EXAMPLE 3.5.   If a least-order system gives

$$G(s) = \begin{bmatrix} \dfrac{1}{s+1} & 0 \\ \dfrac{1}{s-1} & \dfrac{1}{s+1} \end{bmatrix} \tag{3.56}$$

then the pole at $s = 1$ is lost when forming $|I+LGKF|$ if L, K, F are diagonal.

We regard this as a fortuitous loss of the second kind: if for example

$$F = \begin{bmatrix} 1 & 1 \\ 0 & 1 \end{bmatrix}$$

and $L = K = I$, then the pole at $s = 1$ appears in $|I+GF|$.

EXERCISE 3.5. The least-order system shown in Fig. 3.7 is asymptotically stable when $f_1 = f_2 = 0$. Find the return difference matrix when $f_1 = f_2 = k_1 = k_2 = 1$ and show that the system is then asymptotically stable. [Note that the roots of $s^3 + as^2 + bs + c$ are in the open left half-plane if $a > 0$ and $ab > c > 0$.]

EXERCISE 3.6. Show that any decoupling zero of P_K, P_L or P_F is a decoupling zero of P_H. Is the converse true? [No: see SSMVT, Chapter 3, Section 6.1.]

3.2 A decomposition theorem

The question whether a given closed-loop system is stable is answered, in principle, by Theorem 3.1. However, this is not exactly the form in which the problem is posed to the designer. Usually $F = \text{diag}(f_i)$, with the f_i representing loop gains. The interesting question is then: how does stability change as we vary the gains f_i?

To answer this question we should like, if possible, to decompose the stability problem into a number of sub-problems, one for each f_i. We cannot in general expect these sub-problems to be independent when $Q = LGK$ is not diagonal. One such decomposition is given here, but it is not the one which will prove most useful to us: that is given in Section 5.

First we assume that $F = \text{diag}(f_i)$, with f_i real, $i = 1, 2, ..., k$, and define

$$F_i = \text{diag}(f_1, f_2, ..., f_i, 0, ..., 0) \tag{3.57}$$

With the notation of (1.9)

$$H[Q(s), F_{i-1}] = Q(s)[I_k + F_{i-1} Q(s)]^{-1} \tag{3.58}$$

and we define

$$h_i(s) = h_{ii}[Q(s), F_{i-1}] \tag{3.59}$$

where $h_{ii}[Q, F_{i-1}]$ is element (i, i) of $H[Q, F_{i-1}]$. That is to say, h_i is the transfer function seen between input i and output i when loops $1, 2, ..., i-1$ are closed, with gains $f_1, f_2, ..., f_{i-1}$, and the other loops are open. Then we have the following theorem.

THEOREM 3.2.   With the above notation

$$|I_k + FQ(s)| = \prod_{i=1}^{k} [1 + f_i h_i(s)] = |I_k + Q(s) F| \qquad (3.60)$$

Proof.   Write

$$F_i' = \text{diag} (0, ..., 0, f_i, 0, ..., 0) \qquad (3.61)$$

which gives the identity

$$F_i' Q [I + F_{i-1} Q]^{-1} [I + F_{i-1} Q] = (F_i - F_{i-1}) Q \qquad (3.62)$$

whence

$$F_i' H [Q, F_{i-1}][I + F_{i-1} Q] = F_i Q - F_{i-1} Q \qquad (3.63)$$

Now adding the identity matrix to both sides, and rearranging,

$$\{I + F_i' H [Q, F_{i-1}]\}[I + F_{i-1} Q] = I + F_i Q \qquad (3.64)$$

The element (i, i) of $F_i' H [Q, F_{i-1}]$ is the same as element (i, i) of $F_i H [Q, F_{i-1}]$, which is $f_i h_i(s)$. As all rows of $F_i' H [Q, F_{i-1}]$ except row i are zero, it readily follows on taking determinants in (3.64) that

$$[1 + f_i h_i(s)]|I + F_{i-1} Q| = |I + F_i Q| \qquad (3.65)$$

But $h_1 = q_{11}$, whence $|I + F_1 Q| = (1 + f_1 q_1)$. Then on using (3.65) for $i = 2, 3, ..., k$, and noting (3.41), we obtain (3.60).

Theorem 3.2 shows that we can investigate the stability of the system with all loops closed, by considering what happens as the loops are closed in the order $1, 2, ..., k$. By renumbering the loops, they may of course be closed in any order. As loop i is closed, we have a single-input single-output system to consider, with transfer-function $h_i(s)$. The effect of closing loop i is then expressed by the return difference $1 + f_i h_i$, as in Section 4 of Chapter 2.

It is clear on very general grounds that such an investigation by closing the loops in succession can always be made. The interesting point about equation (3.60) is its remarkably simple form. There might, for example, have been a set of complicated multipliers in the product.

The difficulty in using Theorem 3.2 is that $h_i(s)$ will in general be quite different from $q_{ii}(s)$. It will also be different from the transfer function seen between input i and output i when loops $1, 2, ..., i-1, i+1, ..., k$ are closed. In fact the transfer function between input i and output i will be a complicated function of the gains in all the other loops. Unless we can find some way of putting bounds on such changes, we are therefore unable to design a single-loop compensator for loop i which will be appropriate for various combinations of gains in the other loops. Without such bounds it will also be difficult to ensure that the stability region in the gain space has a suitable shape.

In Sections 4, 5 and 6, a different way of decomposing the stability problem will be given. Theorem 3.2 remains useful, however, when we wish to consider the effect on stability of changing only one loop gain. The appropriate transfer function for such an investigation is that seen in the loop under consideration, with specified gains in the other loops.

EXERCISE 3.7. If

$$Q(s) = \begin{bmatrix} \dfrac{1}{s+1} & \dfrac{1}{s+2} \\ \dfrac{1}{s+3} & \dfrac{1}{s+4} \end{bmatrix}$$

(3.66)

show from a block diagram, or from (3.59), that

$$h_2(s) = \frac{1}{s+4} + \frac{1}{s+2} \begin{bmatrix} \dfrac{-f_1}{1+\dfrac{f_1}{s+1}} \end{bmatrix} \frac{1}{s+3}$$

(3.67)

and confirm (3.60). Determine $h_2(s)$ when $f_1 = 0$ and when $f_1 \to \infty$.

4. Frequency-response criteria for stability

In order to use Theorem 3.1 it is necessary to know whether any zeros of a given polynomial $\phi(s)$ occur in the closed right half-plane. Algebraic tests such as those of Routh or Hurwitz can be used for this purpose [Willems, 1970] but as in the single-input single-output case there are advantages in using the "principle of the argument". This gives not only information about stability, but also an indication of the margin of stability. It will also allow us in some circumstances to determine stability from the diagonal elements of Q and F, even though the off-diagonal elements are nonzero [Section 5].

Let D be a large contour in the s-plane consisting of the imaginary axis from $-iR$ to $+iR$, together with a semicircle of radius R in the right half-plane. The radius R is chosen large enough to ensure that every finite zero of the polynomial $\phi(s)$ defined in Theorem 3.1, if it lies in the open right half-plane, is included in D. If $\phi(s)$ has zeros on the imaginary axis, D is indented into the left half-plane to enclose them, and R is again chosen large enough to ensure that all are inside D. The contour D is always traversed clockwise.

Now let $\phi(s)$ map D into Γ_ϕ. As s goes once clockwise around D, it follows from the "principles of the argument" [Chapter 1, Section 8] that the corresponding point on Γ_ϕ will make N_ϕ clockwise encirclements of the origin, where N_ϕ is the number of zeros of ϕ within D. From the way D was constructed, N_ϕ is equal to the number of zeros which $\phi(s)$ has in the open right half-plane. If this number is zero, the closed-loop system is asymptotically stable.

In this form the criterion is awkward to use. A better form, which leads us towards the simpler results in Section 5.1, is the following. Let $Q = LGK$ have an inverse $\hat{Q}$, and let $|\hat{Q}|$ map D into $\hat{\Gamma}_Q$, while $|\hat{H}|$ maps D into $\hat{\Gamma}_H$. The contour D is now indented to the left at any imaginary pole or zero of $|\hat{Q}|$ or $|\hat{H}|$, and is supposed large enough to enclose all finite poles and zeros, of $|\hat{Q}|$ and $|\hat{H}|$, lying in the closed right half-plane. As s goes once clockwise round D, let $\hat{\Gamma}_Q$ encircle the origin $\hat{N}_Q$ times clockwise, and let $\hat{\Gamma}_H$ encircle the origin $\hat{N}_H$ times clockwise. Then we have the following result.

THEOREM 4.1. Let Q have an inverse $\hat{Q}$ and let the open-loop system have p_0 poles in the closed right half-plane: that is, let $|T_L||T_G||T_K||T_F|$ have p_0 zeros there. Then the closed-loop system shown in Fig. 3.1 and described by equations (3.22) to (3.26) is asymptotically stable if and only if

$$\hat{N}_Q - \hat{N}_H = p_0 \qquad (4.1)$$

Proof. From equations (3.29) and (3.46),

$$\frac{|\hat{Q}|}{|\hat{H}|} = \frac{\pm |T_L||T_G||T_K||T_F|}{|T_H|} \qquad (4.2)$$

and the closed-loop system is asymptotically stable if and only if $|T_H|$ has no zero in the closed right half-plane. When (and only when) this is true, the map by the function on the right-hand side of (4.2) of a contour similar to D, but large enough to include also all zeros of $|T_L|$, $|T_G|$, $|T_K|$, $|T_F|$ and $|T_H|$ lying in the closed right half-plane, encircles the origin p_0 times. But the number of encirclements of the origin by $\hat{\Gamma}_Q$ and by $\hat{\Gamma}_H$ remains unchanged as D is enlarged, whence the result follows.

COROLLARY. The closed-loop system is asymptotically stable if and only if the map of D by $|I + QF|$ encircles the origin $-p_0$ times clockwise. Here D is taken large enough to enclose all finite poles and zeros of $|I + QF|$ lying in the closed right half-plane.

Proof. We have, by (3.29), $|I + QF| = \pm |T_H|/|T_L||T_G||T_K||T_F|$, whence the result. Notice that the Corollary does not require the existence of $\hat{Q}$.

EXERCISE 4.1. Explain why right half-plane zeros of $|T_L|$, $|T_G|$, $|T_K|$, $|T_F|$ or $|T_H|$ outside the contour D do not upset the conclusion in Theorem 4.1. [If these zeros are not poles or zeros of $|\hat{Q}|$ or $|\hat{H}|$, they cancel on the right-hand side of (4.2) and the system is unstable: compare Examples 3.3, 3.4, 3.5.]

EXERCISE 4.2.   Illustrate Exercise 4.1 by means of a system giving

$$Q(s) = \begin{bmatrix} \dfrac{1}{s+1} & 0 \\[2ex] \dfrac{1}{s-10} & \dfrac{1}{s+2} \end{bmatrix} \tag{4.3}$$

5. Diagonal dominance

Several considerations now drive us to put some restriction on the form of F and Q. The first is that the stability criteria in Section 4 are difficult to use. It is not so much the labour of making the computations which constitutes the difficulty—these will anyway be done in a computer. It is rather that insight is lost. Secondly we need somehow to ensure that the asymptotically stable region in the gain space has a suitable form. Thirdly, if we design a single-loop compensator, for one set of gains in the remaining loops, we shall wish it to remain appropriate when these gains are changed to other possible values. That is to say, we should like to restrict the changes in the transfer function seen in a given loop when the gains in the other loops are changed.

Each of these difficulties is overcome if both Q and F are diagonal, because we then have k loops of the kind considered in Chapter 2. This procedure has been suggested and used to a limited extent, but it is too extreme for general use. Instead we shall use the much looser criterion of diagonal dominance. A rational $k \times k$ matrix $Z(s)$ is said to be *diagonally row dominant* on the contour D if $z_{ii}(s)$ has no pole on D, $i = 1, 2, ..., k$, and

$$|z_{ii}(s)| - \sum_{\substack{j=1 \\ j \neq i}}^{k} |z_{ij}(s)| > 0 \quad \begin{array}{l} \text{for } i = 1, 2, ..., k \\ \text{and all } s \text{ on } D \end{array} \tag{5.1}$$

Diagonal column dominance is defined similarly by

$$|z_{ii}(s)| - \sum_{\substack{j=1 \\ j \neq i}}^{k} |z_{ji}(s)| > 0 \quad \begin{array}{l} \text{for } i = 1, 2, ..., k \\ \text{and all } s \text{ on } D \end{array} \tag{5.2}$$

Diagonal dominance on D is defined as follows.

$$\text{For each } s \text{ on } D \begin{cases} \text{either } |z_{ii}(s)| - \displaystyle\sum_{\substack{j=1 \\ j \neq i}}^{k} |z_{ij}(s)| > 0, \quad i = 1, 2, ..., k \\[3ex] \text{or} \quad\quad |z_{ii}(s)| - \displaystyle\sum_{\substack{j=1 \\ j \neq i}}^{k} |z_{ji}(s)| > 0, \quad i = 1, 2, ..., k \end{cases} \tag{5.3}$$

For brevity we shall talk simply of *row dominance, column dominance* and *dominance.* From the definitions it follows that row dominance implies dominance, and column dominance implies dominance.

EXERCISE 5.1.   Show that condition (5.3) can be written

$$\min_{\substack{s \\ s \text{ on } D}} \left\{ \max \left[\min_i \left(|z_{ii}(s)| - \sum_{\substack{j=1 \\ j \neq 1}}^{k} |z_{ij}(s)| \right), \min_i \left(|z_{ii}(s)| - \sum_{\substack{j=1 \\ j \neq 1}}^{k} |z_{ji}(s)| \right) \right] \right\} > 0$$

(5.4)

Hence show that if (5.3) is true, there exists an $\varepsilon > 0$ such that (5.3) remains true when both inequalities are strengthened to read " $\geqslant \varepsilon > 0$" instead of " > 0". [The minimum over s in (5.4) exists because D is a compact set and the function within braces is continuous with respect to s (Rosenbrock and Storey, 1970, Chapter 4, Section 7.1). Put the left-hand side in (5.4) equal to ε].

The consequence of dominance which makes it useful to us is contained in the following theorem.

THEOREM 5.1.   Let $Z(s)$ be dominant on C, which is any closed elementary contour having on it no pole of $z_{ii}(s)$, $i = 1, 2, ..., k$. Let $z_{ii}(s)$ map C into Γ_i, $i = 1, 2, ..., k$, and let $|Z(s)|$ map C into Γ_Z. Let Γ_i encircle the origin N_i times and let Γ_Z encircle the origin N_Z times (all encirclements being clockwise). Then

$$N_Z = \sum_{i=1}^{k} N_i$$

(5.5)

Proof. See Chapter 1, Section 9.

This theorem at once allows us to give a number of different stability theorems, depending upon which matrices we assume to be dominant. For example we have the following. In every case the contour D is assumed to include all finite poles and zeros, lying in the closed right half-plane, of the determinant of each dominant matrix occurring; and also to have on it no pole of any element on the principal diagonal of such a matrix.

THEOREM 5.2.   Let $F = \text{diag}(f_i)$, where the f_i are real and nonzero, and let $F^{-1} + Q$ be dominant on D. Let q_{ii} map D into Γ_i which encircles the point $(-f_i^{-1}, 0)$, N_i times, $i = 1, 2, ..., k$. Then the closed-loop system is asymptotically stable if and only if

$$\sum_{i=1}^{k} N_i = -p_0$$

(5.6)

where p_0 is the same as in Theorem 4.1.

Proof. We notice that Γ_i encircles the point $(-f_i^{-1}, 0)$ as often as the map of D by $f_i^{-1} + q_{ii}$ encircles the origin. Then because $|F^{-1} + Q(s)| = |F^{-1}||I + QF|$, the result follows at once from Theorem 5.1 and the Corollary of Theorem 4.1: note that the definition of D validates the conditions of both theorems.

EXERCISE 5.2. State results similar to Theorem 5.2 when $I + QF$ [resp. $I + FQ$] is dominant on D.

EXERCISE 5.3. Show that column dominance of $F^{-1} + Q$ implies column dominance of $I + QF$ [resp. row dominance of $F^{-1} + Q$ implies row dominance of $I + FQ$]. Comment on the relation between Theorem 5.2 and Exercise 5.2, (a) when F is singular, (b) when $F^{-1} + Q$ is dominant in the generalized sense of (5.3).

Theorem 5.2 is analogous to Nyquist's stability criterion given in Chapter 2, Section 5. For reasons which will appear later, however, we prefer to use the following result when $\hat{Q} = Q^{-1}$ exists.

THEOREM 5.3. Let $\hat{Q}$ and $\hat{H}$ be dominant on D, let $\hat{q}_{ii}$ map D into $\hat{\Gamma}_{qi}$ and let $\hat{h}_{ii}$ map D into $\hat{\Gamma}_{hi}$. Let these encircle the origin $\hat{N}_{qi}$ and $\hat{N}_{hi}$ times respectively. Then with p_0 as in Theorem 4.1, the closed-loop system is asymptotically stable if and only if

$$\sum_{i=1}^{k} \hat{N}_{qi} - \sum_{i=1}^{k} \hat{N}_{hi} = p_0 \tag{5.7}$$

Proof. This follows at once from Theorem 4.1 on noticing that Theorem 5.1 gives

$$\hat{N}_Q = \sum_{i=1}^{k} \hat{N}_{qi} \tag{5.8}$$

and similarly for $\hat{N}_H$.

This theorem is the most convenient one for general use, and a graphical interpretation is given in Section 5.1. Sometimes, however, we can make $\hat{H}$ dominant but not $\hat{Q}$. We then use the following result, which is an obvious consequence of Theorem 5.3.

THEOREM 5.4. Let $\hat{H}$ be dominant on D, and let the map of D by $|\hat{Q}|$ encircle the origin $\hat{N}_Q$ times. With $\hat{N}_{hi}$ and p_0 as in Theorem 5.3, the closed-loop system is asymptotically stable if and only if

$$\hat{N}_Q - \sum_{i=1}^{k} \hat{N}_{hi} = p_0 \tag{5.9}$$

COROLLARY. If $|Q|$ has p_Q poles and z_Q zeros in the closed right half-plane, $\hat{N}_Q$ can be evaluated from $\hat{N}_Q = p_Q - z_Q$, and (5.9) becomes

$$\sum_{i=1}^{k} \hat{N}_{hi} = p_Q - p_0 - z_Q \qquad (5.10)$$

The last result can be used if Q is known algebraically.

EXERCISE 5.3. Show that if Q arises from a least-order system, and if none of its right half-plane zeros coincides with any of its poles, then (5.9) becomes $\sum \hat{N}_{hi} = -z_Q$. [Note that a "zero of Q" is any zero of a numerator polynomial in its McMillan form, and a "pole of Q" is any zero of a denominator polynomial in this form. Under the given conditions $p_Q = p_0$.]

EXERCISE 5.4. Show that if Q arises from a least-order system, and if $z_Q{}'$ is the number of zeros of Q in the closed right half-plane, then (5.9) becomes $\sum_{i=1}^{k} \hat{N}_{hi} = -z_Q{}'$. [Under the given conditions $p_Q - z_Q = p_0 - z_Q{}'$.]

EXERCISE 5.5. Illustrate Exercises 5.3 and 5.4 by means of a least-order system giving

$$Q(s) = \begin{bmatrix} \dfrac{s-10}{(s+1)^2} & 0 \\[3mm] 0 & \dfrac{1}{s-10} \end{bmatrix} \qquad (5.11)$$

[This has $p_0 = 1$, $p_Q = 0$, $z_Q = 0$, $z_Q{}' = 1$.]

5.1 Graphical criteria

The dominance of a rational matrix $Z(s)$ can be checked by an easy graphical construction. Let z_{ii} map D into Γ_i as in Fig. 3.8. Select a value of s on D and with the corresponding point $z_{ii}(s)$ on Γ_i as centre draw a circle of radius.

$$d_i(s) = \sum_{\substack{j=1 \\ j \neq i}}^{k} |z_{ij}(s)| \qquad (5.12)$$

As s goes round D, the corresponding circles sweep out a band, which can be adequately represented by a finite set of circles. We call these bands the *Gershgorin bands*, because their usefulness depends on Gershgorin's theorem. If each of the Gershgorin bands so produced excludes the origin, for $i = 1, 2, \ldots, k$, then Z is row dominant on D. By "excludes the origin" we mean here that none of the circles, for any s on D, has the origin as an interior point or on its circumference.

To check column dominance it is only necessary to use circles of radius

$$d_i'(s) = \sum_{\substack{j=1 \\ j \neq i}}^{k} |z_{ji}(s)| \qquad (5.13)$$

To check dominance, a little more care is needed. For each s, the circles of radius $d_i(s)$ and $d_i'(s)$ are considered for $i = 1, 2, ..., k$. Suppose that for a given s, one of the two sets of k circles (the first with radius $d_i(s)$, the second

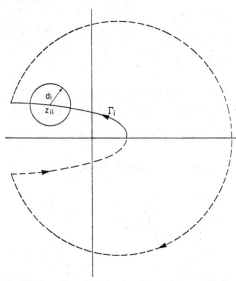

FIG. 3.8.   Graphical criterion for dominance.

with radius $d_i'(s)$) excludes the origin. Suppose also that this is true (with the appropriate set for each s) for all s on D. Then Z is dominant on D. The point to notice is that for given s we must consider either the circles of radius $d_i(s)$, $i = 1, 2, ..., k$, or the circles of radius $d_i'(s)$, $i = 1, 2, ..., k$. We cannot mix row and column circles for the same s, as will be clear from (5.3). The chosen circles (which now are not generally unique) again sweep out a band.

If we wish to apply Theorem 5.2 by means of this graphical construction, we let $Z = Q$. The off-diagonal elements of $F^{-1} + Q$ are just those of Q, so d_i and d_i' are given by (5.12) and (5.13), with $z_{ij}(s)$ replaced by $q_{ij}(s)$. Exclusion of the origin by a band based on $f_i^{-1} + q_{ii}$ is the same as exclusion of the point $(-f_i^{-1}, 0)$ by a band based on q_{ii}. We then obtain the following graphical interpretation of Theorem 5.2.

THEOREM 5.2a.   Let each of the Gershgorin bands swept out by the circles based on q_{ii} exclude the point $(-f_i^{-1}, 0)$, $i = 1, 2, ..., k$. Let these bands encircle the point $(-f_i^{-1}, 0)$, N_i times, $i = 1, 2, ..., k$. Then the closed-loop system is asymptotically stable if and only if (5.6) is true. The Gershgorin bands may have radii $d_i(s)$ (for row dominance) or $d_i'(s)$ (for column dominance) or more generally we may select for each s either $d_i(s)$ or $d_i'(s)$ (for dominance). The values of $d_i(s)$, $d_i'(s)$ are obtained from (5.12), (5.13) by substituting q_{ij} for z_{ij}.

It will be clear that this theorem is a generalized form of the Nyquist criterion. If $k = 1$, dominance is achieved trivially, and Theorem 5.2a is the usual Nyquist criterion, which gives necessary and sufficient conditions for stability. When $k > 1$, Theorem 5.2a gives necessary and sufficient conditions when each band excludes its critical point $(-f_i^{-1}, 0)$. When a band does not exclude its critical point, Theorem 5.2a says nothing.

Theorem 5.2a will be used in Section 9. For the most part, however, we prefer to base our development on Theorem 5.3, which has the following graphical interpretation when $F = \text{diag}(f_i)$ and the f_i are independent of s.

THEOREM 5.3a.   Let each of the Gershgorin bands based on the diagonal elements $\hat{q}_{ii}$ of $\hat{Q}$ exclude the origin and the point $(-f_i, 0)$. Let these bands encircle the origin $\hat{N}_{qi}$ times and encircle the point $(-f_i, 0)$, $\hat{N}_{hi}$ times. Then the closed-loop system is asymptotically stable if and only if

$$\sum_{i=1}^{k} \hat{N}_{qi} - \sum_{i=1}^{k} \hat{N}_{hi} = p_0 \tag{5.14}$$

Here the Gershgorin bands can be chosen as in Theorem 5.2a, with d_i, d_i' now defined by (5.12), (5.13) with z_{ij} replaced by $\hat{q}_{ij}$.

Proof.   When $F = \text{diag}(f_i)$, exclusion of the origin by a band based on $\hat{h}_{ii} = f_i + q_{ii}$ is the same as exclusion of $(-f_i, 0)$ by the corresponding band based on $\hat{q}_{ii}$. A similar remark applies to the number of encirclements.

This theorem has not been quoted in its most general form, because it is implied in the statement of the theorem that the same band is to be used in relation to the origin as to the point $(-f_i, 0)$. It is easy to see that different bands may be used. For example it is good enough if circles of radius d_i based on $\hat{q}_{ii}$ exclude the origin, and circles of radius d_i' based on $\hat{q}_{ii}$ exclude $(-f_i, 0)$, for $i = 1, 2, ..., k$. However, the form given to the theorem is the most useful one in applications. We have assimilated the loop gains into the f_i as in Section 2.1, and consequently we may study the stability as each f_i changes from 0 (meaning that the ith loop is open) to its desired value. It is most convenient to do this without having to redraw the bands, but in critical problems the more general result just mentioned might be useful.

The application of Theorem 5.3a is very easy and is illustrated by Fig. 3.9. If the underlying open-loop system is asymptotically stable we see from Fig.

3.9 that the closed-loop system is asymptotically stable for all combinations of loop gains f_1 and f_2 satisfying $0 \leqslant f_1 < 9.2$ and $0 \leqslant f_2 < 4.0$. (The system is also stable for a range of negative values of f_1 and f_2, but we

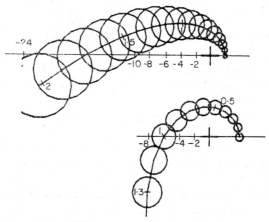

FIG. 3.9. Gershgorin bands for a least-order plant having

$$\hat{G}(s) = \begin{bmatrix} 2s^3 + 6s^2 + 6s + 2 & 2s + 0 \cdot 25 \\ 1 \cdot 5s + 0 \cdot 5 & 4s^4 + 10s^3 + 14s^2 + 10s + 4 \end{bmatrix}$$

restrict attention to negative feedback, which implies $f_i \geqslant 0$.) In the gain space the asymptotically stable region certainly includes the rectangle shown in Fig. 3.10. In particular, if $L = I$ and the operating point is in this rectangle, the system remains stable when either of the measuring instruments fails. If $K = I$, the system remains stable when either of the actuators fails.

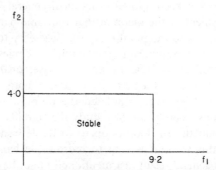

FIG. 3.10.   From Fig. 3.9 it follows that the closed-loop system is asymptotically stable for gains within the rectangle shown. It may be asymptotically stable within a larger region.

EXERCISE 5.6.   Sketch appropriate bands based on $\hat{g}_{11}$ and $\hat{g}_{22}$ when

$$G(s) = \begin{bmatrix} \dfrac{1}{(s+1)^3} & \dfrac{1}{2(s+2)^3} \\[4mm] \dfrac{1}{2(s+1)^3} & \dfrac{1}{(s+2)^3} \end{bmatrix} \tag{5.15}$$

Given that the open-loop plant has least order, find a stability region in the gain space.

EXERCISE 5.7.   Show that for any system giving rise to Fig. 3.9, asymptotic stability at any point in $0 \leqslant f_1 < 9.2$, $0 \leqslant f_2 < 4.0$ implies asymptotic stability everywhere in that region, while instability at any one point in the region implies instability everywhere in the region. [In the text, stability at $f_1 = f_2 = 0$ was assumed to be given.]

6. Ostrowski's theorem

The graphical investigation of dominant systems is completed by the following theorem due to Ostrowski [1952]. Let C be the contour defined in Theorem 5.1. Then we have the following result.

THEOREM 6.1.   Let the rational $k \times k$ matrix $Z(s)$ be row [resp. column] dominant for $s = s_0$ on C. Then $Z(s_0)$ has an inverse $\hat{Z}(s_0)$ and for $i = 1, 2, ..., k$,

$$|\hat{z}_{ii}^{-1}(s_0) - z_{ii}(s_0)| < \phi_i(s_0)\, d_i(s_0) < d_i(s_0)$$

$$[\text{resp. } < \phi_i{}'(s_0)\, d_i{}'(s_0) < d_i{}'(s_0)] \tag{6.1}$$

where

$$\left. \begin{aligned} \phi_i(s_0) &= \max_{\substack{j \\ j \neq i}} \frac{d_j(s_0)}{|z_{jj}(s_0)|} \\ \left[\text{resp } \phi_i{}'(s_0) = \max_{\substack{j \\ j \neq i}} \frac{d_j{}'(s_0)}{|z_{jj}(s_0)|}\right] \end{aligned} \right\} \tag{6.2}$$

Equations (5.12) and (5.13) define d_i and $d_i{}'$.

Proof. This follows by applying Ostrowski's theorem for complex matrices [see Chapter 1, Section 9] to $Z(s)$.

This theorem leads to a number of simple graphical consequences. For

K

example let $F = \text{diag}\,(f_i)$ with the f_i independent of s, and let $\hat{Q} = Q^{-1}$ exist. Then Theorem 5.3a can be extended by the following result.

THEOREM 6.2. Let the conditions of Theorem 5.3a be satisfied. Then for each s on D the diagonal elements h_{ii} of $H[Q, F]$ satisfy

$$|h_{ii}^{-1}(s) - (f_i + \hat{q}_{ii}(s))| < \phi_i(s)\, d_i(s) < d_i(s) \tag{6.3}$$

or

$$|h_{ii}^{-1}(s) - (f_i + \hat{q}_{ii}(s))| < \phi_i'(s)\, d_i'(s) < d_i'(s) \tag{6.4}$$

according as $\hat{H} = F + \hat{Q}$ is row or column dominant at s. The values of ϕ_i or ϕ_i' in (6.3), (6.4) are obtained from (6.2) by substituting h_{jj} for z_{jj}.

Proof. In Theorem 6.1 take $Z = \hat{H} = F + \hat{Q}$, so that $\hat{z}_{ii}^{-1} = h_{ii}^{-1}$ and $z_{ii} = \hat{h}_{ii} = f_i + \hat{q}_{ii}$.

This theorem has the following graphical interpretation. Let us choose a value of i, say $i = j$, and keep $f_1, f_2, ..., f_{j-1}, f_{j+1}, ..., f_k$ constant while we vary f_j. We then have an essentially single-input single-output situation. In the notation of equation (1.9), we have

$$h_{jj}^{-1}[Q, \text{diag}\,(f_1, f_2, ..., f_{j-1}, 0, f_{j+1}, ..., f_k)] + f_j$$
$$= h_{jj}^{-1}[Q, \text{diag}\,(f_1, f_2, ..., f_{j-1}, f_j, f_{j+1}, ..., f_k)] \tag{6.5}$$

Comparing this with (6.3) and (6.4) we see that $h_{ii}^{-1} - f_i$ is just the inverse of the transfer function seen between input i and output i when the ith loop is open ($f_i = 0$) and all other loops are closed with specified gains. Let us call this transfer function $h_i(s)$, that is,

$$h_i(s) = h_{ii}[Q(s), \text{diag}\,(f_1, f_2, ..., f_{i-1}, 0, f_{i+1}, ..., f_k)] \tag{6.6}$$

which differs from the notation used in Section 3.2. Then Theorem 6.2 shows that for each s on D, $h_i^{-1}(s)$ lies in a circle centred on $\hat{q}_{ii}(s)$ and having radius $\phi_i(s)\, d_i(s) < d_i(s)$, (if $\hat{H}$ is row dominant at s) or $\phi_i'(s)\, d_i'(s) < d_i'(s)$ (if $\hat{H}$ is column dominant at s). As s goes round D these circles sweep out bands which lie inside the Gershgorin bands. We shall call these narrower bands the *Ostrowski bands*.

The Ostrowski bands fulfil two functions. First they locate the inverse transfer functions $h_i^{-1}(s)$. If we wish to design a single-loop compensator for the ith loop, we must design it for $h_i(s)$. As the loop gains $f_1, f_2, ..., f_{i-1}, f_{i+1}, ..., f_k$ vary, so $h_i(s)$ will change. As long as dominance is maintained, however, $h_i^{-1}(s)$ lies within the appropriate Ostrowski band, evaluated for the gains $f_1, f_2, ..., f_{i-1}, f_{i+1}, ..., f_k$. Notice particularly that $\phi_i(s)$ and $\phi_i'(s)$ depend on the gains in the other loops, so that the ith Ostrowski band depends on these other gains. The Gershgorin band, however, is independent of the loop gains and gives an outside bound for the Ostrowski band.

The second function of the Ostrowski bands is to determine the stability margins of the loops. Notice that when we vary only one of the f_i we have an essentially single-loop situation. Consequently we may determine appropriate gain and phase margins, or appropriate values of M, if we know $h_i^{-1}(s)$; and this is within the ith Ostrowski band. These criteria are related to the transient response in the same way as was explained in Chapter 2. When the Ostrowski band is narrow enough we may in practice treat it as though it were a single-loop inverse Nyquist plot.

EXERCISE 6.1. Justify the use of the Ostrowski bands to investigate stability margin by reference to Section 3.2. [Notice that if the loops are renumbered so that the one in which we are interested is the last, then the notation here agrees with Section 3.2 for this loop.]

EXAMPLE 6.1. In Fig. 3.9, choose $f_1 = 6, f_2 = 3$. Then the Ostrowski bands are shown in Fig. 3.11. The first intersects the negative real axis at

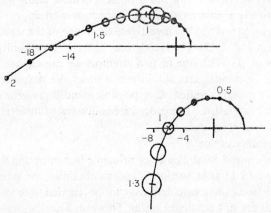

FIG. 3.11.   Ostrowski bands corresponding to Fig. 3.9 when $f_1 = 6, f_2 = 3$.

$-15 \cdot 5$, $-16 \cdot 5$, and the second at $-5 \cdot 2$, -7. If the system is open-loop stable we see that when $f_1 = 6$, the closed-loop system is asymptotically stable for $0 \leqslant f_2 < 5 \cdot 2$ and unstable for $f_2 > 7$. For some f between $5 \cdot 2$ and $7 \cdot 0$ the critical point crosses $h_2^{-1}(s)$, which is within the second Ostrowski band. Similarly for $f_2 = 3$, the system is asymptotically stable for $0 \leqslant f_1 < 15 \cdot 5$ and is unstable for $f_1 > 16 \cdot 5$. In this way we get two points on an inner bound and two points on an outer bound for the stable region in gain space, as shown in Fig. 3.12. By drawing the Ostrowski bands for other values of f_1 and f_2 we can complete these inner and outer bounds as shown. Notice that all this information is implicit in Fig. 3.9.

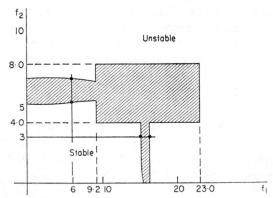

FIG. 3.12.   From Fig. 3.11 we obtain four points on the boundary of the shaded area, within which the stability boundary must lie.

Example 6.1 illustrates how our graphical criteria allow us to ensure that the asymptotically stable region in gain space has an appropriate form. In practice we should not need to investigate the shape of the stable region in the detail shown in Fig. 3.12. The Gershgorin bands show stability for $0 \leqslant f_1 < 9 \cdot 2$, $0 \leqslant f_2 < 4 \cdot 0$. With one or two attempts we can choose a point in this region which gives adequate stability margins. We may then if necessary check stability margins under other possible conditions—for example when one transducer has failed. The procedure is illustrated in detail in Chapter 4.

6.1 Exact stability region

There is, of course, no difficulty of principle in computing the exact values of $h_i^{-1}(s)$ from (6.6) as in Section 2, and so obtaining the stability boundary precisely. Indeed, such calculations can be carried out equally well for systems which are not dominant, using Theorem 3.2.

However, when the system is not dominant, we have no bound such as the Gershgorin band to restrict the change of $h_i(s)$ when the gains $f_1, f_2, \ldots$, $f_{i-1}, f_{i+1}, \ldots, f_k$ are changed. Consequently the shape of the stability region may be very complicated, and therefore difficult to investigate. In such circumstances it may be difficult to ensure stability when some of the loops are open and some closed. Also if a single-loop compensator is designed for $h_i(s)$ with one set of gains in the other loops, there is nothing to show that it will remain appropriate when the other gains are changed.

These difficulties, of course, are the ones which led us to impose the condition of dominance in Section 5. Assuming therefore that the system is dominant, we may still compute $h_i^{-1}(s)$ exactly, if we wish. Experience has shown however that this is not very necessary for two reasons. First, it is usually possible to make the ϕ_i about 1/3. Then $\phi_i\, d_i$ is about 1/9 of $\hat{h}_{ii}$. This locates h_i^{-1} with an accuracy which is usually comparable with the accuracy of $\hat{q}_{ii}$, and there is then little point in refining the calculation of h_i^{-1}. The examples in Chapter 4 illustrate this point.

Secondly, the calculation of the ϕ_i is simple, and they can be estimated quite well by eye. During the preliminary stages of the design, there is therefore no need to make the calculation or display the Ostrowski bands: sufficient guidance can be obtained from the Gershgorin bands. There would be even less point, in these preliminary stages, in calculating the h_i^{-1} exactly.

6.2 Practical application

As in Section 5.2 of Chapter 2, we wish to avoid consideration of the large semicircular arc of D. We achieve this by results similar to those used before.

THEOREM 6.3.   Let $Q(s)$ be strictly proper and let $F(s) = \mathrm{diag}\,(f_i)$, independent of s. Then given any $f_{1i} > 0$, $i = 1, 2, ..., k$, the radius R of the semicircle in the contour D can be made large enough to ensure that no zero of $|T_H(s)|$ lies on this semicircle for any f_i satisfying $0 \leqslant f_i \leqslant f_{1i}, i = 1, 2, ..., k$.

Proof.   By equation (3.29), with $T_F = I_k$,

$$|T_H| = \pm |I_k + QF||T_L||T_G||T_K|\qquad(6.7)$$

Write

$$Q(s) = N(s)/d(s)\qquad(6.8)$$

where $N(s)$ is a polynomial matrix and $d(s)$ is the least common denominator of the elements of Q. Then

$$|I_k + Q(s)\,F| = \frac{|d(s)\,I_k + N(s)\,F|}{[d(s)]^k}\qquad(6.9)$$

Every element of $N(s)\,F$ has degree less than the degree of $d(s)$, because $Q(s)$ is proper. Therefore the right-hand side of (6.7), which is a polynomial, has its term of highest degree independent of $f_1, f_2, ..., f_k$. Hence its roots $s_j(F)$ are continuous functions of $f_1, f_2, ..., f_k$ on the compact region $0 \leqslant f_i \leqslant f_{1i}$, $i = 1, 2, ..., k$, and therefore

$$m(F) = \max_j \left\{ |s_j(F)| \right\}\qquad(6.10)$$

which is also continuous on this region, has an absolute maximum m_0. Then we may choose $R > m_0$.

THEOREM 6.4.   Let the conditions of Theorem 6.3 be satisfied, and let

$$0 \leqslant f_{aj} \leqslant f_{bj} \leqslant f_{1j}, \qquad j = 1, 2, ..., k \qquad (6.11)$$

Let it be possible to choose $R > m_0$ such that the jth Gershgorin disc for $s - iR$ does not include the critical point $(-f_j, 0)$ for $f_{aj} \leqslant f_j \leqslant f_{bj}, j = 1$, $2, ..., k$. Let the dominance condition (5.3) be satisfied by $\hat{H}(i\omega)$ for $0 \leqslant \omega \leqslant R$ and for $F = F_a = \text{diag}(f_{aj})$ and $F = F_b = \text{diag}(f_{bj})$. As f_j goes from f_{aj} to f_{bj} let the critical point make q_j net crossings from left to right of that part of the jth Gershgorin band corresponding to imaginary s. Here the direction of crossing is with respect to the direction in which ω increases along $\hat{\Gamma}_j$. Let $|T_H|$ have p_a poles in the closed right half-plane when $F = F_a$, and have p_b poles there when $F = F_b$. Then

$$p_b - p_a = \sum_{j=1}^{k} q_j \qquad (6.12)$$

Proof. Let $f_j = f_{aj}, j = 2, 3, ..., k$. Then there is a fixed transfer function h_1 between input 1 and output 1, and the mapping of D by h_1^{-1} lies within the first Gershgorin band. Moreover, $h_1^{-1}(iR)$ lies inside a disc which does not include the first critical point for $f_{a1} \leqslant f_1 \leqslant f_{b1}$. As f_1 goes from f_{a1} to f_{b1}, the critical point therefore makes q_1 net crossings from left to right of the mapping by h_1^{-1} of that part of the imaginary axis belonging to D. By Theorem 6.3, the critical point does not cross the mapping by h_1^{-1} of the semicircular arc of D. From the theory of single-loop systems, it therefore follows that the number of poles inside D has increased from p_a to $p_a + q_1$. (Compare Chapter 2, Section 5.1). Now with gains $f_{b1}, f_{a3}, f_{a4}, ..., f_{am}$, there is a fixed transfer function h_2 between input 2 and output 2. The dominance condition is still satisfied, and the mapping of D by h_2^{-1} is therefore within the second Gershgorin band. When f_2 is increased from f_{a2} to f_{b2} it follows that the number of poles inside D increases to $p_a + q_1 + q_2$. The result now follows on considering the loops in succession.

The above results are used with an assumption which we state explicitly in the following way.

ASSUMPTION 6.1.   Those poles which determine stability cross the segment of the imaginary axis between $s = -i\omega_0$ and $s = i\omega_0$, where ω_0 is some specified frequency.

When this assumption is fulfilled we can investigate stability by considering the Gershgorin bands for imaginary s from $s = 0$ to $s = i\omega_1$. Here $\omega_1 \geqslant \omega_0$, and also $\omega_1 \geqslant R$ where R is chosen as in Theorem 6.4. This last condition is satisfied if the Gershgorin discs corresponding to ω_1 do not touch the negative real axis. It ensures that as the jth critical point moves along this axis, the number of crossings of the curve $h_j^{-1}(i\omega)$, $0 \leqslant \omega \leqslant \omega_1$, is the same as the number of crossings of the Gershgorin band.

To be relieved from the need to consider the semicircular arc of D is particularly important to us. Dominance may fail on this arc, and we cannot carry out measurements on the system at the corresponding values of s.

EXAMPLE 6.2.   Let the first row of $\hat{Q}$ be

$$\left\{ \frac{1-s}{(1+s)^2} \qquad \frac{1}{2+s} \right\} \tag{6.13}$$

It is easy to see that the dominance condition is satisfied everywhere on the imaginary axis. But for all real $s > 0 \cdot 28$, the second term is larger in modulus than the first.

EXERCISE 6.2.   Pure time delays are often represented by Padé approximations such as $(1-s\tau)/(1+s\tau)$. How good is the approximation (a) for $s = i\omega$, with ω small, (b) for $s = i\omega$, with ω large, (c) for real positive s? Comment on the suitability of such approximations for investigating stability, with and without the use of Theorem 6.4.

6.3 Reasons for using $\hat{Q}$

We can now give the promised justification for working with $\hat{Q}$ rather than Q. There are three reasons, as follows.

(i) The relation $\hat{H} = F + \hat{Q}$ gives an easy transition from open-loop to closed-loop properties.

(ii) There appears, from practical experience, to be a tendency for $\hat{G}$ to be more dominant than G: see Chapter 4, Section 3 for an example.

(iii) For some given $s = i\omega$, suppose that the critical points $(-f_i, 0)$ in all loops except the jth can be moved so that the distance from $(-f_i, 0)$ to $\hat{q}_{ii}(i\omega)$ becomes indefinitely large. Then the width of the Ostrowski band for the jth loop shrinks to zero at $s = i\omega$. This illustrates a more general result: if in all loops except the jth the gain is so high that the corresponding outputs are held equal to zero when the jth input is sinusoidal with frequency ω, then the transfer function h_j seen between input j and output j at $s = i\omega$ is $\hat{q}_{jj}^{-1}(i\omega)$ [SSMVT, Chapter 5, Section 2.6]. More loosely expressed, as we tighten the other loops* we drive h_j towards $\hat{q}_{jj}^{-1}$ The elements q_{jj} of Q have the opposite property: they are the values attained by h_j as all loop gains go to zero. Since we are interested primarily in the closed-loop behaviour, it is the former property which is most useful.

The third of these reasons is more important than the others. As will be

* Compare Section II, Problems 1 to 3.

seen in Section 9, all our results for $\hat{Q}$ have their analogue for Q. There is also one situation where we cannot use $\hat{Q}$ and have to use Q, namely when Q is initially non-square. Nevertheless the third reason above is strong enough to ensure that we shall use $\hat{Q}$ whenever we can.

7. Achieving dominance

In this Section we shall assume that $k = l = m$, and shall use m for the common value: this is the most usual situation. We return to the general case in Sections 8, 9 and 10. Meanwhile we allow k and l to be general indices.

The preceding Sections have shown the value of dominance in simplifying the multivariable design problem. Once an adequate degree of dominance is achieved, the Ostrowski bands can be used as though they were slightly "fuzzy" inverse Nyquist plots for independent loops. All the single-loop design techniques are then available, with assurance of stability, of adequate stability margin, and of a suitably-shaped stability region in gain space. The important question that remains is whether dominance can be achieved by a simple input compensator (or possibly output compensator, or combined input compensator and output compensator).

We notice first that if we are prepared to let $K(s)$ be sufficiently complicated, we can always achieve dominance, for we can choose $K(s)$ so that $G(s) K(s)$ is diagonal. This, however, is not what we are aiming at. We wish K to be as simple as possible—independent of s if we can achieve this, and sparse as well. (By a sparse matrix we mean one that has few nonzero entries.) In a range of industrial problems it has in fact been found that a constant input compensator (one independent of s) is sufficient to ensure dominance.

Various methods of achieving or increasing dominance are now considered. Some leave more and some less initiative to the designer.

7.1 Elementary operations

In practical applications we shall usually require a matrix $K(s)$ to satisfy the following conditions:

(i) The elements of $K(s)$ should have all their poles in the open left half-plane. This ensures that $K(s)$ can be implemented by an asymptotically stable subsystem.

(ii) In addition, all the zeros of $|K(s)|$ should be in the open left half-plane. Together with (i) this ensures that $K(s)$ is controllable (I) and therefore does not introduce control difficulties associated with nonminimum phase response [compare Exercise 3.1].

We shall assume that $K(s)$ obeys these two conditions, though sometimes we shall make an apparent exception by allowing $K(s)$ to have a pole at the origin. Such a pole can be moved slightly to the left to satisfy condition (i): in fact most systems which are conventially represented with a pole at the origin do have the pole in the open left half-plane [compare Chapter 2, Section 6.2].

Subject to these conditions on $K(s)$ we can show [SSMVT, Chapter 5, Section 7] that $K(s)$ can be written

$$K(s) = K_a K_b(s) K_c(s) \qquad (7.1)$$

where K_a, K_b, K_c are defined in the following way:

(a) K_a is a permutation matrix. That is, in each column and each row of K_a all entries but one are zero, the exceptional entry being 1. The effect of K_a is to interchange the columns of a matrix which it postmultiplies. Such an operation on $G(s)$ is tantamount to renumbering the inputs.

(b) $K_b(s)$ has determinant 1, and can be represented as a product of elementary matrices $K_b^{(k)}(s)$, where

$$K_b^{(k)}(s) = \begin{bmatrix} 1 & 0 & \ldots & 0 & \ldots & 0 & \ldots & 0 \\ 0 & 1 & \ldots & 0 & \ldots & 0 & \ldots & 0 \\ \vdots & \vdots & & \vdots & & \vdots & & \vdots \\ 0 & 0 & \ldots & 1 & \ldots & \alpha_{ij}^{(k)}(s) & \ldots & 0 \\ \vdots & \vdots & & \vdots & & \vdots & & \vdots \\ 0 & 0 & \ldots & 0 & \ldots & 0 & \ldots & 1 \end{bmatrix} \qquad (7.2)$$

Here $\alpha_{ij}^{(k)}(s)$ can occur in any position with $j \neq i$, and is a rational function having all its poles in the open left half-plane. Such a matrix $K_b^{(k)}(s)$ postmultiplying another matrix has the effect of adding to column j a multiple by $\alpha_{ij}^{(k)}(s)$ of column i. Operating on $G(s) K_a$, such a matrix recombines the parallel paths through the system.

(c) $K_c(s)$ is a nonsingular diagonal matrix. All the poles and zeros of the diagonal elements of $K_c(s)$ lie in the open left half-plane. Such a matrix represents a set of m single-loop controllers.

EXAMPLE 7.1. The matrix

$$K(s) = \begin{bmatrix} \dfrac{1-s}{(s+1)^2} & \dfrac{-s}{s+1} \\[3mm] \dfrac{1}{s+1} & 1 \end{bmatrix} \qquad (7.3)$$

satisfies conditions (i) and (ii). It can be written in the form (7.1) with $K_a = I_2$.

$$K_b(s) = \begin{bmatrix} 1 & -1 \\ 0 & 1 \end{bmatrix} \begin{bmatrix} 1 & 0 \\ \dfrac{s+1}{2} & 1 \end{bmatrix} \begin{bmatrix} 1 & \dfrac{2}{s+1} \\ 0 & 1 \end{bmatrix} = \begin{bmatrix} \dfrac{1-s}{2} & \dfrac{-2s}{s+1} \\ \dfrac{s+1}{2} & 2 \end{bmatrix} \qquad (7.4)$$

$$K_c(s) = \begin{bmatrix} \dfrac{2}{(s+1)^2} & 0 \\ 0 & \dfrac{1}{2} \end{bmatrix} \qquad (7.5)$$

Because $K_b(s)$ contains the element $(s+1)/2$, we cannot implement it directly. We can, however, implement $K(s)$ in the form shown in Fig. 3.13. Notice that this system (implemented as shown) does not have least order: an implementation of least order can be obtained if desired.

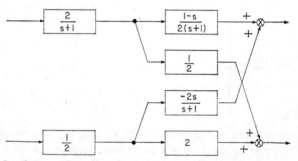

FIG. 3.13.   Implementation of $K(s)$ given by equation (7.3) in a form derived from equations (7.4), (7.5).

The above result shows that any $K(s)$ satisfying conditions (i) and (ii) can be separated into an input compensator $K_a K_b(s)$ and a set of single-loop controllers. The input compensator can be generated by the elementary operations of rearranging columns and of adding multiples of one column to another. We lose no generality by restricting ourselves to these operations, though our insight into the problem may not always be sufficient to give as good an answer in this way as we can achieve in other ways. If we use this approach, we must ensure that the controller which is obtained can finally be implemented. However, Example 7.1 shows that this does not necessarily exclude elementary operations which cannot individually be implemented.

When we work with the inverse matrices, equation (7.1) becomes

$$\hat{K}(s) = \hat{K}_c(s)\,\hat{K}_b(s)\,\hat{K}_a \qquad (7.6)$$

The matrix $\hat{K}_a$ now transposes the rows of any matrix which it premultiplies.

The matrix $\hat{K}_b(s)$ can be represented by successive elementary row operations. Each such operation subtracts, from row i, a multiple by $\alpha_{ij}^{(k)}(s)$ of row j. Correspondingly we can express a matrix $\hat{L}(s)$ in the form

$$\hat{L}(s) = \hat{L}_a\,\hat{L}_b(s)\,\hat{L}_c(s) \tag{7.7}$$

where $\hat{L}_a$ is a permutation matrix and $\hat{L}_b(s)$ is represented by elementary column operations on the matrix it postmultiplies.

The graphical interpretation of these results will become clearer in Chapter 4. Meanwhile the following example illustrates the procedure.

EXAMPLE 7.2. Figure 3.14 shows the *inverse Nyquist array* of a system having $m = 2$. In row 1, $\hat{g}_{12}$ is apparently greater than $\hat{g}_{11}$, and similarly in

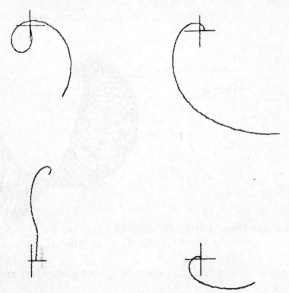

Fig. 3.14.   Inverse Nyquist array, plotted for $0 \leqslant \omega \leqslant 10$.

row 2, $\hat{g}_{21}$ appears to be greater than $\hat{g}_{22}$, like frequencies being compared in every case. If we choose

$$\hat{K}_a = \begin{bmatrix} 0 & 1 \\ 1 & 0 \end{bmatrix} \tag{7.8}$$

we interchange the rows, and the resulting matrix $\hat{Q} = \hat{K}_a\,\hat{G}$ is row dominant for $0 \leqslant \omega \leqslant 10$. This is confirmed by the Gershgorin bands in Fig. 3.15, which are based on rows.

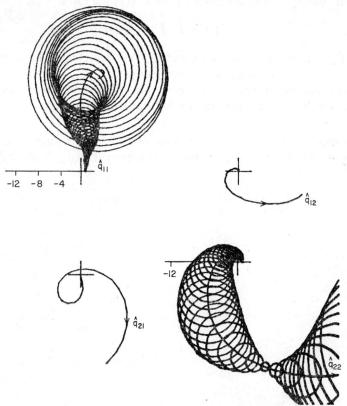

FIG. 3.15.   Inverse Nyquist array and Gershgorin bands for $\hat{Q} = \hat{K}_a \hat{G}$, where $\hat{G}$ is given by Fig. 3.14 and $\hat{K}_a$ by equation (7.8).

The dominance can be further improved by the elementary row operation represented by

$$\hat{K}_b = \begin{bmatrix} 1 & 0 \\ 0.5 & 1 \end{bmatrix} \qquad (7.9)$$

which adds one-half of row 1 to row 2. The first row of Fig. 3.15 remains unaltered by this operation, while the second row of $\hat{Q} = \hat{K}_b \hat{K}_a \hat{G}$ is shown, with its Gershgorin band, in Fig. 3.16.

The system having input compensator K corresponding to the inverse of $\hat{K}_b \hat{K}_a$ allows simple proportional control loops to be set up around it. The performance of the second loop can be further improved by a phase-advance

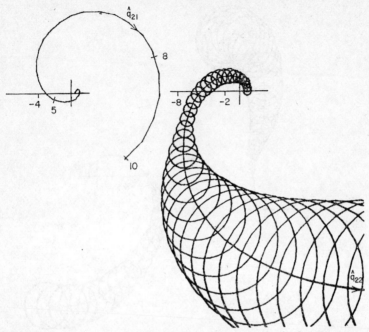

FIG. 3.16. Second row of inverse Nyquist array for $\hat{K}_a \hat{K}_b \hat{G}$ with Gershgorin band, where $\hat{K}_a \hat{G}$ is given by Fig. 3.15 and $\hat{K}_b$ by equation (7.9).

compensator designed by the methods of Chapter 2 for the transfer function $\hat{q}_{22}$ shown in Fig. 3.16. An appropriate compensator is

$$\hat{K}_c(s) = \begin{bmatrix} 1 & 0 \\ 0 & \dfrac{0 \cdot 05s + 1}{0 \cdot 3s + 1} \end{bmatrix} \qquad (7.10)$$

and in interpreting this it should be remembered that we must invert to obtain $K_c(s)$. The resulting system allows gains $f_1 = 5 \cdot 0$ and $f_2 = 3 \cdot 5$, for which the Ostrowski bands are shown in Fig. 3.17. The gain margin in the second loop is appropriate for process control.

In Example 7.2, $\hat{K}(s)$ was built up in the order corresponding to (7.1). This is not necessary: elementary operations can be performed in any order and as often as we choose. Whatever $K(s)$ finally results, it can be decomposed as in (7.1), though whether we choose to carry out the decomposition is a matter of convenience. Usually in practice we aim to have a diagonal matrix $K_c(s)$ of single-loop controllers, and a matrix $K_a K_b$ which is independent of s.

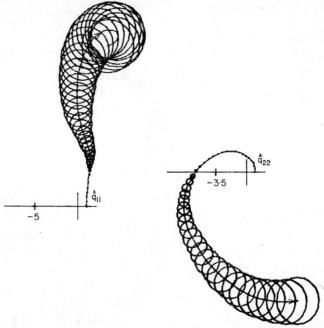

FIG. 3.17.   Ostrowski bands for the compensated plant with $f_1 = 5$, $f_2 = 3 \cdot 5$.

7.2 Pseudo-diagonalization

As was said earlier, a sufficiently complicated $K(s)$ will make GK, and therefore $\hat{K}\hat{G}$, diagonal. If we restrict attention to a subset of all possible matrices $K(s)$—for example to matrices independent of s—we may ask which matrix in this subset makes $\hat{K}\hat{G}$ most nearly diagonal. We should like "most nearly diagonal" to mean, for example, that in each row of $\hat{K}\hat{G}$ the sum of the moduli of the off-diagonal elements, at some chosen s on D, was as small as possible compared with the modulus of the diagonal element. This leads to an awkward computing problem, so following Hawkins [1972] we substitute an alternative meaning.

Choose some $s = i\omega$ on D and consider row j of $\hat{K}\hat{G}(i\omega)$, where K is a constant matrix. The elements $\hat{q}_{jk}(i\omega)$ of this row are

$$\hat{q}_{jk}(i\omega) = \sum_{i=1}^{m} \hat{k}_{ji}\, \hat{g}_{ik}(i\omega) \qquad (7.11)$$

$$= \sum_{i=1}^{m} \hat{k}_{ji}(\alpha_{ik} + i\beta_{ik}) \qquad (7.12)$$

where we have written

$$\hat{g}_{ik}(i\omega) = \alpha_{ik} + i\beta_{ik} \qquad (7.13)$$

Now let us choose $\hat{k}_{j1}, \hat{k}_{j2}, ..., \hat{k}_{jm}$ so that

$$\sum_{\substack{k=1 \\ k \neq j}}^{m} |\hat{q}_{jk}(i\omega)|^2 \tag{7.14}$$

is as small as possible subject to the constraint

$$\sum_{i=1}^{m} \hat{k}_{ji}^{2} = 1 \tag{7.15}$$

Using a Lagrange multiplier λ, this requires us to minimize

$$\phi_j = \sum_{\substack{k=1 \\ k \neq j}}^{m} \left| \sum_{i=1}^{m} \hat{k}_{ji}(\alpha_{ik}+i\beta_{ik}) \right|^2 + \lambda \left\{ 1 - \sum_{i=1}^{m} \hat{k}_{ji}^{2} \right\} \tag{7.16}$$

$$= \sum_{\substack{k=1 \\ k \neq j}}^{m} \left\{ \left[\sum_{i=1}^{m} \hat{k}_{ji} \alpha_{ik} \right]^2 + \left[\sum_{i=1}^{m} \hat{k}_{ji} \beta_{ik} \right]^2 \right\} + \lambda \left\{ 1 - \sum_{i=1}^{m} \hat{k}_{ji}^{2} \right\} \tag{7.17}$$

Taking the partial derivative with respect to $\hat{k}_{jl}$ we obtain

$$\frac{\partial \phi_j}{\partial \hat{k}_{jl}} = \sum_{\substack{k=1 \\ k \neq j}}^{m} \left(2 \left[\sum_{i=1}^{m} \hat{k}_{ji} \alpha_{ik} \right] \alpha_{lk} + 2 \left[\sum_{i=1}^{m} \hat{k}_{ji} \beta_{ik} \right] \beta_{lk} \right)$$
$$- \lambda 2 \hat{k}_{jl} = 0, \quad l = 1, 2, ..., m \tag{7.18}$$

We now introduce the symmetric real matrix

$$A_j = \left(a_{il}{}^{(j)} \right) = \left(\sum_{\substack{k=1 \\ k \neq j}}^{m} [\alpha_{ik} \alpha_{lk} + \beta_{ik} \beta_{lk}] \right) \tag{7.19}$$

which is readily seen to be at least positive semidefinite, so that its eigenvalues are real and non-negative. If we also introduce the row vector

$$\hat{k}_j = (\hat{k}_{jl}) \tag{7.20}$$

we may write (7.18) in the form

$$A_j \hat{k}_j{}^T - \lambda k_j{}^T = 0 \tag{7.21}$$

which is a standard eigenvector problem. Any eigenvector of A_j makes (7.18) true, but since we may write, by (7.17), (7.19), (7.21) and (7.15)

$$\sum_{\substack{k=1 \\ k \neq j}}^{m} |\hat{q}_{jk}(i\omega)|^2 = \hat{k}_j A_j \hat{k}_j{}^T \tag{7.22}$$

$$= \lambda \hat{k}_j \hat{k}_j{}^T \tag{7.23}$$

$$= \lambda \tag{7.24}$$

it follows that to minimize (7.14) we must choose that $\hat{k}_j$ corresponding to the smallest eigenvalue of A_j.

The eigenvector problem (7.21) is not difficult to solve because A_j is real and symmetric. Its solution gives us that jth row in $\hat{K}$, of unit length, which minimizes the sum of squares, of the magnitudes of the off-diagonal elements, of row j of $\hat{K}\hat{G}(i\omega)$.

We may solve a similar problem for each row of $\hat{K}$, using the same or different values of ω for each. In this way we can obtain candidates for $\hat{K}$ which may satisfy our requirements.

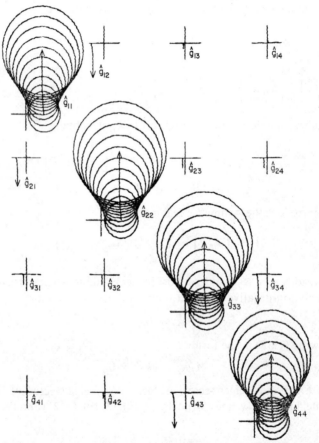

FIG. 3.18. Inverse Nyquist array and Gershgorin bands corresponding to the $G(s)$ defined in equation (7.25). The plots are drawn for $0 \leqslant \omega \leqslant 1$.

EXERCISE 7.1.   Show that if $G(0)$ is finite and nonsingular, and if we choose $\omega = 0$ for each row of K, then the above procedure gives $\hat{K} = G(0)$. [$\hat{G}(0)$ is real; hence show that each A_j has a zero eigenvalue, and use (7.24).]

EXAMPLE 7.3. The transfer function matrix

$$G(s) = \begin{bmatrix} \dfrac{1 \cdot 0}{1+4s} & \dfrac{0 \cdot 7}{1+5s} & \dfrac{0 \cdot 3}{1+5s} & \dfrac{0 \cdot 2}{1+5s} \\[3mm] \dfrac{0 \cdot 6}{1+5s} & \dfrac{1 \cdot 0}{1+4s} & \dfrac{0 \cdot 4}{1+5s} & \dfrac{0 \cdot 35}{1+5s} \\[3mm] \dfrac{0 \cdot 35}{1+5s} & \dfrac{0 \cdot 4}{1+5s} & \dfrac{1 \cdot 0}{1+4s} & \dfrac{0 \cdot 6}{1+5s} \\[3mm] \dfrac{0 \cdot 2}{1+5s} & \dfrac{0 \cdot 3}{1+5s} & \dfrac{0 \cdot 7}{1+5s} & \dfrac{1 \cdot 0}{1+4s} \end{bmatrix} \qquad (7.25)$$

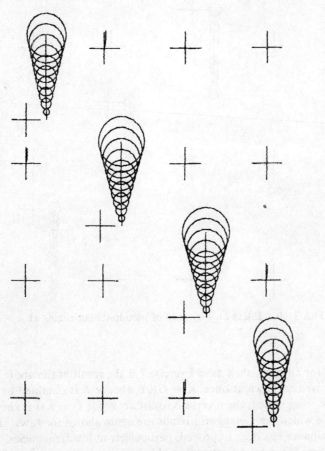

FIG. 3.19. Effect on Fig. 3.18 of diagonalizing at $\omega = 0$.

gives the inverse Nyquist array which is shown, with its Gershgorin bands for the rows, in Fig. 3.18. The system is already dominant, but dominance can be improved by the use of a suitable input compensator K. If we choose

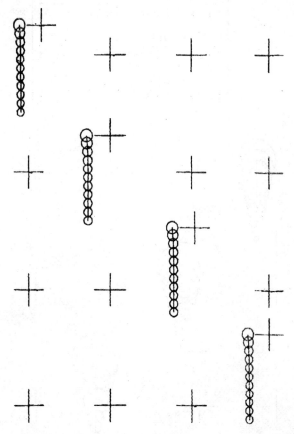

Fig. 3.20. Effect on Fig. 3.18 of pseudo-diagonalizing at $\omega = 0 \cdot 9$.

$\omega = 0$ for all rows, then as in Exercise 7.1 the result of the above procedure can be written down at once, $\hat{K} = G(0)$, whence K is obtained by inversion. With $\hat{K}$ so obtained, the inverse Nyquist array for $\hat{Q} = \hat{K}\hat{G}$ is shown in Fig. 3.19, in which the Gershgorin bands are again shown for rows. The degree of dominance has been improved, particularly at low frequencies.

We can, however, do better than this by suitable choice of ω. After trying several values, we select $\omega = 0 \cdot 9$ for all rows, giving

$$K = \begin{bmatrix} 1 \cdot 469 & -0 \cdot 944 & -0 \cdot 148 & 0 \cdot 050 \\ -0 \cdot 654 & 1 \cdot 814 & -0 \cdot 249 & -0 \cdot 229 \\ -0 \cdot 229 & -0 \cdot 249 & 1 \cdot 814 & -0 \cdot 654 \\ 0 \cdot 050 & -0 \cdot 148 & -0 \cdot 944 & 1 \cdot 469 \end{bmatrix} \qquad (7.26)$$

and the corresponding diagram in Fig. 3.20. The Gershgorin bands in this Figure show that the system has been made virtually noninteracting by the constant input compensator given in (7.26).

7.3 Extension of pseudo-diagonalization

The procedure in Section 7.2 can be generalized in several ways. First, instead of minimizing (7.14), we may minimize the more general function

$$\sum_{r=1}^{N} \left\{ \sum_{\substack{k=1 \\ k \ne j}}^{m} \gamma_r |\hat{q}_{jk}(i\omega_r)|^2 \right\} \qquad (7.27)$$

subject again to (7.15). In (7.27) the γ_r are real and positive, and the quantity to be minimized is a weighted sum of squares, at frequencies ω_1, ω_2, ..., ω_N, of the off-diagonal elements in row j of $\hat{Q}$. An analysis similar to that given before shows that row j of $\hat{K}$ is given again by an eigenvector problem

$$B_j k_j^T - \lambda k_j^T = 0 \qquad (7.28)$$

where

$$B_j = \left(b_{il}^{(j)} \right) = \left[\sum_{r=1}^{N} \gamma_r \left\{ \sum_{\substack{k=1 \\ k \ne j}}^{m} [\alpha_{ik}^{(r)} \alpha_{lk}^{(r)} + \beta_{ik}^{(r)} \beta_{lk}^{(r)}] \right\} \right] \qquad (7.29)$$

and the $\alpha_{ik}^{(r)}$, $\beta_{ik}^{(r)}$ are defined by

$$\hat{g}_{ik}(i\omega_r) = \alpha_{ik}^{(r)} + i\beta_{ik}^{(r)} \qquad (7.30)$$

As before, we choose the eigenvector $\hat{k}_j^T$ corresponding to the smallest eigenvalue of B_j. The same set ω_1, ω_2, ..., ω_N may be used for each row of K, or different sets may be used for different rows.

EXERCISE 7.2.   Derive the result embodied in (7.28) and (7.29).

EXAMPLE 7.4.   A thirty-plate distillation column has the transfer-function matrix

$$G(s) = \begin{bmatrix} \dfrac{0 \cdot 088}{(1+75s)(1+722s)} & \dfrac{0 \cdot 1825}{(1+15s)(1+722s)} \\[4mm] \dfrac{0 \cdot 282}{(1+10s)(1+1850s)} & \dfrac{0 \cdot 412}{(1+15s)(1+1850s)} \end{bmatrix} \qquad (7.31)$$

which relates boil-up and reflux to the temperatures at two points in the column. The inverse Nyquist diagram shows that the system is not dominant. Moreover, the choice $\hat{K} = G(0)$ as in Exercise 7.1 does not achieve dominance. This is shown by Fig. 3.21, in which the Gershgorin bands are derived from rows, and the first row is not dominant.

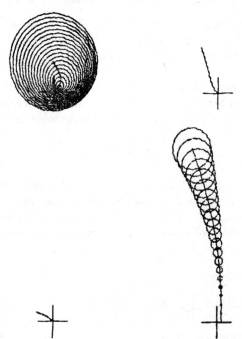

FIG. 3.21.   Inverse Nyquist array and Gershgorin bands for $\hat{Q} = \hat{K}\hat{G}$, where $\hat{G}$ is obtained from equation (7.31) and $\hat{K} = G(0)$. The frequency range is $\omega = 0$, $0 \cdot 001, 0 \cdot 002, ..., 0 \cdot 02$.

The method of Section 7.2 can be used to achieve dominance by suitable selection of ω. However, we illustrate the method of Section 7.3 by selecting a set of 21 frequencies ω_r increasing by steps of $0 \cdot 001$ from $\omega_1 = 0$ to $\omega_{21} = 0 \cdot 02$. With $\gamma_r = 1, r = 1, 2, ..., 21$, we may solve (7.29) for each of the two rows to obtain

$$K = \begin{bmatrix} 0 \cdot 027 & 0 \cdot 094 \\ 0 \cdot 073 & 0 \cdot 394 \end{bmatrix} \qquad (7.32)$$

With this $\hat{K}$, the inverse Nyquist diagram for $\hat{Q} = \hat{K}\hat{G}$ is shown in Fig. 3.22, in which the Gershgorin bands based on rows show that dominance has been achieved for the open-loop system. Dominance is maintained for the closed-loop system, and Fig. 3.23 shows the Ostrowski bands for rows when the

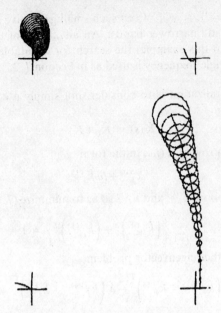

FIG. 3.22. Effect on Fig. 3.21 of pseudo-diagonalizing at 21 frequencies.

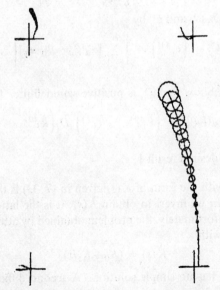

FIG. 3.23. Showing the Ostrowski bands corresponding to Fig. 3.22 when $f_1 = 1$, $f_2 = 1$.

loop gains are $f_1 = 1, f_2 = 1$. Even such small gains give narrow bands, and larger gains give still narrower bands. An advantage of this method is that it can avoid (as in this example) the search for a suitable ω, which may be needed when a single frequency is used as in Section 7.2.

A second generalization is to consider, not simply a constant $\hat{K}$, but the more general form

$$\hat{K}(s) = \hat{K}_0 + \hat{K}_1 s \tag{7.33}$$

If we write the jth row of $\hat{K}(i\omega)$ in the form

$$\hat{k}_j^{(0)} + i\omega \hat{k}_j^{(1)} \tag{7.34}$$

we may seek to choose $\hat{k}_j^{(0)}$ and $\hat{k}_j^{(1)}$ so as to minimize (7.14), subject to

$$\sum_{i=1}^{m} \left\{ \left(\hat{k}_{ji}^{(0)} \right)^2 + \left(\hat{k}_{ji}^{(1)} \right)^2 \right\} = 1 \tag{7.35}$$

This leads to another eigenvector problem

$$D_j \left(\hat{k}_j^{(0)} \quad \hat{k}_j^{(1)} \right)^T - \lambda \left(\hat{k}_j^{(0)} \quad \hat{k}_j^{(1)} \right)^T = 0 \tag{7.36}$$

where

$$D_j = \begin{bmatrix} A_j & \omega C_j \\ \omega C_j & \omega^2 A_j \end{bmatrix} \tag{7.37}$$

with A_j given by (7.19) and C_j by

$$C_j = \left(c_{il}^{(j)} \right) = \left[\sum_{\substack{k=1 \\ k \neq j}}^{m} [\alpha_{ik} \beta_{lk} - \beta_{ik} \alpha_{lk}] \right] \tag{7.38}$$

EXERCISE 7.3. Show that D_j is positive semidefinite. [Prove that

$$\sum_{\substack{k=1 \\ k \neq j}}^{m} |\hat{q}_{jk}(i\omega)|^2 = \left(\hat{k}_j^{(0)} \quad \hat{k}_j^{(1)} \right) D_j \left(\hat{k}_j^{(0)} \quad \hat{k}_j^{(1)} \right)^T \tag{7.39}$$

which implies the desired result.]

One difficulty with the form of $\hat{K}(s)$ given in (7.33) is that its simplicity is generally lost when we invert to obtain $K(s)$: it is the latter which has to be implemented. Unfortunately, the problem obtained by attempting to pseudo-diagonalize $\hat{Q}(s)$ with

$$\hat{K}(s) = (K_0 + K_1/s)^{-1} \tag{7.40}$$

in place of (7.33) has no simple solution. A second difficulty with the $\hat{K}(s)$ obtained from (7.33) is that the corresponding $K(s)$ may have poles or zeros in the open right half-plane. We must check whether this is so, and will ordinarily reject such a $K(s)$. Selection of a different value of ω in (7.14) may then eliminate the difficulty.

The process of generalization represented by (7.27) and (7.33) can obviously be extended. We may take further terms in (7.33), or we may combine the two ideas and use (7.33) with (7.27).

A third direction in which pseudo-diagnonalization can be modified is by using alternative constraints in place of (7.15). Though (7.15) leads to a particularly simple computing problem, it has the disadvantage of doing nothing to ensure that $|\hat{q}_{jj}(i\omega)|$ remains large while the expression in (7.14) is minimized. In some practical examples it has been found that minimization of (7.14) simultaneously leads to small values of $\hat{q}_{jj}$.

To avoid this we may substitute for (7.15) the constraint

$$|\hat{q}_{jj}(i\omega)| = 1 \tag{7.41}$$

An analysis similar to that given before leads to

$$A_j \hat{k}_j{}^T - \lambda E_j \hat{k}_j{}^T = 0 \tag{7.42}$$

instead of (7.21), where A_j is given by (7.19) and E_j is the symmetric matrix

$$E_j = (e_{il}{}^{(j)}) = [\alpha_{ij}\alpha_{lj} + \beta_{ij}\beta_{lj}] \tag{7.43}$$

which is positive semidefinite.

Finally, it is quite possible to adopt a more direct attack, using hill-climbing methods to minimize

$$\sum_{\substack{k=1 \\ k \neq j}}^{m} |\hat{q}_{jk}(i\omega)| / |\hat{q}_{jj}(i\omega)| \tag{7.44}$$

though the sharp ridges of this function may cause difficulty to the hill-climbing method.

7.4 Cancellation of off-diagonal terms

In stating Theorem 5.3a, we assumed for simplicity that F was a diagonal matrix independent of s. In fact the elements f_i of such a matrix usually represent the product of a loop gain with 1 (loop closed) or with 0 (loop open). This was explained in Section 2.1.

Theorem 5.3, on the other hand, is free of any such assumption about F. Since we have $\hat{H} = F + \hat{Q}$, we may therefore use the off-diagonal elements of F to cancel, or partly cancel, the off-diagonal elements of $\hat{Q}$. In this way we may improve the diagonal dominance of $\hat{H}$, but not that of $\hat{Q}$.

This artifice is particularly appealing when we define K as in Exercise 7.1. We then have $\hat{Q}(0)$ diagonal, and may choose $F(0)$ diagonal. Then we may define

$$F(s) = F(0) + F_1(s) \tag{7.45}$$

where $F_1(s)$ has its diagonal elements zero, and its off-diagonal elements chosen to improve the dominance of $\hat{H}$. As $F_1(0) = 0$, $F(s)$ gives transient compensation of the interaction. This transient compensation needs to be chosen with a view to its effect on the dynamical behaviour of the system, which may restrict the scope of the method.

EXAMPLE 7.5. Consider a system having

$$\hat{G}(s) = \begin{bmatrix} s^2 + 8 \cdot 8s + 1 & 2s^2 + 2 \cdot 6s + 2 \\ 2s^2 + 14 \cdot 6s + 2 & 3s^2 + 2 \cdot 4s + 3 \end{bmatrix} \tag{7.46}$$

which is neither row nor column dominant. Making $\hat{Q}(0) = I_2$ we have

$$\hat{Q}(s) = G(0)\hat{G}(s) = \begin{bmatrix} s^2 + 2 \cdot 8s + 1 & -3s \\ 3s & s^2 + 2 \cdot 8s + 1 \end{bmatrix} \tag{7.47}$$

This matrix is not row or column dominant, as is easily seen by choosing $s = i$. If, however, we could choose

$$F = \begin{bmatrix} 1 & 3s \\ -3s & 1 \end{bmatrix} \tag{7.48}$$

we should have $\hat{H}$ diagonal. Such a choice of F is not possible if it involves differentiating the output, though if we can measure the derivative of the output it may serve: see Chapter 2, Exercise 2.2. To avoid the differentiation we may approximate to (7.48) over some band $s = 0$ to $s = i\omega_0$, where ω_0 is large enough to ensure that the terms in s^2 on the diagonal of the matrix in (7.47) dominate the off-diagonal terms. For example we may choose

$$F = \begin{bmatrix} 1 & \dfrac{30s}{s+10} \\ \dfrac{-30s}{s+10} & 1 \end{bmatrix} \tag{7.49}$$

giving

$$\hat{H}(s) = \begin{bmatrix} s^2 + 2 \cdot 8s + 2 & \dfrac{-3s^2}{s+10} \\ \dfrac{3s^2}{s+10} & s^2 + 2 \cdot 8s + 2 \end{bmatrix} \tag{7.50}$$

which is row dominant.

The preceding example is artificial: industrial problems have not so far needed this device. If it is to be used, the sensitivity of the system to changes in $Q(s)$ must obviously be investigated with some care. When the cancelled terms in $F + \hat{Q}$ are individually large, a small change in Q may totally alter the degree of dominance.

8. Sensitivity

The sensitivity of multivariable control systems can be investigated by means similar to those used in Chapter 2. For example if a disturbance $\bar{d}$ enters the system, we can again find the disturbance $\bar{d}_1$ deferred to the output: it is now a k-vector. Equation (8.1) of Chapter 2 is then replaced by

$$\bar{z} = \bar{d}_1 + Q\bar{e} \tag{8.1}$$

$$= \bar{d}_1 + Q(\bar{v} - F\bar{z}) \tag{8.2}$$

$$\bar{z} = (I + QF)^{-1} Q\bar{v} + (I + QF)^{-1} \bar{d}_1 \tag{8.3}$$

The matrix

$$S(s) = (I + Q(s) F(s))^{-1} \tag{8.4}$$

now expresses the sensitivity of the output to the disturbance $\bar{d}_1$. By equation (1.6), if $\hat{Q}(s) = Q^{-1}(s)$ exists,

$$S(s) = H(s) \hat{Q}(s) \tag{8.5}$$

In the same way, when $Q^{-1}(s)$ exists, equation (8.5) of Chapter 2 becomes

$$\hat{H} = F + \hat{Q} \tag{8.6}$$

whence

$$\delta\hat{H} = \delta\hat{Q} \tag{8.7}$$

We now have, to the first order,

$$\delta(H^{-1}) = -H_0^{-1} \delta H H_0^{-1} \tag{8.8}$$

$$\delta(Q^{-1}) = -Q_0^{-1} \delta Q Q_0^{-1} \tag{8.9}$$

Q_0 and H_0 being datum values. Hence (8.7) gives

$$\delta H H_0^{-1} = H_0 Q_0^{-1} \delta Q Q_0^{-1} \tag{8.10}$$

$$= S(\delta Q) Q_0^{-1} \tag{8.11}$$

where S is given by (8.4) or (8.5), evaluated in the datum condition. Equation (8.11) corresponds to equation (8.8) of Chapter 2.

Now compare an open-loop system with transfer function

$$Q Q_0^{-1} H_0 \tag{8.12}$$

where H_0, Q_0 are datum values, with a closed-loop system having

$$H = (I+QF)^{-1} Q \qquad (8.13)$$

and perturb Q for given input $\bar{v}$. The change in the output of the first system is

$$\delta\bar{z}_1 = \delta QQ_0^{-1} H_0 \bar{v} \qquad (8.14)$$

while for the second it is, by (8.11),

$$\delta\bar{z}_2 = \delta H\bar{v} \qquad (8.15)$$

$$= S(\delta Q)Q_0^{-1} H_0 \bar{v} \qquad (8.16)$$

Consequently the effect of feedback is to alter the change in output from $\delta\bar{z}_1$ to $S(s)\,\delta\bar{z}_1$, where $S(s)$ is again given by (8.4) or (8.5), evaluated in the datum condition.

The expressions given above are less informative than those in Chapter 2, because it is less easy to see when the elements of S will be small. The following transformation assists in this respect when we are using the inverse Nyquist array. From (8.5)

$$S = H(\hat{H}-F) \qquad (8.17)$$

$$= I-HF \qquad (8.18)$$

If $\hat{H}$ is dominant we can obtain estimates of $h_{ii}^{-1}(s)$ from the Ostrowski bands. If in addition $F = \operatorname{diag}(f_i)$, then we have from (8.18)

$$s_{ii}(s) = 1-f_i/h_{ii}^{-1}(s) \qquad (8.19)$$

which is readily estimated from the computer display. For any s which makes the Ostrowski circle small, (8.19) can be approximated by

$$s_{ii}(s) = 1-\frac{f_i}{\hat{h}_{ii}(s)} \qquad (8.20)$$

$$= 1-\frac{f_i}{f_i+\hat{q}_{ii}(s)} \qquad (8.21)$$

$$= \frac{\hat{q}_{ii}(s)}{\hat{h}_{ii}(s)} \qquad (8.22)$$

which is the same result as would be obtained for a single isolated loop.

9. The direct Nyquist array

Up to this point we have concentrated heavily on the inverse Nyquist array, for reasons which were given in Section 6.3. All the theorems which we have stated for the inverse Nyquist array, however, have analogues which are valid for the direct Nyquist array. The basic stability criterion has in fact been given in its direct form in Theorem 5.2a, and the direct result obtained from Ostrowski's theorem will be given below.

Our reason for now considering the direct theorems is that we are sometimes presented with plants having non-square $G(s)$. Before loops can be closed around the plant, the number of inputs must be made equal to the number of outputs, and this is itself part of the design problem. Obviously we cannot invert $Q(s)$ unless it is square, so that the part of the design procedure which derives a square $Q(s)$ from a non-square $G(s)$ is outside the scope of the inverse Nyquist methods.

The most usual situation in which we meet a non-square $G(s)$ is when more measurements are available (or can easily be made available) than there are manipulated variables; that is, when $m > l$. If the aim is to control certain specified outputs, then these may fix the measurements which it is appropriate to use. If, however, the aim is primarily to stabilize the plant, then we may ask which l of the m available measurements will be most effective. More generally we may choose l linear combinations of the m measurements, and may use these to close the l loops. Even when l of the m outputs are indicated by the control objectives, it may still be better to use all m outputs to achieve a fast-acting stable system, and then use cascade control on the specified outputs [Chapter 2, Section 2].

An alternative situation, which is less common, is where $l > m$. Then m of the available inputs, or m linear combinations of them, can be chosen in order to give m control loops. We shall speak mainly of the situation where $m > l$, but with appropriate changes the results apply also when $l > m$.

In section 6, we did not give the application of Ostrowski's theorem to the direct Nyquist plots, but only to the inverse plots as in Theorem 6.2. We therefore first develop the analogous result. We suppose that $G(s)$ is $m \times l$, and $L(s)$ is $l \times m$, so that $Q(s) = L(s) G(s)$ is $l \times l$. Alternatively, when $l > m$, we let $K(s)$ be $m \times l$ so that $Q(s) = G(s) K(s)$ is $m \times m$. The matrix F is the same size as $Q(s)$. As we do not require k for a special purpose in this Section, we allow it to represent a general index.

THEOREM 9.1. Let $F = \text{diag}(f_i)$ where the f_i are real numbers. Let the matrix $F^{-1} + Q(s)$ be dominant on D, and write $h_i(s)$ for element (i, i) of the matrix.

$$H[Q(s), \text{diag}(f_1, f_2, ..., f_{i-1}, 0, f_{i+1}, ..., f_l)] \tag{9.1}$$

where the notation is defined by equation (1.8). Then for each s on D,

$$|q_{ii}(s) - h_i(s)| < \phi_i(s) d_i(s) < d_i(s) \tag{9.2}$$

or

$$|q_{ii}(s) - h_i(s)| < \phi_i'(s)\, d_i'(s) < d_i'(s) \tag{9.3}$$

according as $F^{-1} + Q$ is row or column dominant at s. Here d_i, d_i', ϕ_i, ϕ_i' are defined by (5.12), (5.13) and (6.2), with Z replaced by $F^{-1} + Q(s)$.

Proof. Assume row dominance and write $F^{-1} = \hat{F}$, and

$$R(s) = I_l + FQ(s) \tag{9.4}$$

so that

$$F^{-1} + Q(s) = \hat{F}[I_l + FQ(s)] = \hat{F}R(s) \tag{9.5}$$

Then Theorem 6.1 shows that $(\hat{F}R)^{-1}$ exists, whence $\hat{R}$ exists, and

$$|(\hat{r}_{ii}(s)f_i)^{-1} - (f_i^{-1} + q_{ii}(s)|) < \phi_i(s)\, d_i(s) < d_i(s) \tag{9.6}$$

Now equation (1.7) shows that $H(s)$ defined by (9.1) is

$$H = Q[I_l + \text{diag}(f_1, f_2, \ldots, f_{i-1}, 0, f_{i+1}, \ldots, f_l)\, Q]^{-1} \tag{9.7}$$

where we have suppressed s. Write

$$F' = \text{diag}(0, \ldots, 0, f_i, 0, \ldots, 0) \tag{9.8}$$

and notice that $R - F'Q$ is row dominant, and therefore has an inverse by Theorem 6.1. Then from (9.7),

$$I_l + F'H = I_l + F'Q[I_l + FQ - F'Q]^{-1} \tag{9.9}$$

$$= I_l - [R - F'Q][R - F'Q]^{-1} + R[R - F'Q]^{-1} \tag{9.10}$$

$$= [I_l - F'Q\hat{R}]^{-1} \tag{9.11}$$

The ith row of $F'Q\hat{R}$ is the same as the ith row of $FQ\hat{R}$, and from (9.4),

$$FQ\hat{R} = [I_l + FQ]\,\hat{R} - \hat{R} = I_l - \hat{R} \tag{9.12}$$

Hence the matrix to be inverted in (9.11) is

$$\begin{bmatrix} 1 & 0 & \ldots & 0 & \ldots & 0 \\ 0 & 1 & \ldots & 0 & \ldots & 0 \\ \vdots & \vdots & & \vdots & & \vdots \\ \hat{r}_{i1} & \hat{r}_{i2} & \ldots & \hat{r}_{ii} & \ldots & \hat{r}_{il} \\ \vdots & \vdots & & \vdots & & \vdots \\ 0 & 0 & \ldots & 0 & \ldots & 1 \end{bmatrix} \tag{9.13}$$

Then equating elements (i, i) on each side of (9.11) we have

$$1 + f_i h_i = \hat{r}_{ii}^{-1} \tag{9.14}$$

and on using this, (9.6) becomes

$$|h_i(s) - q_{ii}(s)| < \phi_i(s)\, d_i(s) < d_i(s) \tag{9.15}$$

which proves the first part of the theorem. The second part is proved in a similar way from the formula

$$H = [I_l + Q \,\mathrm{diag}\,(f_1, f_2, ..., f_{i-1}, 0, f_{i+1}, ..., f_l)]^{-1}\, Q \tag{9.16}$$

The graphical interpretation of Theorem 9.1 is analogous to that of Theorem 6.2. When loops $1, 2, ..., i-1, i+1, ..., l$, are closed, with gains $f_1, f_2, ..., f_{i-1}, f_{i+1}, ..., f_l$, but loop i is open, the transfer function seen between input i and output i is $h_i(s)$: observe that the notation in Section 3.2 was different. When $F^{-1} + Q(s)$ is dominant on D, $h_i(s)$ lies inside a circle of radius $\phi_i(s)\, d_i(s)$ centred on $q_{ii}(s)$, if the row condition in (5.3) is satisfied at s on D. If the column condition in (5.3) is satisfied at s, $h_i(s)$ lies inside a circle of radius $\phi_i'(s)\, d_i'(s)$ centred on $q_{ii}(s)$. Consequently, as the gains in the other loops are changed, $h_i(s)$ remains inside the Gershgorin band (defined by circles with radius d_i or d_i' as appropriate at each s) provided that the critical point $(-f_j^{-1}, 0)$ in each other loop remains outside its Gershgorin band. For any specified gains in the other loops, $h_i(s)$ can be located more accurately by its Ostrowski band, provided again that the critical points for the other loops are outside their Gershgorin bands.

Notice that ϕ_i in (9.2) or ϕ_i' in (9.3) now becomes small as the gains in the other loops tend to zero. This is what we expect, as h_i must equal q_{ii} when all the other loops are open. The contrast with the result in Section 6.3 illuminates again the reasons for working with $\hat{Q}$ when this can be done.

EXERCISE 9.1. Show that if $Q(s)$ is strictly proper, (9.2) or (9.3) is true for some specified $i = k$ even if $(-f_k^{-1}, 0)$ is inside the kth Gershgorin band. [All that is needed for the proof is that some value f_{k0} of f_k exists for which $(-f_{k_0}^{-1}, 0)$ is outside the kth Gershgorin band. When $Q(s)$ is strictly proper this is always true. For (9.2) or (9.3) to be true for $j \neq k$, we must of course have $(-f_k^{-1}, 0)$ outside its Gershgorin band.]

9.1 Design procedure

Suppose now that a plant is given with $m \times l$ transfer function matrix $G(s)$, and $m > l$. That is, there are more measurements than manipulated variables. We wish if we can to find an $l \times m$ matrix L, independent of s, such that $Q(s) = LG(s)$ permits l closed loops with satisfactory performance. To this end, we seek to make $Q(s)$ dominant. We should prefer to do this with a matrix L having as many zero columns as possible: that is, we prefer to use less than m measurements if we can.

The $m \times l$ Nyquist array can be presented graphically by the computer.

We may then seek to combine rows by the elementary operations defined in Section 7.1. That is, we interchange rows, or we add a multiple of one row to another, the multiplier being a rational function with its poles in the open left half-plane. By such operations we seek to produce an $m \times l$ matrix $Q_a(s)$ of the form

$$Q_a(s) = \begin{bmatrix} Q(s) \\ Q_b(s) \end{bmatrix} = \begin{bmatrix} L_{11} & L_{12} \\ L_{21} & L_{22} \end{bmatrix} \begin{bmatrix} G_1(s) \\ G_2(s) \end{bmatrix} \tag{9.17}$$

in which $Q(s)$ is $m \times m$ and is dominant on D. Then the appropriate matrix L is $(L_{11} \quad L_{12})$, which is $l \times m$.

Alternatively we may generate L by a process of pseudo-diagonalization similar to that described in Section 7.2. We write

$$q_{jk} = \sum_{i=1}^{m} l_{ji} g_{jk}, \quad j, k = 1, 2, \dots, l \tag{9.18}$$

and seek to choose $l_{j1}, l_{j2}, \dots, l_{jm}$ so that

$$\sum_{\substack{k=1 \\ k \neq j}}^{l} |q_{jk}|^2 \tag{9.19}$$

is as small as possible subject to

$$\sum_{i=1}^{m} l_{ji}^2 = 1 \tag{9.20}$$

If l_j is the row vector $(l_{j1}, l_{j2}, \dots, l_{jm})$, we find that l_j is the solution of

$$A_j l_j^T - \lambda l_j^T = 0 \tag{9.21}$$

corresponding to the smallest eigenvalue λ of the $m \times m$ symmetric matrix

$$A_j = \left[a_{il}^{(j)} \right] = \left[\sum_{\substack{k=1 \\ k \neq j}}^{l} [\alpha_{ik} \alpha_{lk} + \beta_{ik} \beta_{lk}] \right] \tag{9.22}$$

in which α_{ik}, β_{ik} are defined by

$$g_{ik} = \alpha_{ik} + i\beta_{ik} \tag{9.23}$$

EXERCISE 9.2. Obtain the above result as in Section 7.2.

This procedure may be carried out at any chosen $s = i\omega$, and ω may be different for each row. As in Section 7.3 the procedure may be generalized in various ways. Because of the greater freedom provided by the increased number of outputs, we are likely to achieve a better result from (9.21) when $m > l$ than when $m = l$. The same is true when the alternative method based on elementary operations is used.

EXERCISE 9.3. Show that if $m \geqslant 2l-1$, the procedure for pseudo-diagonalizing with L at $s = i\omega$ always generates a matrix which is diagonal at $s = i\omega$. [Write

$$A_j = (\alpha \quad \beta) \begin{bmatrix} \alpha^T \\ \beta^T \end{bmatrix} \tag{9.24}$$

where α, β are suitably defined matrices, each $m \times (l-1)$. Show that when $m \geqslant 2l-1$, A_j has a zero eigenvalue, and compare Exercise 7.1.]

Probably little more needs to be said about the design procedure. If $Q(s)$ can be made dominant on D, then Theorem 9.1 locates the transfer functions $h_i(s)$ within the Ostrowski bands. If these are narrow enough, they will allow single-loop controllers to be designed. Similar methods can be used when $l > m$, in which case we design an $m \times l$ input compensator K.

10. Multivariable circle criteria

In the preceding Sections, it has been assumed that the system was linear and time-invariant. For single-input single-output systems these restrictions were partially removed in Section 11 of Chapter 2. We now give a similar generalization for dominant multivariable systems. Proofs will be omitted because they would be inconveniently long, and the reader is referred to the original papers.

As before, let $Q(s) = L(s)\,G(s)\,K(s)$ be the $k \times k$ transfer function matrix in the forward path, which is assumed strictly proper, but let feedback be

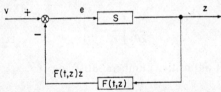

FIG. 3.24. System with nonlinear time-dependent feedback matrix. The multivariable system S is linear and time-invariant, and has strictly proper transfer function matrix $Q(s)$.

applied via a diagonal matrix F which depends upon t and the output z (see Fig. 3.24)

$$F(t, z) = \text{diag}\,[f_i(t, z)] \tag{10.1}$$

where for all t and z, and $i = 1, 2, ..., k$,

$$0 < \alpha_i \leqslant f_i(t, z) \leqslant \beta_i, \quad \alpha_i < \beta_i \tag{10.2}$$

Notice that $f_i(t, z)$ may depend on all the elements of z, and that it multiplies the output signal, so that

$$v_i - e_i = f_i(t, z)\, z_i \qquad (10.3)$$

Notice also that by redefining the loops as in Section 2.1 we may consider a set of nonlinear time-dependent gains at any point in the system.

The transfer function matrix $Q(s)$ arises from a dynamical system

$$T_Q(s)\, \check{\xi}_Q = U_Q(s)\, \bar{e}$$

$$\bar{z} = V_Q(s)\, \check{\xi}_Q + W_Q(s)\, \bar{e} \qquad (10.4)$$

which if we wish can be decomposed as in Section 3.1 into subsystems corresponding to L, G and K. We do not assume that the system (10.4) has least order. Let the system (10.4) have p_0 poles in the closed right half-plane: that is, let $|T_Q(s)|$ have p_0 zeros there.

Gershgorin row bands based on the maps by the q_{ii} of a contour D can be defined just as they were for Theorem 5.2a. So also can Gershgorin column bands, but Theorem 10.1 below has not been proved for the more general type of dominance corresponding to condition (5.3). The contour D is suitably indented and chosen large enough to ensure that every pole of $q_{ii}(s)$, $i = 1, 2, ..., k$, which lies in the closed right half-plane is inside D. The critical points are now replaced by critical discs: the ith critical disc has centre at

$$-\left[\frac{1}{2\alpha_i} + \frac{1}{2\beta_i}\right] \qquad (10.5)$$

and has radius

$$\frac{1}{2\theta_i}\left[\frac{1}{\alpha_i} - \frac{1}{\beta_i}\right] \qquad (10.6)$$

Here the θ_i are a set of positive numbers satisfying

$$\sum_{i=1}^{k} \theta_i^2 \leqslant 1 \qquad (10.7)$$

The terminology is illustrated by Fig. 3.25.

With this notation we have the following theorem [Rosenbrock, 1973b].

THEOREM 10.1. For some θ_i, $i = 1, 2, ..., k$, satisfying (10.7), let the least distance, between the ith critical disc and the Gershgorin row [resp. column] band centred on the map by q_{ii} of D, be greater than $\varepsilon > 0$, $i = 1, 2, ..., k$. Let this be true for all contours D' satisfying the conditions for D and having $R' \geqslant R$. Let the ith Gershgorin row [resp. column] band encircle the ith critical disc N_i times clockwise as s goes once clockwise around D. Then if

$$\sum_{i=1}^{k} N_i = -p_0 \qquad (10.8)$$

the closed-loop system corresponding to (10.3), (10.4) is uniformly asymptotically stable in the large [Chapter 1, Section 7].

EXERCISE 10.1. As in Theorem 10.1, let $Q(s)$ be row [resp. column] dominant, not only on D but also on every D' having $R' \geqslant R$. Show that the condition "every pole of $q_{ii}(s)$, $i = 1, 2, ..., k$, lying in the closed right half-

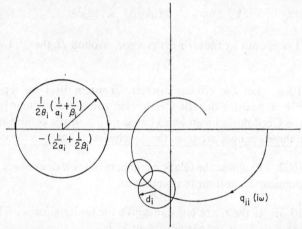

FIG. 3.25. Gershgorin row band and critical disc. Only two Gershgorin circles have been shown. The Gershgorin band is generated by all such circles for s on D.

plane is inside D" implies the condition "every pole of $Q(s)$ and zero of $|Q(s)|$ lying in the closed right half-plane is inside D" [Compare the proof of Theorem 9.4 in Chapter 1.]

It will be seen that this theorem gives only a sufficient condition in (10.8) when the other conditions are met. Otherwise it reduces to a form resembling Theorem 5.2a when the f_i in (10.3) become constant. Then we may take the $\beta_i - \alpha_i$ arbitrarily small, and the critical discs tend to the critical points. In Theorem 10.1 the numbers θ_i can be chosen as we wish: if a set of θ_i can be found for which the conditions of the theorem are true, then the conclusion follows. We can therefore reduce the radius of any one disc at the expense of another.

The θ_i nevertheless are inconvenient, as they weaken the theorem. It has not so far been possible to obtain a stronger theorem for systems which

M

are row [resp. column] dominant, but Cook [1973b], by introducing a new dominance condition (*mean dominance*) allows us to give the following result.

Let the ith critical disc have its centre as before at the point given by (10.5), but let its radius be

$$\frac{1}{2}\left[\frac{1}{\alpha_i} - \frac{1}{\beta_i}\right] \tag{10.9}$$

Define the ith *Gershgorin mean disc* for each s on D to be the disc having its centre at $q_{ii}(s)$ and having radius equal to the mean of the radius of the Gershgorin row disc at s and the Gershgorin column disc at s. Explicitly, the radius of the Gershgorin mean disc is

$$d_i''(s) = \frac{1}{2}\left\{ \sum_{\substack{j=1 \\ j \neq i}}^{k} |q_{ij}(s)| + \sum_{\substack{j=1 \\ j \neq i}}^{k} |q_{ji}(s)| \right\} \tag{10.10}$$

Call the band swept out by these discs, as s goes around D, the ith *Gershgorin mean band*.

THEOREM 10.2. Let the critical discs in Theorem 10.1 be replaced by those just defined, and let the ith Gershgorin row [resp. column] band be replaced by the Gershgorin mean band based on q_{ii}. If the conditions of the theorem with these changes are true, the conclusion follows.

EXERCISE 10.2. Examine the relationship between row dominance, column dominance, dominance, and mean dominance.

EXERCISE 10.3. If the f_i are constant, give the limiting form of Theorem 10.2 as $\alpha_i \to f_i$, $\beta_i \to f_i$. [Compare Problem 33.]

Corresponding results can also be stated in terms of the inverse plots, though now we have to be a little more careful in ensuring adequate clearance between the Gershgorin bands and the critical discs. The contour D is suitably indented and chosen large enough to ensure that every pole of $\hat{q}_{ii}(s)$, $i = 1, 2, ..., k$, if it lies in the closed right half-plane, is inside D. The Gershgorin row [resp. column] bands based on the maps by the $\hat{q}_{ii}$ of D are defined exactly as they were for Theorem 5.3a. As before, Theorem 10.3 has not been proved for the more general type of dominance defined by condition (5.3). The critical discs now have their centres at

$$-\frac{\alpha_i + \beta_i}{2} = -\gamma_i \tag{10.11}$$

and have radii

$$\frac{\beta_i + \alpha_i}{2\theta_i} \tag{10.12}$$

The θ_i are defined as before to satisfy (10.7), and we have [Rosenbrock, 1973b].

THEOREM 10.3.   For some θ_i, $i = 1, 2, ..., k$ satisfying (10.7), let the ith Gershgorin row [resp. column] band based on $\hat{q}_{ii}$ exclude the origin. Let the least distance, between the Gershgorin disc centred on $\hat{q}_{ii}(s)$ and the critical disc centred on $-\gamma_i$ be greater than $\varepsilon|\gamma_i + \hat{q}_{ii}(s)| > 0$. Let this be true for $i = 1, 2, ..., k$ and for all s on D', where D' satisfies the conditions for D and has $R' \geqslant R$. Let the ith Gershgorin row [resp. column] band encircle the origin $\hat{N}_{qi}$ times clockwise, and the ith critical disc $\hat{N}_{ci}$ times clockwise, as s goes once clockwise around D. Then if

$$\sum_{i=1}^{k} \hat{N}_{qi} - \sum_{i=1}^{k} \hat{N}_{ci} = p_0 \tag{10.13}$$

the closed-loop system defined by (10.3), (10.4) is uniformly asymptotically stable in the large.

The relation between this theorem and Theorem 5.3a is again very close. Notice that we have used $\hat{N}_{ci}$ instead of $\hat{N}_{hi}$ in order to avoid suggesting that the closed-loop system has a transfer function. Again the θ_i are inconvenient, and Cook [1973b] allows us to give the following result.

Let the centre of the ith critical disc, as in Theorem 10.3, be given by (10.11), but let the radius be

$$\frac{1}{2}(\beta_i - \alpha_i) \tag{10.14}$$

Define the ith Gershgorin mean disc at s on D to be the disc with centre $\hat{q}_{ii}(s)$ and radius

$$d_i'' = \frac{1}{2}\left\{ \sum_{\substack{j=1 \\ j \neq i}}^{k} |\hat{q}_{ij}(s)| + \sum_{\substack{j=1 \\ j \neq i}}^{k} |\hat{q}_{ji}(s)| \right\} \tag{10.15}$$

As s goes round D these discs sweep out a band which we call the ith Gershgorin mean band.

THEOREM 10.4.   Let the critical discs in Theorem 10.3 be replaced by those just defined, and let the ith Gershgorin row [resp. column] band be replaced by the Gershgorin mean band centred on $\hat{q}_{ii}$. If the conditions of the theorem, with these changes, are true then the conclusion follows.

The theorems given above can be used directly in some special problems: an example is given in Section 4 of Chapter 4. However that example also shows that the theorems may sometimes be too conservative to be helpful. In addition there are many problems where a model obtained from the physics and chemistry of the process contains a number of nonlinear elements (without memory) interconnected by a mesh of linear (or sometimes non-linear) dynamical elements. These lie outside the scope of the theorems, as would also most nonlinear models obtained by experimental identification procedures. For such systems, some generalization of the describing function is probably the most hopeful approach [Lighthill and Mees, 1973.]

Nevertheless, the theorems have an importance in their bearing on earlier results. As will be emphasized in Chapter 4, no engineering problem ever satisfies the conditions of any mathematical theorem which the engineer applies. The engineer has to judge whether the discrepancies between his assumptions and the reality will invalidate his conclusions. We can regard the theorems of this Section as giving an important reassurance about the effect of certain types of nonlinearity or time-dependence. Within certain limits these will not invalidate our conclusions, nor the general form of our stability criterion.

11. Problems

(1) Let a system give

$$
\left.\begin{array}{l}
\bar{y}_1 = g_{11}(s)\,\bar{u}_1 + g_{12}(s)\,\bar{u}_2 \\[2mm]
\bar{y}_2 = g_{21}(s)\,\bar{u}_1 + g_{22}(s)\,\bar{u}_2
\end{array}\right\} \tag{11.1}
$$

Then let $\bar{u}_2$ be determined so that $\bar{y}_2 = 0$ even though $\bar{u}_1 \neq 0$. Show that this requires

$$
\bar{u}_2 = g_{22}^{-1}\,g_{21}\,\bar{u}_1 \tag{11.2}
$$

and that then

$$
\bar{y}_1 = \hat{g}_{11}^{-1}\,\bar{u}_1 \tag{11.3}
$$

where $\hat{g}_{11}$ is element $(1, 1)$ of $\hat{G} = G^{-1}$. Deduce that a feedback loop from $\bar{y}_2$ to $\bar{u}_2$, as it is made more effective, will drive the transfer function seen between input 1 and output 1 towards the value $\hat{g}_{11}^{-1}(s)$. Compare with Section 6.3.

(2) Generalize the result in Problem 1 to systems with m inputs and m outputs. [Compare SSMVT, Chapter 5, Section 2.6.]

(3) Illustrate Problem 1 with the example

$$
G(s) = \begin{bmatrix} \dfrac{1}{s+1} & \dfrac{2}{s+3} \\[4mm] \dfrac{1}{s+1} & \dfrac{1}{s+1} \end{bmatrix} \tag{11.4}
$$

by writing down $H(s)$ as a function of f_1 and f_2, and then allowing f_2 to become large.

(4) Let all the poles of $G(s)$ in Problem 1 lie in the open left half-plane, but

let $|G(s)|$ have a zero in the open right half-plane. Suppose that it is possible to use arbitrarily high gain f_2 between y_2 and u_2 without instability. Show that for sufficiently large f_2, the transfer function from $\bar{u}_1$ to $\bar{y}_1$ will be non-minimum phase.

(5) Illustrate Problem 4 by the $G(s)$ given in (11.4).

(6) Write $G(s) = L(s)M(s)N(s)$, where $M(s)$ is the McMillan form of $G(s)$, and $L(s)$, $N(s)$ are unimodular matrices. Let $|G(s)|$ have one or more zeros in the closed right half-plane, and consider what this implies for the numerator zeros in $M(s)$. If $G(s)$ is $m \times m$, and $r \leqslant m$ elements on the principal diagonal of $M(s)$ have a zero $s = s_0$ in the open right half-plane, put $s = s_0$ and show that there are at most $m-r$ independent paths through the system when $s = s_0$. [By "$m-r$ independent paths" we mean a set of $m-r$ inputs and $m-r$ outputs such that the corresponding $(m-r) \times (m-r)$ minor is nonzero for the given s.]

(7) In the McMillan form of the $m \times m$ transfer function matrix $G(s)$, let r elements on the principal diagonal have zeros in the closed right half-plane and let $m-r$ elements have no zero there. Let $K(s)$ be an $m \times m$ rational matrix having all its poles in the open left half-plane. If $G(s)K(s)$ is diagonal, show that at most $m-r$ elements on the principal diagonal of $G(s)K(s)$ are free of zeros in the closed right half-plane.

(8) Show by the example

$$G(s) = \begin{bmatrix} \dfrac{1-s}{(s+1)^2} & \dfrac{1}{2s+1} \\ 0 & \dfrac{1}{s+1} \end{bmatrix} \qquad (11.5)$$

that in Problem 7 the upper bound $m-r$ to the number of elements on the principal diagonal of $G(s)K(s)$ which are free of zeros in the closed right half-plane, cannot necessarily be achieved. [Show that $k_{21}(s) = 0$ and $k_{22}(s) = -g_{11}(s)k_{12}(s)/g_{12}(s)$, and study the implications for $G(s)K(s)$.]

(9) Let the McMillan form of the $m \times m$ transfer function matrix $G(s)$ have an element on the principal diagonal with a zero at $s = 0$. Show that it is not possible to make $y = c$, where c is any given constant m-vector, by application of a constant input vector u.

(10) Illustrate Problem 9 by finding the input u which makes $y = \begin{bmatrix} 1 \\ 0 \end{bmatrix}$ when

$$G(s) = \begin{bmatrix} \dfrac{s}{(s+1)^2} & 0 \\ 0 & \dfrac{1}{s} \end{bmatrix} \qquad (11.6)$$

Note that $|G(0)| \neq 0$.

(11) Let the rational $m \times m$ matrix $G(s)$ have its inverse $\hat{G}(s)$ dominant on the imaginary axis. Show that $g_{ii}^{-1}(i\omega)\,\hat{g}_{ii}^{-1}(i\omega)$ lies inside a circle with centre 1 and radius $r(i\omega) < 1$. Hence show that $g_{ii}(i\omega)\,\hat{g}_{ii}(i\omega)$ lies inside a circle in the right half-plane containing the point $(1, 0)$. [Use Theorem 6.1 with $Z = \hat{G}$.]

(12) In Problem 11, assume that $G(s)$ is dominant rather than $\hat{G}(s)$, and show that the same result is obtained. [Use Theorem 6.1 with $Z = G$.]

(13) From Theorem 3.1 and from Problem 15 of Chapter 2, show how Routh's criterion may be used to investigate the stability of a multivariable feedback system. What will be the advantages and disadvantages compared with the graphical methods of Section 5?

(14) Show how Fig. 3.4 could be obtained from the Routh or the Hurwitz criterion.

(15) The rational functions form a field, and consequently a rational $k \times k$ transfer function matrix $Q(s)$ has eigenvalues $\lambda(s)$ (which in general are not rational) defined by

$$|\lambda_i(s)\, I_k - Q(s)| = 0 \qquad (11.7)$$

Find the eigenvalues of the matrix $G(s)$ defined by (11.4).

(16) If the feedback matrix $F = \alpha I_k$ show from (11.7) that the eigenvalues of $Q(s)\,F$ are $\alpha\lambda_i(s)$, where $\lambda_i(s)$ are the eigenvalues of $Q(s)$.

(17) If the $\lambda_i(s)$ are defined by (11.7), show that

$$|I_m + \alpha Q(s)| = \prod_{i=1}^{k} [1 + \alpha\lambda_i(s)] \qquad (11.8)$$

Suggest a way of investigating the stability of a multivariable system with $F = \alpha I_k$, as a function of α, by plotting the k mappings of a contour D by the k eigenvalues $\lambda_i(s)$ when these eigenvalues are rational.

(18) If $Q(s)$ is dominant on D, use Gershgorin's theorem to bound $|\lambda_i(s) - q_{ii}(s)|$ for s on D, where the $\lambda_i(s)$ are rational and are defined by (11.7). Compare with Theorem 5.2a when $F = \alpha I$.

(19) If $\hat{Q}(s)$ is dominant on D, find a bound for $|\hat{\lambda}_i(s) - \hat{q}_{ii}(s)|$ for s on D, where the $\hat{\lambda}_i(s)$ are the eigenvalues of $\hat{Q}$ and are assumed to be rational. Compare with Theorem 5.3a when $F = \alpha I$.

(20) The right-hand side of (11.8) bears a superficial resemblance to the product in (3.60). Comment on the differences between them.

(21) Show that if $F + \hat{Q}(s)$ is $k \times k$ and is dominant on D, and $0 < \hat{q}_{ii}(0) \ll f_i$, $i = 1, 2, \ldots, k$, then $\phi_i(0)$ in Theorem 6.2 is approximately

$$\phi_i(0) \doteq \max_{\substack{j \\ j \neq i}} \left(\frac{d_j(0)}{f_j} \right) < \max_{\substack{j \\ j \neq i}} \left(\frac{q_{ii}(0)}{f_j} \right) \ll 1 \qquad (11.9)$$

Find the corresponding result for a dominant $F^{-1} + Q(s)$ with $0 < f_i^{-1} \ll$ $q_{ii}(0)$, $i = 1, 2, ..., k.$ Interpret the results in terms of the respective Ostrowski bands when the loop gains are high for $s = 0$.

(22) In applications the transfer functions $h_i(s)$ in Theorem 9.1 will often have a fairly simple form, but quite complicated behaviour is possible. Show that if $\alpha \gg 1$ and

$$Q(s) = \begin{bmatrix} \dfrac{1}{s+1} & \dfrac{0\cdot 9e^{-\alpha s}}{s+1} \\[3mm] \dfrac{0\cdot 9}{s+1} & \dfrac{1}{s+1} \end{bmatrix} \qquad (11.10)$$

then $h_1(i\omega)$ exhibits a complicated behaviour, when f_2 is large, while remaining inside the Ostrowski band. [Note that Ostrowski's theorem is true for this non-rational $Q(s)$.]

(23) Construct an example to illustrate for Theorem 6.2 the point corresponding to the one made in Problem 22.

(24) Show that if

$$Q(s) = \begin{bmatrix} \dfrac{s+4}{2s+5} & \dfrac{s+1}{2s+5} \\[3mm] \dfrac{s+3}{2s+5} & \dfrac{s+2}{2s+5} \end{bmatrix} \qquad (11.11)$$

then $\hat{Q}(s)$ is row dominant on a suitable contour D. Sketch the Gershgorin bands and show that if $Q(s)$ arises from a least-order system, the corresponding closed-loop system is stable for all $f_1 \geqslant 0$ and $f_2 \geqslant 0$.

(25) Is the matrix

$$\hat{Q}(s) = \begin{bmatrix} 2-s & s+1 \\ s+3 & s+4 \end{bmatrix} \qquad (11.12)$$

dominant on a suitable large contour D? Show that the corresponding system is open-loop unstable and cannot be stabilized by any $f_1 > 0$ and $f_2 > 0$. [Note $\hat{Q}(i\omega)$ is dominant and use Theorem 6.4.]

(26) Is the matrix

$$\hat{Q}(s) = \begin{bmatrix} 2-s & s+1 \\ 3-s & s+4 \end{bmatrix} \qquad (11.13)$$

dominant on a suitable contour D? Is it dominant for imaginary s? Can Theorem 6.4 be used to investigate closed-loop stability?

(27) Sketch the Gershgorin row bands for $\hat{Q}(s)$ when

$$Q(s) = \begin{bmatrix} \dfrac{s+4}{(s+1)(s+5)} & \dfrac{1}{s+5} \\ \dfrac{s+3}{(s+1)(s+5)} & \dfrac{2}{s+5} \end{bmatrix} \tag{11.14}$$

and investigate the closed-loop stability.

(28) Sketch the Gershgorin column bands for $Q(s)$ given in (11.14) and investigate the closed-loop stability as in Section 9.

(29) Estimate the Ostrowski bands for Problems 27 and 28. Compare their widths when f_1 and f_2 are large.

(30) Sketch the Gershgorin row bands for $\hat{Q}(s)$ when

$$Q(s) = \begin{bmatrix} \dfrac{s+4}{(s+1)(2s+5)} & \dfrac{1}{2s+5} \\ \dfrac{s+3}{(s+2)(2s+5)} & \dfrac{1}{2s+5} \end{bmatrix} \tag{11.15}$$

and investigate the closed-loop stability.

(31) Show that if the elements of an $m \times m$ complex matrix Z satisfy

$$|z_{ii}| - \sum_{\substack{j=1 \\ j \neq i}}^{m} \tfrac{1}{2}(|z_{ij}| + |z_{ji}|) > 0, \quad i = 1, 2, ..., m \tag{11.16}$$

then Z is nonsingular. [Let $Y = \text{diag}(z_{ii}/|z_{ii}|)$ and $X = \tfrac{1}{2}(Y^*Z + Z^*Y)$ where the star denotes the complex conjugate transpose. From (11.16) and Gershgorin's theorem show that X is nonsingular. Hence if v is any nonzero complex vector, $v^*Xv > 0$. But with Euclidean norms,

$$||Zv|| \, ||v|| = ||Zv|| \, ||Yv|| \geqslant v^*Xv > 0.]$$

(32) Show that if the mean dominance condition (11.16) is substituted for the dominance condition in Theorem 9.4 of Chapter 1, then the result still follows.

(33) Show that the conclusion of Theorem 5.1 holds if dominance of $Z(s)$ on C is replaced by mean dominance of $Z(s)$ on C, where mean dominance is defined by (11.16). Use this result to obtain new theorems corresponding to Theorems 5.2, 5.2a, 5.3, 5.3a.

(34) Show that if there exist real numbers $\lambda_i > 0$, $i = 1, 2, ..., m$ such that

$$|z_{ii}| - \sum_{\substack{j=1 \\ j \neq i}}^{m} \frac{\lambda_j}{2\lambda_i} (|z_{ij}| + |z_{ji}|) > 0 \quad i = 1, 2, ..., m \qquad (11.17)$$

then Z is nonsingular. Hence generalize the results in Problem 33. [Let $\Lambda = \text{diag}(\lambda_i)$ and consider $\Lambda Z \Lambda$. See Cook [1973b] for the connection with Theorem 10.2.]

Chapter 4

Design examples

1. Introduction

Chapter 2 gave a brief account of frequency-response methods for designing single-input single-output control systems, with a strong emphasis on interaction between the designer and the computer. In Chapter 3, a way of extending these methods to multivariable systems was given, using the idea of diagonal dominance.

Apart from the emphasis on computer-aided design, the methods of Chapter 2 are well-known and have been extensively tested. They are highly successful, and were never displaced by the more algorithmic methods arising from state-space theory. The methods of Chapter 3, on the other hand, are relatively new. For this reason it is important to know how they perform on a wide range of industrial problems. More than 25 such problems have in fact been studied since 1969, and in general the methods have had the same kind of success as the earlier methods for single-input single-output systems. In almost all cases, it has been found that diagonal dominance is easy to achieve, and can be obtained by a compensating matrix independent of s.

In the present Chapter, four typical multivariable problems are considered. They have been chosen to illustrate different aspects of the design procedure, and the different requirements which can arise from engineering considerations. For reasons of industrial security it has been necessary to disguise some of the details, but in all essential respects the examples are authentic.

2. Pressurized flowbox

In the Fourdrinier paper-making machine, a suspension of pulp in water (stock) is pumped into a flowbox (or headbox), there being less than 1 % by weight of pulp in the water. At the base of the flowbox is a slice (or sluice) through which the stock flows onto an endless wire-mesh belt. In a large machine this belt may be travelling at 2000 ft. per minute or more, and the web of paper forms on its upper surface as the water in the stock drains through the wire. Drainage is assisted by vacuum boxes and rolls, and the damp web is removed from the wire, pressed, and dried by steam-heated rolls. A diagrammatic sketch is shown in Fig. 4.1.

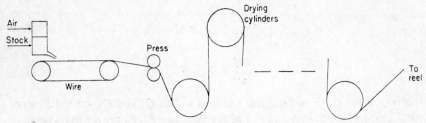

FIG. 4.1.   Diagrammatic sketch of a Fourdinier paper-making machine.

The stock flowing through the slice has a horizontal velocity depending on the head above the slice. As the stock meets the wire a shearing action is set up, depending on the relative velocities of stock and wire. This action is important because it affects the degree to which fibres are aligned and so influences the properties of the paper. At the same time, the amount of stock dispensed to the wire through the slice governs the basis weight of the paper; that is, the weight per unit area. The level of stock in the flowbox affects the flow pattern inside it and therefore the distribution of pulp on the wire.

In order to achieve the required velocity of stock from the slice without excessive depth of liquid, the flowbox can be pressurized with air. The slice is adjusted manually to give the required distribution of flow. Then automatic control may be applied during the operation of the machine to keep the stock in the flowbox at the desired level and to keep the total head above the slice at the value which gives the desired flow through it. The flows of air and stock to the flowbox can each be manipulated, and we therefore have a two-input two-output control system.

An elementary mathematical model of the process can be obtained in the following way [Smith, 1969]. The flow Q_0 through unit width of the slice is

$$Q_0 = C(2gH)^{\frac{1}{2}} \tag{2.1}$$

where C is the effective slice jet thickness and H is the total head over the slice: this is

$$H = L + P - P_0 \tag{2.2}$$

where L is the stock level above the slice, and P, P_0 are the absolute pressures (expressed as equivalent head of stock) of air in the box and outside: P_0 is assumed constant. The air in the box obeys the equation

$$PV = MRT/M_w \tag{2.3}$$

where V is the air volume per unit width, M is the mass of air per unit width, T is the air temperature which is assumed constant, R is the gas constant and M_w is the molecular weight for air. The accumulation of stock and of air within the box are described by the differential equations

$$A\frac{dL}{dt} = Q_1 - Q_0 \qquad (2.4)$$

$$\frac{dM}{dt} = F_1 - F_0 \qquad (2.5)$$

where A is the stock surface area per unit width, Q_1 and Q_0 are the flows of stock per unit width into and out of the box, and F_1, F_0 are the mass flows of air per unit width into and out of the box.

These equations are now linearized by writing $Q_1 + q_1$ in place of Q_1, and similarly for the other variables, and then neglecting products of small quantities. We thus obtain from (2.1)

$$Q_0 + q_0 = C(2gH)^{\frac{1}{2}}\left(1 + \frac{h}{H}\right)^{\frac{1}{2}} \qquad (2.6)$$

$$\doteqdot Q_0\left(1 + \frac{h}{2H}\right) \qquad (2.7)$$

$$q_0 \doteqdot \frac{Q_0}{2H}h \qquad (2.8)$$

In a similar way (2.3), (2.4) and (2.5) lead to the linearized equations

$$h = l + p \qquad (2.9)$$

$$Vp - APl = \frac{RT}{M_w}m \qquad (2.10)$$

$$A\frac{dl}{dt} = q_1 - q_0 \qquad (2.11)$$

$$\frac{dm}{dt} = f_1 - f_0 = f_1 - kp \qquad (2.12)$$

where in (2.10) we have used $v = -Al$, and in (2.12) we have assumed f_1 to be the manipulated flow into the box and f_0 to depend on p.

EXERCISE 2.1.   Find an expression from which k may be calculated. [Air flows out of the box through an orifice having a pressure ratio less than 2, whence

$$F_0 = \alpha \left[\frac{2g(P-P_0)}{\gamma} \right]^{\frac{1}{2}}$$

where α is a constant and γ is the air density, which is proportional to P. Hence

$$F_0 = \beta\sqrt{(1-P_0/P)}$$

where β is another constant, which can be evaluated from the steady-state values of F_0, P_0 and P. Now find $\partial F/\partial P$.]

Equations (2.8) to (2.12) illustrate the comments in Section 1 of Chapter 1. They are not in state-space form, and even in this very simple example some thought is needed to bring them into that form. On the other hand it is easy to write down a polynomial system matrix. We note that the system variables are q_0, h, l, p, m, and that the input and output vectors are

$$u = \begin{bmatrix} u_1 \\ u_2 \end{bmatrix} = \begin{bmatrix} q_1/Q_0 \\ f_1/F_1 \end{bmatrix}, \qquad y = \begin{bmatrix} y_1 \\ y_2 \end{bmatrix} = \begin{bmatrix} q_0/Q_0 \\ l/L \end{bmatrix} \qquad (2.13)$$

which for convenience have been made dimensionless. Then after taking Laplace transforms with zero initial conditions we may write (2.8) to (2.13) in the single equation

$$\left[\begin{array}{ccccc|cc} 1 & -Q_0/2H & 0 & 0 & 0 & 0 & 0 \\ 0 & 1 & -1 & -1 & 0 & 0 & 0 \\ 0 & 0 & -AP & V & -RT/M_w & 0 & 0 \\ 1 & 0 & As & 0 & 0 & Q_0 & 0 \\ 0 & 0 & 0 & k & s & 0 & F_1 \\ \hline -1/Q_0 & 0 & 0 & 0 & 0 & 0 & 0 \\ 0 & 0 & -1/L & 0 & 0 & 0 & 0 \end{array} \right] \begin{bmatrix} q_0 \\ h \\ l \\ p \\ m \\ \hline -u_1 \\ -u_2 \end{bmatrix} = \begin{bmatrix} 0 \\ 0 \\ 0 \\ 0 \\ 0 \\ \hline -y_1 \\ -y_2 \end{bmatrix} \qquad (2.14)$$

Because of the form of the vectors, we see from Section 2.1 of Chapter 1 that the matrix in (2.14) is a polynomial system matrix for the flowbox. No thought is needed to write down the system matrix, and if desired it can now be manipulated by strict system equivalence to give state-space equations. These manipulations can in fact be done in a routine way in a computer. So also can the manipulations which give $G(s)$ or $\hat{G}(s)$: these can be obtained directly from (2.14) without putting the equations into state-space form.

To obtain $\hat{G}(s)$ by hand, the easiest procedure is to simplify the system matrix $P(s)$ in (2.14) by means of the elementary operations permitted under strict system equivalence (Chapter 1, Section 4). By row operations we bring

$P(s)$ as near as we can to upper triangular form, the successive stages being

$$\left[\begin{array}{ccccc|cc} 1 & -Q_0/2H & 0 & 0 & 0 & 0 & 0 \\ 0 & 1 & -1 & -1 & 0 & 0 & 0 \\ 0 & 0 & -AP & V & -RT/M_w & 0 & 0 \\ 0 & Q_0/2H & As & 0 & 0 & Q_0 & 0 \\ 0 & 0 & 0 & k & s & 0 & F_1 \\ \hline 0 & -1/2H & 0 & 0 & 0 & 0 & 0 \\ 0 & 0 & -1/L & 0 & 0 & 0 & 0 \end{array}\right] \quad (2.15)$$

$$\left[\begin{array}{ccccc|cc} 1 & -Q_0/2H & 0 & 0 & 0 & 0 & 0 \\ 0 & 1 & -1 & -1 & 0 & 0 & 0 \\ 0 & 0 & -AP & V & -RT/M_w & 0 & 0 \\ 0 & 0 & As+Q_0/2H & Q_0/2H & 0 & Q_0 & 0 \\ 0 & 0 & 0 & k & s & 0 & F_1 \\ \hline 0 & 0 & -1/H & -1/2H & 0 & 0 & 0 \\ 0 & 0 & -1/L & 0 & 0 & 0 & 0 \end{array}\right] \quad (2.16)$$

$$\left[\begin{array}{ccccc|cc} 1 & -Q_0/2H & 0 & 0 & 0 & 0 & 0 \\ 0 & 1 & -1 & -1 & 0 & 0 & 0 \\ 0 & 0 & -AP & V & -RT/M_w & 0 & 0 \\ 0 & 0 & 0 & \dfrac{Q_0(AP+V)+2HVAs}{2HAP} & \dfrac{-RT(As+Q_0/2H)}{APM_w} & Q_0 & 0 \\ 0 & 0 & 0 & k & s & 0 & F_1 \\ \hline 0 & 0 & 0 & \dfrac{-(AP+V)}{2HAP} & \dfrac{RT}{2HAPM_w} & 0 & 0 \\ 0 & 0 & 0 & \dfrac{-V}{APL} & \dfrac{RT}{APM_wL} & 0 & 0 \end{array}\right]$$

$$(2.17)$$

Now it is easy to obtain $\hat{G}(s)$ from equation (2.11) of Chapter 1,

$$\hat{G}(s) = \begin{bmatrix} 1 & \dfrac{AL}{Q_0} s \\[3mm] \dfrac{2Hk}{F_1} + \dfrac{2HVM_w}{F_1\,RT} s & -\dfrac{Lk}{F_1} - \dfrac{(AP+V)M_w L}{F_1\,RT} s \end{bmatrix} \tag{2.18}$$

$$= \begin{bmatrix} 1 & N_1\,s \\[2mm] N_2 + N_3\,s & -(N_4 + N_5\,s) \end{bmatrix} \tag{2.19}$$

Premultiplication of $\hat{G}(s)$ by $\hat{K} = G(0) = \hat{G}^{-1}(0)$ will give a matrix $\hat{Q}(s)$ which is diagonal when $s = 0$,

$$\hat{Q}_1(s) = \begin{bmatrix} 1 & 0 \\[2mm] \dfrac{N_2}{N_4} & \dfrac{-1}{N_4} \end{bmatrix} \hat{G}(s) \tag{2.20}$$

$$= \begin{bmatrix} 1 & N_1\,s \\[2mm] -\dfrac{N_3}{N_4} s & 1 + \dfrac{N_1 N_2 + N_5}{N_4} s \end{bmatrix} \tag{2.21}$$

Johnston [1969] who obtained this result, remarks that N_3 is generally less than $N_1 N_2 + N_5$, so that the second row satisfies the condition for dominance. Notice that this conclusion depends on the choice of y and u. If these had been chosen with different scaling factors (e.g. $y_1 = q_0/2Q_0$), or had not been made dimensionless, the entries in $\hat{G}$ would have been changed in value. However, it is easy to see from the relation $u = \hat{G}y$ that a change in the units used to measure y_1 (for example) corresponds to multiplying the first column of $\hat{G}$ by a constant. This can be done by means of an appropriate diagonal matrix $\hat{L}$, which, if the feedback matrix F is also diagonal, can later be moved round the loop. We conclude that any change of units needed to agree with Johnston's analysis can be produced by diagonal matrices $\hat{K}$, $\hat{L}$, which do not essentially change the solution obtained.

To improve the first row, Johnston suggests that a multiple, by $N_1 N_4/(N_1 N_2 + N_5)$, of the second row should be subtracted from the first.

This gives

$$\hat{Q}_2(s) = \begin{bmatrix} 1 + \dfrac{N_1\,N_3}{N_1\,N_2 + N_5}\,s & -\dfrac{N_1\,N_4}{N_1\,N_2 + N_5} \\[3ex] -\dfrac{N_3}{N_4}\,s & 1 + \dfrac{N_1\,N_2 + N_5}{N_4}\,s \end{bmatrix} \tag{2.22}$$

and the first row satisfies the dominance criterion if $N_1\,N_4 < N_1\,N_2 + N_5$.

Mardon *et al* [1966] give data for a flowbox which is 13 ft wide, 2·63 ft high, and 6·7 ft along the axis of the machine. Their data can be converted into the present notation to give

$$Q_0 = 0\cdot84 \ \text{ft}^3/\text{sec ft.}$$
$$H = 5\cdot7 \ \text{ft.}$$
$$A = 6\cdot7 \ \text{ft}^2 \ \text{per ft.}$$
$$P = 38\cdot2 \ \text{ft head.}$$
$$P_0 = 34 \ \text{ft head.}$$
$$V = 7\cdot6 \ \text{ft}^3 \ \text{per ft.}$$
$$R/M_w = 0\cdot82 \ \text{ft head ft}^3/\text{lb} \ °\text{R.}$$
$$T = 550°\text{R.}$$
$$k = 1\cdot35 \times 10^{-4} \ \text{lb/sec ft head per foot.}$$
$$F_1 = 1\cdot28 \times 10^{-3} \ \text{lb/sec per foot.}$$
$$L = 1\cdot5 \ \text{ft.}$$

EXERCISE 2.2.   Verify the value given for R/M_w. [One cubic foot of air at 1 atmosphere and 0°C weighs 0·0807 lb. Convert pressure to ft head of water and temperature to °R and evaluate R/M_w from $PV = MT(R/M_w)$.]

Using the above values we obtain

$$N_1 = 12$$
$$N_2 = 1\cdot2$$
$$N_3 = 150$$
$$N_4 = 0\cdot158$$
$$N_5 = 730$$

whence

$$\hat{G}(s) = \begin{bmatrix} 1 & 12s \\[1ex] 1\cdot2 + 150s & -(0\cdot158 + 730s) \end{bmatrix} \tag{2.23}$$

$$\hat{Q}_1(s) = \begin{bmatrix} 1 & 12s \\[1ex] -950s & 1 + 4700s \end{bmatrix} \tag{2.24}$$

$$\hat{Q}_2(s) = \begin{bmatrix} 1+2\cdot42s & -0\cdot0025 \\ -950s & 1+4700s \end{bmatrix} \tag{2.25}$$

This has a satisfactory degree of dominance in the second row, while interaction in the first row is negligible.

EXERCISE 2.3. Convert the data given above into *MKS* units. Does this change $\hat{Q}_2$?

The above analysis is interesting for several reasons. It was the first application of diagonal dominance, and was carried out without the use of a computer. This is possible because the plant model is particularly simple. For the same reason the effect of the design parameters upon interaction can be seen directly from equation (2.22).

However, the form of (2.25) indicates that we should proceed with some caution. The zeros of $|\hat{Q}_2(s)|$ are the poles of the transfer function matrix, and as the system has least order they are the poles of the open-loop system. Because $\hat{Q}_2$ is nearly triangular these poles are very nearly $-1/4700$ and $-1/2\cdot42$. Notice that these cannot be associated individually with the specific physical mechanisms upon which the model was based. They can however be associated with modes of the system.

The pole at $-1/4700$ indicates a time constant of $1\cdot3$ hr, for which the assumptions of the analysis are likely to be valid. The other pole, indicating a time constant of $2\cdot42$ sec, must however be suspect. In deriving the model we assumed isothermal compression of the air, and we neglected the inertia of the water and also the time-constant associated with the control valves. Attention to these factors will modify the existing poles, particularly the one at $-1/2\cdot42$. It will also introduce further poles into the model, some of which will probably have modulus comparable to $1/2\cdot42$. For example if no special precautions are taken a pneumatic control valve may have a time constant of 1 or 2 sec. These factors will also change $\hat{G}$ and will affect the interaction. Our conclusion must be that the elementary model given above needs to be extended if it is to give a true indication of the dynamic behaviour of the system.

3. Boiler furnace

This problem arose in the control of the furnace of a boiler. Four sets of heating coils were enclosed in a common furnace enclosure, and four sets of burners were inserted into the furnace. Each set of burners was directed at one of the sets of heating coils, but heat naturally spilled over to adjacent coils. Fig. 4.2 shows a sketch of the system, which was symmetrical.

N

In the plant as built, the outlet temperature of each of the heating coils was measured, and the heat input to each set of burners was manipulated. This gave a four-input four-output system. When the plant was designed, experience with a previous boiler led to the conclusion that interaction would

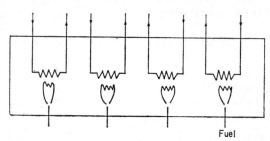

FIG. 4.2.   Diagrammatic sketch of boiler furnace.

prevent stable control with four independent loops. Accordingly one measured temperature was used to control all four sets of burners. Manual trims were provided for three of the sets of burners, and the operator used these, as best he could, to control the three remaining temperatures. With this arrangement control was poor, and an investigation was begun in order to improve it.

With such a system, the easiest test signal to inject is a step. Step responses were obtained, and for economy only those responses were measured which were expected to be different. That is, it was assumed that the geometric symmetry of the system would be reflected in corresponding symmetry properties of $G(s)$. By this assumption the number of paths for which step responses had to be measured was reduced from 16 to 8, the explicit relations which were assumed being

$$\left.\begin{aligned}
g_{11} &= g_{44} \\
g_{22} &= g_{33} \\
g_{12} &= g_{43} \\
g_{13} &= g_{42} \\
g_{14} &= g_{41} \\
g_{21} &= g_{34} \\
g_{23} &= g_{32} \\
g_{24} &= g_{31}
\end{aligned}\right\} \qquad (3.1)$$

Some of the step responses were measured for positive- and negative-going steps, and for different operating conditions. Examination of these showed obvious nonlinearity, both the gain and response-time varying by up to 2:1. Mid-range responses were chosen, and were fitted by first-order transfer functions. In this way the elements of $G(s)$ were found, and the result was

$$G(s) = \begin{bmatrix} \dfrac{1\cdot0}{1+4s} & \dfrac{0\cdot7}{1+5s} & \dfrac{0\cdot3}{1+5s} & \dfrac{0\cdot2}{1+5s} \\[2ex] \dfrac{0\cdot6}{1+5s} & \dfrac{1\cdot0}{1+4s} & \dfrac{0\cdot4}{1+5s} & \dfrac{0\cdot35}{1+5s} \\[2ex] \dfrac{0\cdot35}{1+5s} & \dfrac{0\cdot4}{1+5s} & \dfrac{1\cdot0}{1+4s} & \dfrac{0\cdot6}{1+5s} \\[2ex] \dfrac{0\cdot2}{1+5s} & \dfrac{0\cdot3}{1+5s} & \dfrac{0\cdot7}{1+5s} & \dfrac{1\cdot0}{1+4s} \end{bmatrix} \qquad (3.2)$$

No great accuracy was justified in view of the nonlinearity, and the values shown are drastically rounded. Some comments on this point will be made later.

The interaction shown by (3.2) is obviously large; $G(s)$ is by no means dominant on the imaginary axis as is shown by Fig. 4.3. Here the Gershgorin bands are based on rows, but the situation for columns is similar. Nevertheless, when $\hat{G}(s)$ is evaluated on the imaginary axis it is found as in Fig. 4.4 that a fairly high degree of dominance exists: this illustrates a remark in Section 6.3 of Chapter 3. Not only is $\hat{G}(s)$ dominant, for s on the imaginary axis, but the dominance can be readily improved. This system was in fact considered in Example 7.3 of Chapter 3, and Fig. 3.20 shows the result of pseudo-diagonalizing at $\omega = 0\cdot9$. In view of the uncertainties in $G(s)$, the resulting $\hat{Q}(s)$ may be regarded for practical purposes as diagonal. There would certainly be no point at all in going further and applying, for example, the methods of noninteracting control [see the references in the Appendix for Chapter 3, Section 4] which seek to make $Q(s)$ exactly diagonal.

At this point the situation was as follows. On the basis of a somewhat doubtful model the uncompensated system has the inverse Nyquist array shown in Fig. 4.4. The plant is known by observation to be open-loop stable, and Fig. 4.4 shows that four independent loops can be closed around the plant, without difficulties arising from interaction. Indeed, the figure indicates that stability will be retained for large gains, though the model is not sufficiently reliable at high frequencies to indicate just how high the gains may be made. This is because no attempt was made to carry the model beyond a first-order approximation.

If the input steps from which $G(s)$ was obtained had been small enough, this result would at least prove that we should have asymptotic stability in some neighbourhood of the state corresponding to the chosen operating condition. In fact the inputs were not small, because this would have introduced difficulties in measurement and would have required more effort and expense. Nevertheless, as the size of the input step is changed, we expect the frequency response fitted to the output to change continuously. In the same way, we expect the frequency response to change continuously as the operating condition of the plant is changed.

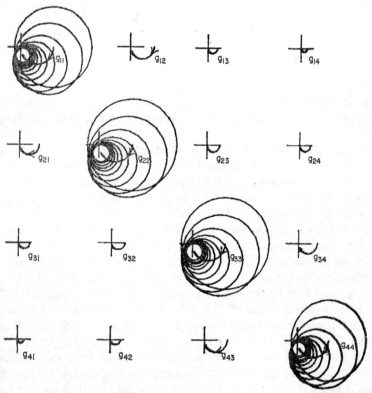

FIG. 4.3. Nyquist array and Gershgorin row bands corresponding to $G(s)$ in equation (3.2), with $0 \leqslant \omega \leqslant 1$.

Continuous changes starting from the situation shown in Fig. 4.4 might fairly rapidly lead to a non-dominant system. Similar continuous changes starting from Fig. 3.20 should permit us to retain dominance over a wider range. There is of course no certainty in such arguments, but there is some degree of probability.

Further analysis in such a situation is not very profitable. Even if we had a nonlinear model, it is unlikely that the nonlinearities would be of such a kind that we could apply the circle criteria of Chapter 3, Section 10.2. Simulation would then be the only way of proceeding. This would still be subject to uncertainties arising from inaccuracies in the model.

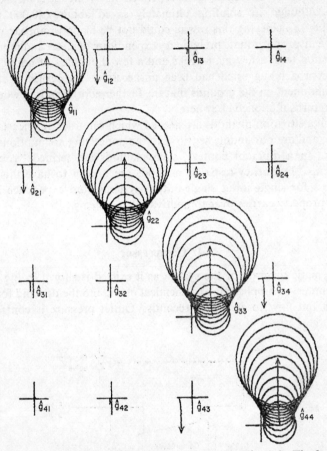

FIG. 4.4.   Inverse Nyquist array for the same plant as in Fig. 4.3. The frequencies run from $\omega = 0$ to $\omega = 1$.

Accordingly it was recommended that four independent control loops should be set up on the plant. If these proved unsatisfactory, then the multivariable compensator obtained in Example 7.3 of Chapter 3 should be tried. Some expense was involved in each of the steps, but enough confidence was felt as a result of the above work to justify this expenditure.

During the next routine shutdown of the plant, four independent control loops were installed. These were put onto automatic control without difficulty, and control was good. The multivariable compensator was therefore not required.

This example illustrates a common practical situation. No very large amount of effort or money could be expended on solving the control difficulty, because although its solution ultimately saved about £40,000 p.a., the probability of achieving this saving could not be made to appear very high without a disproportionate preliminary expenditure of effort and money. The investigation took a few man-weeks and a few thousands of pounds. If the simple approach suggested had been unsuccessful, the project would have been abandoned, on the grounds that the further effort required would bring greater returns if applied elsewhere.

In such a situation methods are needed which can tolerate uncertainties in the data, and are not unduly sensitive to the underlying assumptions such as linearity. In a different context, such methods are termed "robust" by statisticians. Frequency-response methods are known to have this kind of robustness for single-input single-output systems, and experience indicates that the property carries over to multivariable systems.

4. Compressor

A schematic diagram of the system as it existed is shown in Fig. 4.5. A large compressor supplies air to a chemical plant, and the demand for air can fall from full flow to zero in 8 seconds. Outlet pressure is controlled by

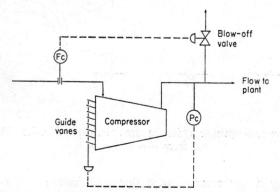

FIG. 4.5. Schematic diagram of industrial compressor.

manipulating the guide vanes of the compressor. To prevent surge, a blow-off valve is opened when the flow at the inlet drops below 20% of full flow.

With the blow-off valve closed, we have a single-input single-output closed-loop control system. In this configuration the system could be set to give good control, using a standard pneumatic controller. When the blow-off valve opens, the system has two inputs (guide-vane signal u_1 and blow-off valve signal u_2) and two outputs (pressure y_1 and flow y_2). This multivariable system went unstable as the gains in the two loops were increased, and useful gains could not be achieved, in both loops simultaneously, without instability.

Sinusoidal disturbances were injected into the two inputs, and the frequency-responses were measured through all four paths with the blow-off valve open. These were fitted by transfer-functions, using an on-line version of Levy's method with graphic display. In order to avoid complicated rational functions, the transfer functions of the paths were allowed to have time delays. The resulting transfer function matrix was

$$G(s) = \begin{bmatrix} \dfrac{0 \cdot 1133 e^{-0 \cdot 715s}}{1 \cdot 783 s^2 + 4 \cdot 48s + 1 \cdot 0} & \dfrac{0 \cdot 9222}{2 \cdot 071s + 1 \cdot 0} \\[4mm] \dfrac{0 \cdot 3378 e^{-0 \cdot 299s}}{0 \cdot 361 s^2 + 1 \cdot 09s + 1 \cdot 0} & \dfrac{-0 \cdot 321 e^{-0 \cdot 94s}}{0 \cdot 104 s^2 + 2 \cdot 463s + 1 \cdot 0} \end{bmatrix} \qquad (4.1)$$

The subsequent analysis could have been carried out using the measured frequency-responses, without fitting an expression such as (4.1). It would then have been necessary to interpolate, however, and we regard (4.1) simply as a way of summarizing the measurements and interpolating between them. Irrational entries in (4.1) do not mean that the plant necessarily had an irrational transfer function: they simply allow us to use more compact expressions. These remarks illustrate the discussion in Section 10 of Chapter 2.

EXERCISE 4.1. We might have used Padé approximations to the time delays in (4.1) in order to retain a rational $G(s)$. For example $e^{-0 \cdot 94s}$ could have been replaced by $(1 - 0 \cdot 47s)/(1 + 0 \cdot 47s)$. Show that without the discussion in Section 6.2 of Chapter 3 such expressions might give us considerable difficulty. [Compare Example 6.2 of Chapter 3.]

The inverse Nyquist array is shown in Fig. 4.6. Without plotting the Gershgorin circles it is already evident that $\hat{G}$ is not dominant. Indeed, in each row the off-diagonal element is larger than the element on the principal diagonal. This suggests that the loops should be crossed: y_2 to u_1 and y_1 to u_2. Pressure would then, however, be controlled by the blow-off valve, which would be effective but highly extravagant. Clearly it is uneconomic to have the blow-off valve open except when necessary to prevent surge. Such engineering considerations are easily taken into account by the present method, but are very difficult to include in more algorithmic approaches.

Our final system must behave in a satisfactory way both when the blow-off valve is open, when $G(s)$ in (4.1) applies, and also when the blow-off valve is closed. A linearized model in this last situation will have $\bar{u}_2 \equiv 0$. If, therefore we choose as our principal loops (Chapter 3, Section 2.1) those defined by $\bar{u}_1$ and $\bar{u}_2$, we can study the stability under both conditions simultaneously. When the blow-off valve is open, f_2 will have its design value.

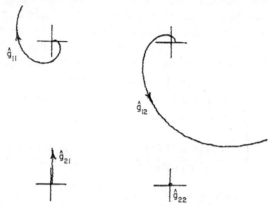

FIG. 4.6.   Inverse Nyquist array corresponding to equation (4.1), plotted for
$$0 \leqslant \omega \leqslant 10.$$

When the blow-off valve is closed, we simply put $f_2 = 0$. These considerations lead us to design an output compensator L, rather than an input compensator K, as shown in Fig. 4.7. In this figure the closed-loop inputs $\bar{w}_1$, $\bar{w}_2$ and outputs $\bar{z}_1, \bar{z}_2$ are the ones which will be implicit in our design procedure: that is, $H(s)$ will relate $\bar{z}$ to $\bar{w}$. However, when the design is complete we will move L round the loop.

We start the design of L by diagonalizing at zero frequency (compare Exercise 7.1 of Chapter 3). That is to say, we choose

$$\hat{L}_1 = G(0) = \begin{bmatrix} 0\cdot 113 & 0\cdot 9222 \\ 0\cdot 3378 & -0\cdot 321 \end{bmatrix} \tag{4.2}$$

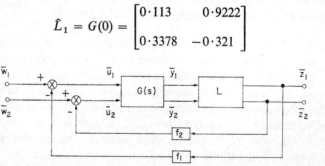

FIG. 4.7.   Block diagram of system considered in the design procedure for control
of an industrial compressor.

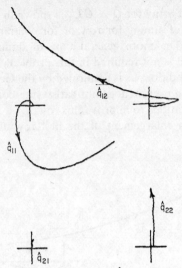

FIG. 4.8. Inverse Nyquist array for $\hat{Q} = \hat{G}\hat{L}_1$, with $\hat{G}$ obtained from (4.1) and $\hat{L}_1$ from (4.2). The frequency range is $0 \leqslant \omega \leqslant 10$.

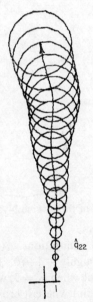

FIG. 4.9. Gershgorin row band for $\hat{q}_{22}$ in Fig. 4.8. The Gershgorin circles are at $\omega = 0\cdot 5, 1\cdot 0, ..., 10$.

The inverse Nyquist array for $\hat{Q} = \hat{G}\hat{L}_1$ is shown in Fig. 4.8. We have at this point the choice of aiming for row or for column dominance, and we choose the former. The more general type of dominance considered in Section 5 of Chapter 3 is not required in this problem. Row 2 already satisfies the dominance condition, as is confirmed by the Gershgorin band shown in Fig. 4.9. Row 1, however, does not satisfy the condition, and we shall carry out further operations to improve this row.

Fig. 4.10 shows an enlargement of the first row of the inverse Nyquist

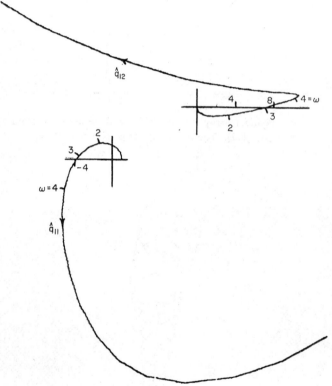

FIG. 4.10.   First row of the inverse Nyquist array in Fig. 4.8.

array, with further frequency calibrations. At $\omega = 3$ we notice that $\hat{q}_{12}$ is roughly $8 + i0$, while $\hat{q}_{11}$ is roughly $-4 + i0$. If we add $2\hat{q}_{11}$ to $\hat{q}_{12}$ we shall reduce the latter to a small value when $\omega = 3$, which will make the Gershgorin band for $\hat{q}_{11}$ narrow at the point where it crosses the negative real axis. As we shall use an output compensator to achieve this modification, we shall at the same time add $2\hat{q}_{21}$ to $\hat{q}_{22}$. Figure 4.8 shows that dominance of the second row will also be improved by this modification, the result of which is shown in Fig. 4.11. The expected effect has been achieved at $\omega = 3$, and because we have a great deal in hand in the second row, we may scale the second column by $0 \cdot 4$ to give Fig. 4.12. An enlargement of the Gershgorin band for $\hat{q}_{11}$ is shown in Fig. 4.13.

The open-loop plant was known by observation to be stable, so that $p_0 = 0$ in Theorem 5.3a of Chapter 3. If we make the Assumption 6.1 of Chapter 3, with $\omega_0 = 10$, we may conclude that the system is asymptotically

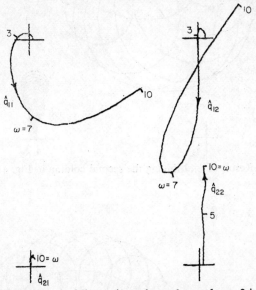

FIG. 4.11.   Result of adding twice column 1 to column 2 in Fig. 4.8.

stable for all gains in the first loop from 0 to at least $3 \cdot 5$, and for all positive gains in the second loop, in all combinations. Once again we remind the reader that a model which suggests that stability will be retained for arbitrarily high gains is obviously over-simplified. If we wished to use extremely large values of f_2, we should clearly have to extend the model and reconsider the value which we assumed for ω_0. Nevertheless we may expect to be able to use quite high values of gain in the second loop. This is particularly useful because the second loop must respond quickly to prevent surge when the demanded flow is falling.

EXERCISE 4.2.   Show that the assumption made above with $\omega_0 = 10$ implies that the Gershgorin band for $\hat{q}_{22}$ never crosses the negative real axis.

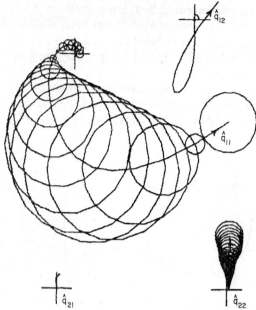

FIG. 4.12.   Result of multiplying the second column in Fig. 4.11 by 0·4.

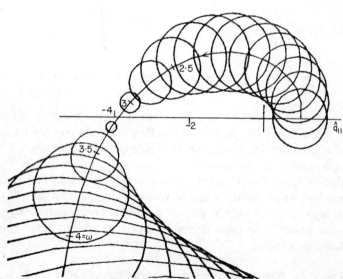

FIG. 4.13.   Gershgorin band for $\hat{q}_{11}$ in Fig. 4.12.

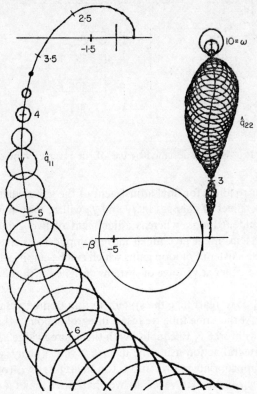

FIG. 4.14. Ostrowski row bands corresponding to Fig. 4.12. A critical disc has been added.

If we choose a gain of 5 in the second loop and a gain of $1 \cdot 5$ in the first loop, the Ostrowski bands are as shown in Fig. 4.14. The gain margin in the first loop is about $2 \cdot 6$. The corresponding value of $\hat{L}$ is readily found from

$$\hat{L} = \hat{L}_1 \hat{L}_2 \hat{L}_3 = \begin{bmatrix} 0 \cdot 113 & 0 \cdot 942 \\ 0 \cdot 338 & -0 \cdot 318 \end{bmatrix} \begin{bmatrix} 1 & 2 \\ 0 & 1 \end{bmatrix} \begin{bmatrix} 1 & 0 \\ 0 & 0 \cdot 4 \end{bmatrix} \quad (4.3)$$

where $\hat{L}_1$ was given above, $\hat{L}_2$ represents the addition of twice column 1 to column 2, and $\hat{L}_3$ represents the scaling of column 2. The resulting L is

$$L = \begin{bmatrix} -1 \cdot 016 & 3 \cdot 301 \\ 2 \cdot 427 & -0 \cdot 814 \end{bmatrix} \quad (4.4)$$

and the system is shown in Fig. 4.15.

The gains f_1 and f_2 could be assimilated in a single matrix FL, but it is

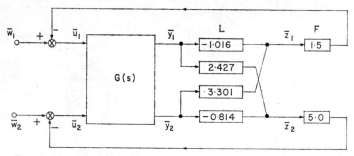

FIG. 4.15.   System designed by use of the inverse Nyquist array.

probably better to allow for final adjustment of the gains when the plant is in operation. The effect of changes in f_1 and f_2 will be very much as expected for two independent loops, whereas adjustment of two gains at a different point in the system might give much more complicated behaviour owing to interaction. The existence of loop gains which can be empirically adjusted in a simple way is a further advantage of systems designed with the aid of diagonal dominance.

The final step is to rearrange the system so that desired values of y_1 and y_2 can be put in. At the same time we insert integral action in the first loop at a point where it will force y_1 to equality with the desired value v_1. To study the effect of this integral action using the inverse Nyquist array, we should have to multiply an appropriate matrix into $\hat{G}$ (on the right) or $\hat{L}$ (on the left) since it occurs between them. However, as we shall later make a simulation, we may rely on the fact that if the integral action time is relatively long, it will not seriously affect the stability margin of the system. No integral action is used in the second loop, as the error in this loop is nonzero in normal operation and it is important to avoid integral saturation (Chapter 2, Section 6.2). The final system is shown in Fig. 4.16.

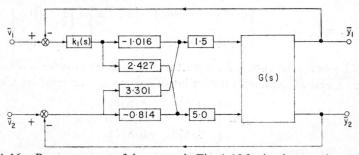

FIG. 4.16.   Rearrangement of the system in Fig. 4.15 for implementation. Integral action has been added in the pressure control loop by means of $k_1(s) = 1 + 1/sT_i$.

EXERCISE 4.3. Justify moving the sign changes in the feedback loops from their positions in Fig. 4.15 to those in Fig. 4.16. [Note that $-I$ commutes with any matrix.]

Up to this point we have adopted a simplified view of the system. We have assumed that the linearized behaviour expressed by $G(s)$ continues to hold in all operating conditions, and that the blow-off valve has one of two positions. In fact the blow-off valve in some operating conditions will open and close during the course of a transient response, so that the flow response will be nonlinear. For example, when the mean flow is about 20 % and the valve is on the point of opening, its flow characteristic will have the form sketched in Fig. 4.17.

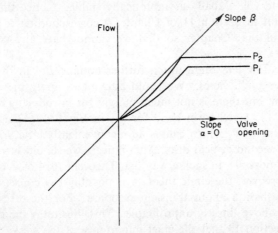

FIG. 4.17.   Form of the flow response of the blow-off valve when it is on the point of opening. Two characteristics are shown for pressures p_1 and $p_2 > p_1$.

This valve characteristic may be moved into the feedback path if we neglect any dynamic effects associated with the valve actuator. Notice that the flow through the valve depends not only on the signal to the valve, but also on the pressure, which is permitted by (10.2) in Chapter 3. The valve characteristic can be included in a sector between two lines with slopes $\alpha_2 = 0$ and a suitable $\beta_2 > 0$ as shown in Fig. 4.17. Theorem 10.3 of Chapter 3, as we have stated it, requires $\alpha_2 > 0$, but an inspection of the original paper [Rosenbrock, 1973b] will show that this condition can be relaxed when we are dealing with inverse Nyquist plots. The same is true for the single-loop theorem given in Section 11 of Chapter 2.

COMPUTER-AIDED CONTROL SYSTEM DESIGN

EXERCISE 4.4. Show that if the dynamics of the valve actuator cannot be ignored, they must be moved round the loop to the output of the plant, and this will modify the transfer function matrix in the forward path.

Assuming for the moment that there is no other nonlinearity in the system, we need only the single-loop version of the circle criterion, which was given in Section 11 of Chapter 3. Accordingly we may insert a critical disc in Fig. 4.14 as shown, with its diameter on the segment of the real axis from $-\alpha_2 = 0$ to $-\beta_2$. If $h_2(s)$ is the transfer function between input 2 and output 2 with the first loop closed, then $h_2^{-1}(i\omega)$ must avoid the critical disc. Since the graph of $h_2^{-1}(i\omega)$ is inside the Ostrowski band, this is clearly true. Provided that the map by $h_2^{-1}(s)$ of the semicircular arc of the contour D also avoids the critical disc we can use the circle theorem to conclude that the nonlinear system is globally asymptotically stable. Notice that we do not have any result in Section 11 of Chapter 2 corresponding to the result in Section 5.2 of that Chapter so that we cannot base any conclusion on $h_2^{-1}(i\omega)$ alone.

In the actual system there was a further nonlinearity in the mechanical linkage to the guide vanes. We could attempt to apply the multivariable circle theorem, but there is not much margin for introducing a critical disc which avoids the Gershgorin band for $\hat{q}_{11}$ in Fig. 4.13. This in turn will demand a value of θ_2 which causes an inconveniently large increase in the radius of the second critical disc. Alternatively we should have to redesign the system, if possible, in such a way that Theorem 10.4 of Chapter 3 could be used. Moreover, the circle theorem is possibly too conservative, and it gives no information about transient response. For these reasons further work on the above lines is unprofitable. This illustrates the conclusion in Chapter 3, Section 10 that the chief importance of the circle theorem is to show that the inverse Nyquist array is not unduly sensitive to nonlinear elements in the feedback paths.

At this stage, therefore, a full nonlinear simulation of the final system was made. This showed that the stability of the system, its speed of response, and the transient behaviour would all be satisfactory.

One final point should be made. During the design procedure we had before us a closed-loop inverse transfer function matrix $\hat{H}(s)$ for the linearized system, which we made to a considerable extent noninteracting. The corresponding $H(s)$ relates $\bar{z}_1$ and $\bar{z}_2$ to $\bar{w}_1$ and $\bar{w}_2$ in Fig. 4.15. The closed-loop transfer function relating $\bar{y}_1$ and $\bar{y}_2$ to $\bar{u}_1$ and $\bar{u}_2$ in Fig. 4.16 will be quite different. If we had been designing a servo system, with severe requirements on the closed-loop response, the procedure followed here might not have been suitable. What we have, however, is a regulator problem. The chief requirements are stability in all operating conditions, satisfactory pressure control without offset, and fast response of the blow-off valve. All three of these requirements were met.

5. Unstable batch process

This particular batch process was in operation, but its control was giving difficulty. It was a two-input two-output multivariable system, intended to stabilize the open-loop unstable plant. Operators complained of drift after several hours of operation.

The open-loop system, which was highly nonlinear, had been analysed theoretically to obtain a linearized model

$$
\left.\begin{array}{c}
\dot{x} = Ax + Bu \\
y = Cx
\end{array}\right\} \tag{5.1}
$$

with

$$
A = \begin{bmatrix}
1 \cdot 38 & -0 \cdot 2077 & 6 \cdot 715 & -5 \cdot 676 \\
-0 \cdot 5814 & -4 \cdot 29 & 0 & 0 \cdot 675 \\
1 \cdot 067 & 4 \cdot 273 & -6 \cdot 654 & 5 \cdot 893 \\
0 \cdot 048 & 4 \cdot 273 & 1 \cdot 343 & -2 \cdot 104
\end{bmatrix} \tag{5.2}
$$

$$
B = \begin{bmatrix}
0 & 0 \\
5 \cdot 679 & 0 \\
1.136 & -3 \cdot 146 \\
1 \cdot 136 & 0
\end{bmatrix} \tag{5.3}
$$

$$
C = \begin{bmatrix}
1 & 0 & 1 & -1 \\
0 & 1 & 0 & 0
\end{bmatrix} \tag{5.4}
$$

which lead to

$$
G(s) =
$$
$$
\begin{bmatrix}
29 \cdot 2s + 263 \cdot 3 & -(3 \cdot 146s^3 + 32 \cdot 67s^2 + 89 \cdot 93s + 31 \cdot 81) \\
5 \cdot 679s^3 + 42 \cdot 67s^2 - 68 \cdot 84s - 106 \cdot 8 & 9.43s + 15 \cdot 15
\end{bmatrix}
$$
$$
\div (s^4 + 11 \cdot 67s^3 + 15 \cdot 75s^2 - 88 \cdot 31s + 5 \cdot 514) \tag{5.5}
$$

The data have been transformed by a change of basis and of time scale. The matrix A has two eigenvalues with positive real part, and two with negative real part. The open loop system is therefore unstable, with $p_0 = 2$. It is also easy to show that the system has least order. Furthermore, $|G(s)|$

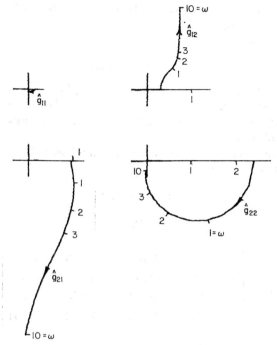

FIG. 4.18.   Inverse Nyquist array corresponding to $G(s)$ given by equation (5.5).

has no zero in the closed right half-plane, but has two poles there. Analysis of the existing control scheme showed that it placed three poles in the left half-plane, but one remained in the right half-plane close to the origin. The resulting instability, with a very long time-constant, was the cause of the difficulty in control. The operators were in fact endeavouring to stabilize an unstable system by manual adjustment.

Figure 4.18 shows the inverse Nyquist array corresponding to (5.5), which immediately suggests the input compensator

$$\hat{K} = \begin{bmatrix} 0 & -1 \\ 1 & 0 \end{bmatrix} \qquad (5.6)$$

This simply crosses over the two loops and reverses the sign of the gain in the (new) first loop. In contrast to the situation in Section 4, there was no engineering objection to this transposition. Then the array for $\hat{Q} = \hat{K}\hat{G}$ is shown in Fig. 4.19, together with the Gershgorin bands based on the rows. Dominance has been achieved in the second row, but not in the first for small gains. Moreover, $p_0 = 2$ whereas the sum of the encirclements of the origin

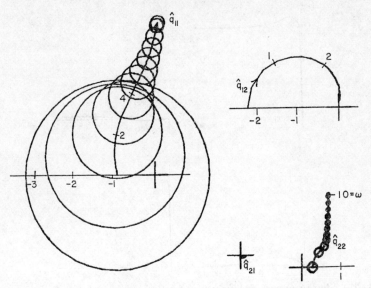

FIG. 4.19.   Compensated system obtained from Fig. 4.18, with Gershgorin bands.

shown by $\hat{q}_{11}$ and $\hat{q}_{22}$, when suitably completed, is only 1. We therefore know that open-loop dominance cannot be achieved, unless rather severe modifications are made so that $\hat{q}_{11}$ and $\hat{q}_{22}$ between them give two encircle-ments of the origin (Chapter 3, Corollary to Theorem 5.4).

Because of this last fact we do not attempt to achieve dominance for $f_1 = f_2 = 0$, but use the Corollary of Theorem 5.4, Chapter 3. We know from what was said above that $p_Q = 2$, $z_Q = 0$, and the condition for closed-loop asymptotic stability is

$$\sum_{i=1}^{2} \hat{N}_{hi} = p_Q - p_0 - z_Q = 0 \qquad (5.7)$$

This is satisfied for $f_1 > 3 \cdot 44$, $f_2 > 0$. Consequently we can stabilize the system by ensuring that f_1 is sufficiently large. Choosing $f_1 = 5$, $f_2 = 2$, and adding integral action in the two loops to eliminate offset, we obtain the step responses shown in Fig. 4.20. This control system was implemented on the plant and behaved in a satisfactory way, as predicted by the linear analysis.

The apparent triviality of this example is deceptive. The Company con-cerned had made a previous investigation using optimal control theory with a quadratic performance criterion. As only three independent physical measurements could be made, the performance criterion was varied until the coefficients relating to the fourth (physically impracticable) measurement were small. These coefficients were replaced by zero, and stability was

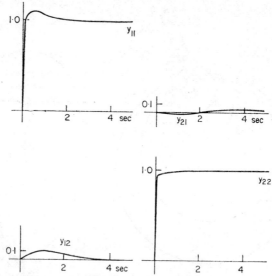

FIG. 4.20. Step-responses for system corresponding to Fig. 4.19, with $f_1 = 5$, $f_2 = 2$: y_{ij} is the response at output i to a unit step at input j. The time scale is correct for Fig. 4.19, but does not correspond to real time.

checked. This gave a stabilizing control, but it required a further instrument and a 3×2 matrix for feedback. As the control system was pneumatic these changes were not easy to implement. Furthermore, empirical attempts to stabilize the plant had been made by crossing the two loops, but an appropriate pair of gains to stabilize the plant had not been found. With an unstable plant having long time constants, it is not easy to explore the gain space experimentally.

Subsequent work showed that better speed of response could be achieved by adding one further nonzero element in K. This was not implemented, however, as control with the matrix given in (5.6) was found to be satisfactory. The contrast between algorithmic methods (such as optimal control, or pole assignment), and methods which allow the designer to choose a solution according to criteria such as simplicity of implementation will be clear from this example.

6. Comments on the examples

The preceding design examples show that satisfactory designs can be achieved by the methods we have described. Being design methods, rather than algorithmic methods adapted to synthesis, they allow the designer considerable freedom to include constraints (for example, efficiency in Section 4) or to pursue other requirements (simplicity of implementation, Sections 3, 5).

They also show that in every problem the performance criteria are likely to be different, and that these have an effect on the course of the design procedure.

Another point to be noted is that in practical applications we are always using our methods outside their area of mathematical validity. This is true, when a sufficiently detailed view is taken, of all design (or synthesis) methods, and indeed of all engineering, and good design methods should be tolerant of such discrepancies. The task of recognizing when discrepancies are likely to affect the conclusions is one of the chief responsibilities of the engineer.

In the above examples, nonlinearity of the plant was the major discrepancy, and incorrect representation of high-frequency behaviour was a second. It was known in each example that the nonlinearities were smooth and allowed a local linearization. In each case, a design based on the local linearization was found to be satisfactory. This is important, because the problem of accurately characterizing ("identifying") a nonlinear plant from measurements is probably insoluble in most industrial situations. The incorrect representation of high-frequency behaviour was recognized by our refusal to exploit the apparently unlimited gains permitted in some examples.

Besides the examples described, applications have been made to the following problems: Diesel-engine test-bed; Aircraft gas turbines; Turboprop engine; Aircraft lateral stability; Slender delta-wing aircraft autopilot; VSTOL aircraft autopilot; Gas generator sets; Marine boiler; Automotive gas turbine; Automotive diesel engine; Helicopter flight control; Mersey river barrage; Distillation columns; Power-station boiler; Rotary drier; Ammonia plant; Multiple-effect evaporator; Stirred tank reactor. Details of some of these designs have been published, and references are given in the Appendix.

7. Problems

(1) Examine the criteria which the multivariable control systems in Sections 2 to 5 had to satisfy. Which of these were peculiar to multivariable systems and which would also apply to single-input single-output systems? Which would be expected to apply to most multivariable systems, and which were special to the system considered?

(2) Include the dynamic behaviour of the two control valves in Section 2 and examine the effect on $\hat{G}$. [Replace G by GG_1, where

$$G_1(s) = \begin{bmatrix} \dfrac{1}{1+\alpha s} & 0 \\ 0 & \dfrac{1}{1+\beta s} \end{bmatrix} \tag{7.1}$$

represents the dynamic behaviour of the valves.]

(3) If $\hat{G}(s)$ is row dominant, and $\hat{K}(s)$ is a diagonal matrix, show that $\hat{Q}(s) = \hat{K}(s)\,\hat{G}(s)$ is also row dominant. Show on the other hand that if $\hat{H}(s) = F+\hat{G}(s)$ is row dominant it does not follow that $F+\hat{Q}(s)$ is row dominant.

(4) Illustrate Problem 4 by the example

$$\hat{G}(s) = \begin{bmatrix} 1+s & s \\ s & 1+s \end{bmatrix} \tag{7.2}$$

$$\hat{K}(s) = \begin{bmatrix} (1+s)^2 & 0 \\ 0 & 1 \end{bmatrix} \tag{7.3}$$

$$F = \begin{bmatrix} 8 & 0 \\ 0 & 1 \end{bmatrix} \tag{7.4}$$

(5) In the light of Problems 3 and 4, examine the effect of the valve dynamics in Problem 2 on the compensation needed. [Take for example $\alpha = 1$, $\beta = 1/2$, and use the numerical values given in (2.23).]

(6) In equation (4.3) of Chapter 1, let $M(s)$, $N(s)$, $X(s)$, $Y(s)$ be rational matrices. Show that $P(s)$ and $P_1(s)$ then give rise to the same transfer function matrix. [This transformation is a specialization of "system equivalence", SSMVT, Chapter 2, Section 3.3.]

(7) Show that the transformation defined in Problem 6 is generated by the following operations:

(i) Multiply any one of the first r rows (resp. columns) by a rational function, not identically zero.

(ii) Add a multiple, by a rational function, of any one of the first r rows (resp. columns) to any other row (resp. column).

(iii) Interchange any two among the first r rows (resp. columns).

(8) Show that by means of the row operations in Problem 7 all entries below the principal diagonal in the first r columns of $P(s)$ can be reduced to zero, so that $P(s)$ becomes a rational matrix

$$P_1(s) = \begin{bmatrix} T_1(s) & U_1(s) \\ 0 & W_1(s) \end{bmatrix} \tag{7.5}$$

with $T_1(s)$ upper triangular. Show that $W_1(s) = G(s)$, the transfer function matrix given by $P(s)$. [Note that $G_1 = 0.T_1^{-1}V_1 + W_1$ and use the result in Problem 6.]

(9) Apply the method suggested in Problem 8 to find $G(s)$ from (2.14).

(10) Try to invert the $G(s)$ given in (3.2) by hand calculation. [This is very tedious and liable to error. It illustrates the need for a computer.]

(11) Heat is supplied to a metal bar at one end and removed at the other. Divide the bar into isothermal blocks, with heat flow between them proportional to the temperature difference. Laplace transform with zero initial conditions and show that $sI-A$ is column dominant on the imaginary axis. [Compare Rosenbrock, 1962.]

(12) Show that if a plate-type distillation column distilling a binary mixture is modelled with the simplest possible assumptions, the resulting $sI-A$ is column dominant on the imaginary axis. [Compare Rosenbrock, 1962.]

(13) Let $sI-A$ be column dominant on the imaginary axis, as in Problems 11 and 12. Show that if we had $B = I$, $C = I$, then $\hat{G}(s)$ would be column dominant. [We never have $B = C = I$, but there may be some clue here to the tendency for $\hat{G}$ to be more dominant than G. Compare Section 3.]

(14) Examine the behaviour of

$$e^{-s\tau}, \quad \frac{1-s\tau/2}{1+s\tau/2}, \quad \frac{1}{(1+s\tau/10)^{10}} \tag{7.6}$$

(a) on the imaginary axis.
(b) on the positive real axis.
What do you conclude about the possibility of saying, from frequency-response tests, whether $\hat{G}(s)$ for a given plant is dominant on the semicircular arc of D?

(15) In Section 4, show that efficiency requires us to leave a signal path between pressure measurement and guide vanes. Is this the only requirement?

(16) Examine the problem which would arise if we used integral action in the flow control loop in Section 4.

(17) Would the problem in Section 5 have been easier to analyse if the time-constants had been shorter? (As an extreme example, consider a plant with an 8 hr unstable time constant under shift operation).

(18) Find an easy way of checking that the system (5.2) to (5.4) has least order. [Does the denominator in (5.5) vanish when $s = -263 \cdot 3/29 \cdot 2$? What do you conclude? Compare SSMVT, Chapter 3, Section 5.1.]

(19) The system (5.2) to (5.4) has least order, and has two poles in the closed right half-plane, and $|G(s)|$ has no zero in the closed right half-plane. Does it follow that $|G(s)|$ has two poles in the closed right half-plane? [No. Why?]

(20) From the facts given in Problem 19, does it follow that the McMillan form of $G(s)$ has two poles in the closed right half-plane? (Yes. Why?)

Appendix

Notes and references

Results used in the book have usually been derived in a systematic way on the basis described in Chapter 1. Where these results are not original, the derivation is therefore usually different from that first given. In such cases the relation to known results is given here. Where the results used are quoted in the form which will be found in the literature, references are usually given at the appropriate point in the text.

Chapter 1

Some references for this Chapter are given below: further references will be found in SSMVT.

Section 2. The terminology "strictly proper" differs from that ("proper") used in SSMVT. It now seems to be accepted terminology to use "strictly proper" in this way, while "proper" is used to mean that $G(s)$ tends to a finite limit as $s \to \infty$.

Section 3. The significance of the condition "T, V relatively (right) prime" has been made clearer by the work of Forney (1974, see also Rosenbrock, 1974a).

Section 3.1. For a concise statement of results concerning zeros of a system, see Rosenbrock (1973c). For the relationship with other definitions based on state-space methods, see Davison and Wang (1973).

The condition given at the end of this Section is due to Kalman, Ho and Narendra (1962). A treatment in terms of system matrices is given in SSMVT, Chapter 4, Section 2.

Section 4. The transformation of system similarity was extensively investigated by Kalman (1963a) under the name "algebraic equivalence". Strict system equivalence is due to Rosenbrock (1967a, b) and is related to Howitt transformations (Newcomb, 1966, p. 328).

The results concerning strict system equivalence in the last two paragraphs are due to Rosenbrock (1967b, SSMVT, Chapter 3, Section 3, respectively). The second generalizes a fundamental result proved by Ho and Kalman (1966) and by Youla and Tissi (1966).

Section 5. The algorithm for reduction to least order was first given in Rosenbrock (1968).

Section 6. If the system equations are not in the form (2.8), there are severe difficulties in the way of using the term "controllable (p.s.)", and it is better to use relative primeness as in Section 3. (See Rosenbrock, 1974a, 1974b, 1974c.)

Section 9. Theorem 9.4 forms the basis of the design method in Chapter 3, and is due to Rosenbrock (1969, 1970b). It is related to Rouché's theorem.

Chapter 2

Section 1.1.   For an account of the development of frequency-response design methods, see Bode (1960).

Section 4.   Theorems 4.1 and 4.2 are usually given only for systems of least order, but the restriction is quite unnecessary.

Section 5.   Theorem 5.1 is due to Nyquist (1932), but has been generalized to cover systems which do not have least order. As $q(s)$ depends only on the least-order part of the system giving rise to it, it may seem surprising that the stability of a system not having least order can be investigated by using the Nyquist plot of $q(s)$. The clue lies of course in the number p_0: only if the system has least order can p_0 be obtained from $q(s)$. Otherwise p_0 is obtained from the system equations, and it is here that we introduce knowledge of any system poles in the closed right half-plane, even if the corresponding modes are decoupled from input or output (Chapter 1, Section 3.2).

Section 5.2.   Theorem 5.3 is apparently new (but see Callier and Desoer, 1972) although it has been assumed implicitly by every designer who has used a Nyquist diagram. Similarly, Assumption 5.1 makes explicit something which all designers have tacitly accepted.

Example 5.5 was used by Luntz (1970) to disclose the difficulty mentioned here.

Section 6.   Graphical displays of Nyquist or root locus plots have been widely implemented. The displays presented here were obtained using part of a much larger suite of programmes available on a PDP-10 (see the notes on Chapter 4).

Section 8.   For an introduction to sensitivity analysis, see Tomović (1963).

Section 10.   Later work by Callier and Desoer (1972, 1973) allows the open-loop system to have poles in the closed right half-plane and extends the results to multi-variable systems.

Section 11.   Lur'e (1951) was concerned with nonlinear engineering systems, and solved a number of significant problems by using Laipunov's stability theory (Willems, 1970, Chapter 2, where further references are given). Intensive efforts were then devoted to finding Liapunov functions for general classes of nonlinear systems, but without any very notable success (see for example Letov, 1961). By quite different methods, Popov (1961) found a frequency-response criterion, and this rapidly led to a solution of the Liapunov problem (Yakubovich, 1962; Kalman, 1963b; see also Aizerman and Gantmacher, 1964). Popov's criterion is relatively awkward to use, and the less sharp but more convenient (and more general in that it applies also to time-dependent systems) circle criterion was obtained at about the same time by Sandberg (1964), Narendra and Goldwyn (1964) and others (see Brockett, 1970, p. 227). Theorems 11.1 and 11.2 go beyond the usual statements of the circle theorem in not requiring the linear system to have least order.

Section 11.1.   An introduction to the describing function is given by Ogata (1970). A more extended account will be found in Gelb and VanderVelde (1968).

Chapter 3

A simple account of the inverse Nyquist array method has been given by Munro (1972c).

Section 2.   The need for stability when one or more loops in the closed-loop system is opened was pointed out in Rosenbrock (1966). The idea of the gain space occurs briefly in Chen (1968) and was developed independently and more fully by MacFarlane (1970b). The examples shown in Figs. 4.4 and 4.5 were studied by Belletrutti (1972).

Section 3.   No complete account is given here of nonminimum phase effects in multivariable systems. The subject has not been intensively studied, but some information is given in Section 11, Problems 4 to 10, and in Rosenbrock (1966).

Section 3.1.   A simpler version of Lemma 3.1 was given by Popov (1964); also by Chen (1968) and Hsu and Chen (1968) who consider only systems of least order. Equation (3.45) is the formula usually quoted.

Section 3.2.   Theorem 3.2 was given by Rosenbrock (1972) and independently by Mayne (1973), who used it as the basis of a design procedure. The proof given here is due to Barnett (1972).

Section 4.   For accounts of "noninteracting control", in which Q and F are both made diagonal, see for example Tsien (1954), Kavanagh (1957), and Chatterjee (1960).

Section 5.   Diagonal dominance was introduced by Rosenbrock (1969, 1970b, 1971). Those accounts treat only the case $p_0 = 0$, the generalization to $p_0 > 0$ being given by McMorran (1970a).

Section 6.   Theorem 6.2 was rediscovered by Rosenbrock (1970a) and subsequently located in Ostrowski (1952) by A. Rowe. Its use for design purposes was introduced by Rosenbrock (1971).

The determination of stability margin as in Example 6.1 is due to Rosenbrock (unpublished). The result was subsequently obtained by Hawkins and McMorran (1971, 1973) using another result of Ostrowski's.

Section 7.1.   The result following eqn. (7.1) is due to Rosenbrock (1969). Without this result we could not be sure that elementary operations of the types described would be sufficient to obtain the most general controller in which we are interested.

Sections 7.2, 7.3.   The method embodied in (7.42) was suggested by Rosenbrock (1970c). Hawkins (1972) developed the other results in these Sections, implemented them on the computer, and applied them to a range of industrial problems. MacFarlane (private communication) arrived independently at (7.42) by quite different methods.

Section 7.4.   This technique was suggested by Rosenbrock (1971).

Section 8.   The treatment here is based on McMorran (1971): see also Cruz and Perkins (1964).

Section 9.   The problem of designing control systems for a nonsquare $G(s)$ is still an open one, requiring more work.

Theorem 9.1 was given by Rosenbrock (1973a). The method of proof given here is based on the treatment by Barnett (1972) of Theorem 3.2.

Section 10.   Theorems 10.1 and 10.3 were given by Rosenbrock (1973b) and were improved as in Theorems 10.2, 10.4 by Cook (1973b). As suggested in Exercise 10.3 and Problem 33, mean dominance is a further type of dominance which can be used in the earlier stability criteria. Its use has not so far been explored in practical problems.

The earlier paper by Freedman, Falb and Zames (1969) is also interesting but the version of the multivariable circle theorem given there is not well adapted to applications.

Problems.   Problem 2 gives a result obtained by Bristol (1966), Rosenbrock (1966) and, in a different form, by Mayne (1973). Problems 4 to 8 also relate to Rosenbrock (1966).

Problems 11 and 12 may be compared with Bristol (1966) where the numbers $g_{ii}(0) \hat{g}_{ii}(0)$ are proposed as measures of interaction.

Problems 15 to 17 contain the basis of an extensive development by MacFarlane (1970a, 1970c; MacFarlane and Rosenbrock, 1970; Belletrutti and MacFarlane,

1971; MacFarlane and Belletrutti, 1973). When $F = \alpha I$ and the eigenvalues λ_i or $\hat{\lambda}_i$ exist and have suitable properties it is easy to get the sufficiency part of Theorems 5.2a, 5.3a. The necessity part is more difficult, but has been studied (also for $F = \alpha I$) by Barman and Katzenelson (1973). The results obtained in this way fall short of what has been proved in Chapter 3: in particular the eigenvalues cannot in general be associated uniquely with the feedback loops, so that it is not possible to consider any feedback matrix other than $F = \alpha I$. It is an interesting open question whether the known results can be obtained from the theory of eigenvalues of a rational matrix, but Rosenbrock and Cook (1974) suggest that this is unlikely.

Problems 31 to 34 are based upon Cook (1973b).

Chapter 4

Section 2. Johnston (1969) was the first to apply the methods of Chapter 3 to a technical problem. At that time the method had not been implemented on the computer and calculations had to be made by hand. This limited the amount of detail which could be included in the model, and a more realistic model is being studied by Epton and Kirk (1973, private communication).

Section 3. The initial design work on this example was done by McLeod (1971) using data obtained by Luntz. The solution was later improved by Hawkins (1972) using his pseudo-diagonalization technique.

Section 4. The preliminary design work on this example was done by McLeod (1971), using data obtained by Luntz and in collaboration with Munro (Luntz *et al.*, 1971).

Section 5. For reasons of commercial security the matrices A, B, C have been transformed and time-scaling has been introduced. The design work was done by Munro with the assistance of McMorran and McLeod (Munro, 1972a).

Section 6. The further examples mentioned here have been described as follows.

Aircraft gas turbine: McMorran (1970b)
Automotive gas turbine: Winterbone *et al.*, (1973)
Distillation column: Munro and Ibrahim (1973).

The multivariable frequency response methods were first implemented on a PDP-10 computer, and these programmes are being rewritten (at the University of Connecticut, and at Sir George Williams University, Montreal) for the IBM 360 series and for the CDC 3300 series. Versions of the programme have been implemented independently on much smaller computers.

As implemented on the PDP-10 the inverse Nyquist array method forms part of an extensive suite of programmes which have been described by Luntz *et al.*, (1971) and Munro (1972b).

Problems. The fact mentioned in Problem 13 was noticed by Blumberg (1970) who based a design method on it.

References

Throughout the book, "SSMVT" is used to refer to "State-space and Multivariable Theory", Rosenbrock (1970b) (Nelson).

Ahlfors, L. V., (1966)   Complex Analysis (McGraw-Hill).
Aizerman, M. A. and Gantmacher, F. R., (1964)   Absolute Stability of Regulator Systems (Holden-Day).

Barman, J. F. and Katzenelson, J., (1973) University of California, Berkeley, Memorandum No. ERL-383.

Barnett, S., (1972) Comments on "The stability of multivariable systems", *Trans. IEEE*, AC-17, 745.

Belletrutti, J. J., (1972) Theory and design of multivariable feedback systems, Ph.D. Thesis, UMIST.

Belletrutti, J. J. and MacFarlane, A. G. J., (1971) Characteristic loci techniques in multivariable-control-system design, *Proc. I.E.E.*, 118, 1291–1297.

Blumberg, J. M., (1970) Modelling and control of the cement manufacturing process, Ph.D. Thesis, UMIST.

Bode, H. W., (1945) Network Analysis and Feedback Amplifier Design (van Nostrand).

Bode, H. W., (1960) Feedback—the history of an idea, Proc. Symposium on active networks and feedback systems, Polytechnic Institute of Brooklyn (Polytechnic Press). Reprinted in Selected papers on mathematical trends in control theory, 1964, (Ed. R. Bellman and R. Kalaba), pp. 106–123 (Dover).

Bristol, E. H., (1966) On a new measure of interaction for multivariable process control, *Trans. IEEE*, AC-11, 133–134.

Brockett, R. W., (1970) Finite Dimensional Linear Systems (Wiley).

Callier, F. M. and Desoer, C. A. (1972) A graphical test for checking the stability of a linear time-invariant feedback system, *Trans. IEEE*, AC-17, 773–780.

Callier, F. M. and Desoer, C. A., (1973) Necessary and sufficient conditions for stability, *Trans. IEEE*, AC-18, 295–298.

Chatterjee, H. K., (1960) Multivariable process control, Proc. 1st IFAC Congress, Moscow, Vol. 1, pp. 132–137 (Butterworths).

Chen, C-T, (1968) Stability of linear multivariable feedback systems, *Proc. IEEE*, 56, 821; 828.

Cook, P. A., (1973a) Describing function for a sector nonlinearity, *Proc. I.E.E.*, 120, 143–144.

Cook, P. A., (1973b) Modified multivariable circle theorems, *In* Recent Mathematical Developments in Control, (Ed. D. J. Bell), pp. 367–372 (Academic Press).

Cruz, J. B. and Perkins, W. R., (1964) A new approach to the sensitivity problem in multivariable feedback system design, *Trans. IEEE*, AC-9, 216–223.

Davison, E. J. and Wang, S. H., (1973) The numerical calculation and properties of transmission zeros of linear multivariable time-invariant systems, Univ. Toronto, Control System Report No. 7311.

Desoer, C. A. and Wu, M. Y., (1968) Stability of linear time-invariant systems, *Trans. IEEE*, CT-15, 245–250.

Epton, J. A. G. and Kirk, L. A., (1973) Private communication.

Forney, G. D., (1974) Minimal bases of rational vector spaces, with applications to multivariable linear systems. (To be published.)

Freedman, M. I., Falb, P. L. and Zames, G., (1969). A Hilbert space stability theory over locally compact Abelian groups, *J. SIAM Control*, 7, 479–495.

Gantmacher, F. R., (1959) Applications of the Theory of Matrices (Interscience).

Gelb, A. and VanderVelde, W. E., (1968) Multiple-input describing functions and nonlinear system design (McGraw-Hill).

Hawkins, D. J., (1972) "Pseudodiagonalization" and the inverse-Nyquist-array method, *Proc. I.E.E.*, 119, 337–342.

Hawkins, D. J. and McMorran, P. D., (1971) Diagonal dominance and the inverse Nyquist method, UMIST, CSC Report No. 159, July.

Hawkins, D. J. and McMorran, P. D., (1973)   Determination of stability regions with the inverse Nyquist array, *Proc. IEE*, **120**, pp. 1445–1448.

Ho, B. L. and Kalman, R. E., (1966)   Effective construction of linear state-variable models from input/output functions, *Regehengstechnik*, **14**, 545–548.

Hsu, C-H and Chen, C-T, (1968)   A proof of the stability of multivariable feedback systems, *Proc. IEEE*, **56**, 2061–2062.

Johnston, R. E., (1970)   Non-interacting control of pressurized flow boxes, in Papermaking systems and their control, (Ed. F. Bolam) (Trans. Symposium Brit. Paper and Board Mfrs. Assn., Oxford, 1969), Vol. 2, pp. 509–512.

Kalman, R. E., (1963a)   Mathematical description of linear dynamical systems, *J. SIAM Control*, ser. A, **1**, 152–192.

Kalman, R. E., (1963b)   Liapunov functions for the problem of Lur'e in automatic control, *Proc. Natn. Acad. Sci. U.S.A.*, **49**, 201–205.

Kalman, R. E., Ho, Y. C. and Narendra, K. S. (1963)   Controllability of linear dynamical systems, Contributions to the theory of differential equations, Vol. 1, pp. 189–213 (Interscience).

Kavanagh, R. J., (1957)   Noninteraction in linear multivariable systems, *Trans. A.I.E.E.*, part 2, **76**, 95–100.

Letov, A. M., (1961)   Stability in nonlinear control systems (Princeton University Press).

Lighthill, J. and Mees, A., (1973)   Stability of nonlinear feedback systems, *in* Recent mathematical developments in control, (Ed. D. J. Bell), pp. 1–19 (Academic Press).

Luntz, R. M., (1970)   Approximate transfer functions for multivariable systems, *Electron. Lett.*, **6**, 444–445.

Luntz, R., Munro, N. and McLeod, R. S., (1971)   Computer-aided-design of multivariable control systems, I.E.E. 4th UKAC Convention, Manchester, pp. 59–65.

Lur'e, A. I., (1951)   Some nonlinear problems in the theory of automatic control, Translation published 1957 by H.M.S.O. (London).

Mardon, J., Monahan, R. E., Mehaffey, W. H. and Dahlin, E. B., (1966)   A theoretical and experimental investigation into the stability and control of paper machine headboxes. *Paperi ja Puu*, **48**, 3–14; 301–310. Also **49**, 189–197.

Munro, N., (1972a)   Design of controllers for open-loop unstable multivarable system using inverse Nyquist array, *Proc. I.E.E.*, **119**, 1377–1382.

Munro, N., (1972b)   Conversational mode C.A.D. of control systems using display terminals, I.E.E. International Conference on Computer Aided Design, Southampton, pp. 418–431.

Munro, N., (1972c)   Multivariable systems design using the inverse Nyquist array, Computer Aided Design, Vol. 4, pp. 222–227.

Munro, N. and Ibrahim, A., (1973)   Computer aided design and multivariable sampled-data systems, I.E.E. Conference on Computer Aided Control System Design, Cambridge, pp. 133–148.

MacFarlane, A. G. J., (1970a)   Commutative controller: a new technique for the design of multivariable systems, *Electron. Lett.* **6**, 121–123.

MacFarlane, A. G. J., (1970b)   Multivariable-control-system design techniques: a guided tour, *Proc. I.E.E.*, **117**, 1039–1047.

MacFarlane, A. G. J., (1970c)   Return-difference and return-ratio matrices and their use in analysis and design of multivarable feedback control systems, *Proc. I.E.E.*, **117**, 2037–2049.

MacFarlane, A. G. J. and Belletrutti, J. J., (1973)   The characteristic locus design method, *Automatica*, **9**, 575–588.

MacFarlane, A. G. J. and Rosenbrock, H. H., (1970)   New vector-space structure for dynamical systems, *Electron. Lett.*, **6**, 162–163.

McLeod, R. S., (1971)   The computer-aided design of multivarable control systems, Ph.D. Thesis, UMIST.

McMorran, P. D., (1970a)   Extension of the inverse Nyquist method, *Electron. Lett.*, Vol. 6, pp. 800–801.

McMorran, P. D., (1970b)   Design of gas-turbine controller using inverse Nyquist method, *Proc. I.E.E.*, **117**, 2050–2056.

McMorran, P. D., (1971)   Parameter sensitivity and inverse Nyquist method, *Proc. I.E.E.*, **118**, 802–804.

Mayne, (1973)   Design of linear multivariable systems, *Automatica*, **9**, pp. 201–207.

Newcomb, R. W., (1966)   Linear multiport synthesis (McGraw-Hill).

Nyquist, H., (1932)   Regeneration theory, Bell System Tech. J., Vol. 11, pp. 126–147. Reprinted in Selected papers on mathematical trends in control theory, 1964, (Eds. R. Bellman and R. Kalaba), pp. 83–105 (Dover).

Ogata, K., (1970)   Modern control engineering, Chapter 11 (Prentice-Hall).

Ostrowski, A. M., (1952)   Note on bounds for determinants with dominant principal diagonal, *Proc. Am. Math. Soc.*, **3**, 26–30.

Popov, V. M., (1961)   Absolute stability of nonlinear systems of automatic control, *Automation and Remote Control*, **22**, 857–875.

Popov, V. M., (1964)   Hyperstability and optimality of automatic systems with several control functions, *Rev. Roum. Sci. Tech., Electrotechn. Energ.*, **9**, 629–690.

Rosenbrock, H. H., (1962)   A Lyapunov function with applications to some nonlinear physical systems, *Automatica*, **1**, 31–53.

Rosenbrock, H. H., (1966)   On the design of linear multivariable control systems, Proc. 3rd IFAC Congress, London, Vol. 1, Book 1, Paper 1A (Instn. Mech. Engrs., London).

Rosenbrock, H. H., (1967a)   Transformation of linear constant system equations, *Proc. I.E.E.*, **114**, 541–544.

Rosenbrock, H. H., (1967b)   On linear system theory, *Proc. I.E.E.*, **114**, 1353–1359.

Rosenbrock, H. H., (1968)   Computation of minimal representations of a rational transfer-function matrix, *Proc. I.E.E.*, **115**, 325–327.

Rosenbrock, H. H., (1969)   Design of multivariable control systems using the inverse Nyquist array, *Proc. I.E.E.*, **116**, 1929–1936.

Rosenbrock, H. H., (1970a)   Two theorems concerning the inverse Nyquist array, UMIST., CSC Report No. 90, (unpublished).

Rosenbrock, H. H., (1970b)   State-space and multivariable theory (Nelson).

Rosenbrock, H. H., (1970c)   Research note on the achievement of diagonal dominance, UMIST Control Systems Centre Report No. 116.

Rosenbrock, H. H., (1971)   Progress in the design of multivariable control systems, *Measurement and Control*, **4**, 9–11.

Rosenbrock, H. H., (1972)   The stability of multivariable systems, *Trans. I.E.E.E.* AC-17, 105–107.

Rosenbrock, H. H., (1973a)   Bounds for transfer functions in multivarable systems, *Trans. I.E.E.E.*, **AC-18**, 54–56.

Rosenbrock, H. H., (1973b)   Multivariable circle theorems, in Recent mathematical developments in control, (Ed. D. J. Bell), pp. 345–365 (Academic Press).

Rosenbrock, H. H., (1973c)   The zeros of a system, *Int. J. Control*, **18**, 297–299; see also Correction, *ibid.*, 1974, **20**, 525–527.

Rosenbrock, H. H., (1974a)   Order, degree and complexity, *Int. J. Control*, **19**, 323–331.

Rosenbrock, H. H., (1974b)   Structural properties of linear dynamical systems, *Int. J. Control*, **20**, 191–202.

Rosenbrock, H. H., (1974c)   Redundancy in linear, time-invariant finite-dimensional systems, IFAC Symposium on Multivariable Technological Systems, Manchester, 18–19 Sept.

Rosenbrock, H. H. and Cook, P. A., (1974)   Stability and the eigenvalues of $G(s)$, *Int. J. Control* (to be published).

Rosenbrock, H. H. and Storey, C., (1970).   Mathematics of dynamical systems (Nelson).

Routh, E. J., (1877)   Stability of a given state of motion (MacMillan, London).

Smith, B. W., (1970)   Designing for control, in Papermaking systems and their control, (Ed. F. Bolam) (Trans. Symposium Brit. Paper and Board Mfrs. Assn., Oxford, 1969), Vol. 1, pp. 44–65.

SSMVT: see Rosenbrock, H. H., (1970b).

Thaler, G. J. and Brown, R. G., (1960).   Analysis and design of feedback control systems (McGraw-Hill).

Tomović, R., (1963)   Sensitivity analysis of dynamic systems (McGraw-Hill).

Tsien, H. S., (1954).   Engineering cybernetics, Chapter 5 (McGraw-Hill).

Westcott, J. H., (1952)   The development of relationships concerning the frequency bandwidth and the mean square error of servo systems from properties of gain-frequency characteristics, in Automatic and manual control, pp. 45–64 (Butterworths).

Willems, J. L., (1970)   Stability theory of dynamical systems (Nelson).

Winterbone, D. E., Munro, N. and Lourtie, P. M. G., (1973)   A preliminary study of the design of a controller for an automotive gas turbine, *Trans. A.S.M.E.*

Yakubovich, V. A., (1962)   The solution of certain matrix inequalities encountered in the theory of automatic control, *Dokl. Akad. Nauk SSSR*, **143**, 6. [Referenced by Aizerman and Gantmacher (1964).]

Youla, D. C. and Tissi, P., (1966)   *n*-port synthesis via reactance extraction, Part I, I.E.E.E. International Convention Record.

Ziegler, J. G. and Nichols, N. B., (1942)   Optimum settings for automatic controllers, *Trans. A.S.M.E.*, **64**, 759–768.

Subject Index